FACING TWO WAYS

WAYS

The Story of My Life

By

BARONESS SHIDZUÉ ISHIMOTO

Illustrated

FARRAR & RINEHART · INCORPORATED

On Murray Hill   *New York*

CONTENTS

Contents

LIST OF ILLUSTRATIONS

PART ONE

MY PEACEFUL CHILDHOOD IN HALF-
WESTERNIZED TOKYO

I

My Father and Mother

I WAS born into a samurai family of Tokyo, so I began life as a member of a caste. Today there is less significance in such a fact, but when I was born it still meant a good deal as Japan had thrown off feudalism only thirty years before. At the time of my birth, the four classes—the samurai, tillers of the earth, artisans and traders—were still distinct. Thus, for generations my ancestors had been loyal retainers of a daimyo, one of whose descendants is the present Count Abe. Lord Abe's feudal estate was located in the middle west of Japan proper, on the coast of the Inland Sea, a place of beautiful scenery and mild climate. On a neighboring estate lived the daimyo whose retainers' loyalty is immortalized in the popular play, *Chushingura,* or *The Forty-Seven Ronin.*

Daimyos were heads of feudal clans, and in the days of the Tokugawa shogunate Japan was divided into about three hundred of these. The rank of each daimyo was calculated by the amount of rice his land produced. For instance, the measurement of rice crops from the lands which belonged directly to the Tokugawa Central Government called Ten-Ryo (the Land of Heaven), measured eight million koku,[1] and the former lands of Prince Shimazu, Marquis Mori, and Marquis Mayeda, the three wealthiest daimyos of the time, counted about one million koku each. Our family's daimyo, Lord Abe, was of the middle rank, owning about one hundred thousand koku worth of land around his Fukuyama Castle, whose noble outline, with

[1] One koku is five bushels.

3

its snow-white plaster walls supporting a succession of heavy-gabled, mild-sloping roofs, their gray tiles framed against the blue sky, can still be seen from the train windows, if one knows where to look.

Every samurai family belonged to one of the three hundred daimyos and rendered him civil and military service. The daimyo's income, chiefly in the form of rice, was allotted from his treasury to the families in his service according to their rank in the economic and social hierarchy within the clan, and for generations the income was inherited by the samurai descendants with almost no change in the amount from the beginning to the end of the Tokugawa period. The eldest son became the head of the family after the death or retirement of his father and the samurai rights were all dependent on this heir. In case a father had no son, all the family privileges were lost. An heir was of the utmost importance, therefore, and many concubines were retained to assure the birth of a son. Following the arrival of a boy, babies were coldly received into the family, if at all, for they would only impoverish it by consuming its strictly limited income. These children were plainly distinguished from the heir and were called "Cold Rice." They had to be satisfied with cold, leftover food, while the heir enjoyed the freshly cooked, warm rice.

The stern moral code of this daimyo and samurai class, called "Bushido," which has been made widely known to the Western world by Dr. Inazo Nitobe, bore a good many resemblances to the moral code of Western chivalry. Both stood for honor and the defense of the weak. The starting point of samurai training was the cultivation of this sense of honor and protection. The Bushido code taught the samurai that the worst thing he could possibly do was to bring shame on the lord and on his own family. "Harakiri," an honorable suicide by disemboweling, was encouraged, and when a samurai felt that he had committed a dishonorable act he killed himself to compensate for it.

Another typical attitude of life as revealed in this Bushido moral code was stoicism, coming from Buddhist teachings. The Japanese samurai renounced personal desire of any kind. This was appropriate in a country so poorly endowed with natural resources. Bushido was well practiced in the days of feudalism. Warriors did not have to worry about their livelihood: they had only to consider how to behave according to conventions.

However, after the Meiji political restoration which was completed in 1868, feudalism was replaced by a new social system based on modern industrialism. The samurai suddenly lost their security of living, whether they had heirs or not, and had no training with which to meet the new social order. Their traditional moral principle—"Deprecate the material value of things, and be loyal to thy lord"—was a positive handicap as feudalism was being undermined by Western materialism. The samurai conception that it was shameful to work for direct material remuneration made the starved warrior sit passively at a table heaped with plates of wooden fish, put there just for show, and pretend he had eaten enough by using a toothpick in a satiated manner. The toothpick, which often horrifies the visitor from the West, has a long and honorable history.

My father, Ritaro Hirota, who was born two years before the Meiji restoration, faced difficulties and privations in his boyhood, and was one of those who struggled in the tide of this great social change. But the samurai class soon developed ambition, and my father was urged to study at the Imperial University of Tokyo, which was being organized on the Western basis of education. Only a selected few could secure the privilege of entry. There he studied science to be a mechanical engineer. In my father's boyhood, students had learned their history and literature from Chinese books, and modern science through European languages. As paper manufacturing and printing in those days were still done in the old-fashioned way, father could not afford expensive books. He copied from cover to cover the whole volume of a Chinese-Japanese dictionary that he needed so much. This is only one instance of the great efforts made by the students of early reconstruction days.

Out from the university my father pulled his boat up the stream of awakening industry, where this young inexperienced engineer was well received. The hectic years in establishing factories, with new machines of high efficiency, changed our land of the Lotus Dream into a country of whistles and smoking chimneys. How many huge chimneys have I seen rising around high temple towers and against the picturesque green hills of the seashore! My father would proudly tell me that these were his great contribution to industrial Japan, at which I would smile, saying to myself, "That couldn't be helped in those days!"

The marriage of my father to my mother was, of course, not a love match. According to the Japanese custom, it was arranged by the parents as a family affair, or indeed, an affair of two families. Both belonged to the samurai caste and the honorable marriage was effected by a go-between who satisfied the families concerned that the standards of culture and family tradition were well balanced. Although my father, as an engineer with Western training, had an outward appearance of modernity, psychologically he was controlled by the feudal code of the old regime. He stayed in a mental world with my grandfather, who dared not step out from this conservatism, feeling great pride in his family traditions.

This samurai pride may be said to have been the motive power of the mid-Meiji reaction against the swift and superficial westernization of Japan: the basis of national consciousness, crying for the abolition of extraterritorial rights and other ill-considered treaties with the Western countries.

Thus my father, wearing a Western suit and hat, understanding English well, designing factories in modern style, was in his private life thoroughly imbued with the feudalistic ideology. He was during my childhood, and he still is, a samurai, not with the sword girded at his side, but with the engineer's ruler in his pocket.

My father has had very regular habits all through his life. He does not like to use the word "about," while Japanese usually speak and act with the "about." He acts with the precision his ruler and scales indicate, the only exception being when he gives his order to the maids at dinner table. He may say that he likes to measure his sake (rice wine) a little more generously than precisely, with a sly glance at mother's face. He is gifted in music and likes to play the bamboo flute and sing folk songs. But, according to his stoic samurai principle, he believes that the encouragement of pleasure will ruin the nation and refrains from singing too much or playing too long on his favorite bamboo flute.

During the Tokugawa period, literature, art, music and drama—the things that perpetuate the humane side of life—were regarded as evils by the ruling class except as it directed them. The plays which grew out of the old marionette shows persisted as popular entertainment, and the acting, costuming, subtlety of dramatic expression and power of emotional appeal in the Kabuki theater are highly esteemed to this day by the people at large. But only the classical No drama with its extremely reserved action and ultrarefined taste was permitted for the enjoyment of the samurai class in former times.

The No are religious dramas, inculcating Buddhist morals. They were developed by the great masters of the art in the fourteenth and fifteenth centuries and were inherited generation after generation by the families who founded the No schools, such as "Kanze" or "Hosho," under the patronage of the daimyo or samurai class. The leading performers play in skillfully carved masks appropriate to the characters portrayed, and their words are chanted or intoned to a particular kind of musical accompaniment—flutes, large drums and tsuzumi (hand drums), descriptive and explanatory passages being sung by the chorus. The dancers, masked and gorgeously robed in sweeping garments, move, from the beginning to the end of the play, through a series of stately posturings, each of which is prescribed by tradition. The No drama had its own comedy, though of a formal nature—the Kyogen, or short farces, performed by way of relief. They now appear on No programs, ridiculing everything in heaven and earth, displaying the humorous aspects of the servant problem, of marital relations, the iniquities of priests. But to repress one's feelings to the limit of endurance became second nature to the Japanese. It is highly appreciated as a samurai virtue, but often misunderstood by people who do not know the background of Japanese culture and interpret restraint as a denial of emotions. My father's ancestry spoke through his relation to the arts. He and mother usually responded to the solemn effect of the No, although father occasionally hummed a little passage from Kyogen, cheerful and a little red in the face from his rice wine after supper.

When my mother came into my father's house as a young bride, she entered the family of his parents, brothers, sisters, cousins, student servants,[1] and housemaids of various ages, more than twenty in number. Soon after my father, in his twenty-third year, was graduated from the university, my grandfather retired as active head of the household and father became the legal chief. His first salary of sixty yen a month ($30) was just about enough to support this big family, including the expense of sending his younger brothers and cousins to the Imperial University from which he himself had been graduated. The cost of living was about one-tenth of what it is at present, but it was hard for my mother to manage the family finances even though each member of the group was brought up with the samurai habits of extreme thrift.

[1] The student servant is an old Japanese institution. During the Tokugawa period, students usually lived with masters, waiting on them with the utmost humility. In present-day Japan, many poor boys become servants and thus work their way through colleges or universities.

It was a great extravagance, for instance, to purchase a bicycle for my father's younger brothers to ride in turn instead of their having to walk all the way to the school which was located far from home. Only after long discussions did they get permission to buy one. Later my father entered the Takata Trading Company, at that time one of the largest foreign trading firms in Japan, all of which were busy importing machines for the industrialization of Japan. He was highly valued for his knowledge of mechanics. He was successful in the business field; especially so when he showed his acumen by promptly purchasing munitions to meet the urgent demands of the Japanese army and navy during the Russo-Japanese War. He was in London during the war to prosecute this great undertaking. Later his service was recognized by the government when he was decorated by the Emperor—a rare treat for one who was not a direct official of the imperial government. The honorable degree of Doctor of Engineering was conferred on my father by the Imperial University of Tokyo, and although he has now retired from business, he enjoys his chair at the university, giving lectures there. He is still head of the Hirota family, which numbers nearly a hundred members.

My mother is rather tall for a Japanese. Her skin is smooth as ivory, and her hair is long and thick. She is intelligent, modest, unselfish, and always thoughtful of the other members of the family. She is particular about her manners, and impresses everybody she meets with her graceful dignity. Strict with herself, and formal, she plays the part of a samurai's wife, majestically, as if in a dramatic performance. She rises earlier and retires later than anybody else in the family. She has never allowed herself to enjoy a lazy Sunday morning in bed, and the sickbed is the only place for her to rest. Nobody ever saw her sit in a relaxed manner: she is always erect, wearing her kimono tightly with her heavy sash folded on her back. Even on hot summer days her thick black hair is dressed in the old-fashioned married lady's style. I remember how I loved, when a little girl, to stay in mother's boudoir watching her hair being dressed.

Lafcadio Hearn, in his delicate style, described Japanese hairdressing: "volutes, jets, whirls, eddyings, foliations, each passing into the other blandly like the linking of brush-strokes in the writing of a Chinese master! Far beyond the skill of the Parisian *coiffeuse* is the art of the kamiyui [professional hairdresser]. From the mythical era of the race, Japanese ingenuity has exhausted itself in the invention and the improvement of pretty devices for the dressing of women's hair; and probably there have never been so many beautiful fashions of wearing it in any other country as there have been in Japan." [1]

This formality will remain with us forever just as Kabuki plays will be appreciated even when talkies and revues seem to have taken the whole ground in the world of amusement. Japanese girls now spend their schooldays in the so-called "foreign style" uniform with their hair cut short. They frequently wear the American garb, but as soon as they are engaged and begin to prepare for the wedding, they let their hair grow, to conform to the beautiful shimada—the bride's style. No girl could look ungraceful when she leaves the hairdresser's hands.

To come back to my mother's dressing room where she sits patiently in front of her mirror for an hour or more once in every three days when the kamiyui comes to her house to arrange her hair. The kamiyui sends the maiden apprentice first, who cleans, steams, perfumes the hair, and finally combs it with instruments of various kinds, changing gradually from rough to fine ones. When this has been done, the kamiyui arrives. With a comb which has a sharp hairpin at the end, she separates mother's hair into five sections, and twists it in the marumage— the dignified married woman's fashion. Then the hair is tied with new white strings especially made for the purpose, and a

[1] *Glimpses of Unfamiliar Japan*, p. 419.

big round knot is fixed on the top with four parts around it, puffed out, stiffened with oil and sometimes lined with black paper. On her black hair mother usually wears stringed red coral beads, or green jade ones inherited from her mother, a bit of dark blue tied-and-dyed crepe beneath the center knot, and a gilded and lacquered ornamental comb besides a hairpin or two of the same sort in front and on the sides.

My mother uses polite words only, never liking to pick up the vulgar words spoken in the street. She never betrays unpleasant feelings. "Endurance" and "repression" are her greatest ideals. She says to me, "Endurance a woman should cultivate more than anything else. If you endure well in any circumstances, you will achieve happiness." She never loses her temper with the servants, but is always dignified and gentle, however stupid or slow they may be. She hates ordinary theatergoing. Her stoic principle makes her regard a place of amusement as inappropriate for a samurai's wife; consequently, I was never allowed to go to a theater until I was married and had left her jurisdiction. However, she makes one exception, attending the drama *Chushin-gura,* a true samurai play. She is absorbed in the moral spirit of this story of loyalty rather than in the artistic qualities of the play, and for days and days after she has seen a performance she will say, "Kichi-emon [the name of the well-known actor particularly good as Yurano-suke, the hero] must have been sorry to undergo such horrible disgrace"; she cannot distinguish the actor from the living character.

My mother has accomplished all that is required of a wise parent and a good wife according to the standards of her generation. She has managed the household admirably, and has brought up her six children well. She herself attended a Canadian mission school in Tokyo, which was considered a place of progressive education for Japanese girls. There she studied English and domestic science in Western style. This helped her a good deal in understanding father as befitted the wife of a progressive businessman. But her missionary education did not make her thoroughly Christian; nor did it greatly affect her way of thinking, for she was reluctant to be converted into the alien religion and stuck to the old moral code which maintains that submission is the utmost womanly virtue. She was faithful to the old family system, humbly serving her parents-in-law and sisters- and brother-in-law.

And yet when I grew old enough to learn music as a part of the training of girlhood she insisted on my learning the piano instead of the koto (thirteen-stringed harp), because she remembered how hard it had been for her to play the koto every day to please her mother-in-law whether she was in a musical mood or not. Nevertheless, she did not wish her daughters to be exempt from the matter of pleasing mothers-in-law, as she believed that the performance of this obligation makes a woman's virtues brighter. Having inculcated this in her children she dared to have her eldest daughter marry into a family with a mother-in-law who was said to be especially difficult to please.

My mother was especially assiduous in educating her children. She made every effort to further their development but her feudal concept of "man first, woman to follow" was clearly seen in her treatment of her sons and daughters. Of course the daughters took sex discrimination for granted, as they did not know anything else. Mother has never understood the moral beauty of romantic love between man and woman. She regards it as indicative of wild feelings which can be allowed to exist only among vulgar people. "Unselfishness, sacrifice and endurance for woman. That is all-sufficient," my honorable mother maintains.

II

Family Manners and Customs

SINCE prefeudal times in Japan the third day of the third month has been the day for the Peach Blossom Festival. On this occasion a pair of candles burn in the delicately framed paper lanterns, on the top of a five-shelved stand covered with scarlet cloth, throwing soft light and shadow on the snow-white faces of the Doll Prince and Princess, crowned and dressed in gorgeous brocades and set on their lacquer-framed throne. An ancient court is resurrected. Artificial plants of pink cherry and yellow orange blossoms are placed on both sides of the throne on the top shelf. Three graceful dolls dressed in white brocade silk robes with red hakama-skirts are the court ladies, and as such are placed below the royal dolls. Beside them are arranged the austere ministers of the Left and the Right together with the household servants. Five musicians with flutes and drums are placed on the middle shelf. The display includes great numbers of miniature household utensils, furniture, dressing mirrors, bureaus, a whole cooking and dinner set, tea set, flower carriages and even ox-drawn carts, all gilded and lacquered. A white and black toy Pekingese is there with a handsomely uniformed maid-in-waiting. Every detail reveals exquisite workmanship in a style derived from ancient times. This festival is celebrated for the girls of the family. They invite their friends to the party and the mother entertains these small guests, who try their best to behave gracefully before the Doll Prince and Princess. I was born on the eve of this festival— my parents' first daughter.

My father was away at the moment and not, as ordinarily, for business reasons. He was paying one of his rare visits to a performance at the No theater, of which he was so fond. Greatly impressed by the austere play of *Shidzuka,* his mind was occupied, on the way home, with the story of this ancient woman of beauty and courage. When he arrived, to his surprise and joy he was told that a daughter had been added to the household. On the seventh day afterward the family welcomed their latest child with a red-rice-and-tai-fish feast [1] and the name of "Shidzué," for the heroine of the No play, was given her by her father, who blessed the infant and expressed the wish that she might have a bright future and be brought up to be as brave as her ancient namesake.

As the legend goes Lady Shidzuka was the beloved fiancée of the young general Yoshitsune whose brother Yoritomo was the first shogun founder of the feudal government in this island empire eight hundred years ago. Very jealous, the shogun accused his younger brother, General Yoshitsune, of treason. To escape persecution, Yoshitsune fled to a remote mountain. Then the shogun tried to take advantage of Shidzuka. She was ordered to come to the Shrine of Kamakura Hachiman and in the presence of hundreds of warriors demonstrate by her homage the power of their lord. Shidzuka was offended. She defied the shogun's command to betray her lover's hiding place. In her great loyalty to him she performed on the spur of the moment a classic dance and composed impromptu a poem praising the glory of her fiancé, Yoshitsune. This historic event was dramatized in various ways later. My father hoped that I would exemplify this loyalty, naming me Shidzué.

At this time we were living near the Imperial University in Hongo located in the residential quarter reserved for the former retainers of Count Abe's family. The Tokugawa feudal gov-

---

[1] A feast, in which rice boiled with red azuki beans and tai-fish broiled whole are served, is always given on a happy occasion.

ernment ordered all the feudal lords to maintain, besides their castles on their estates, two mansions in Yedo (now Tokyo): an official residence called the Upper Mansion, and a private residence called the Lower Mansion. They were ordered to spend three years on their land and the next three years in their Tokyo residence. This was one of the wise policies of the Tokugawas. It gave no time to any feudal lord to prepare a war against the central government, and it made them all spend money, traveling back and forth with their retinues, expensive daimyo processions. The Upper Mansions of the feudal lords were located outside the beautiful moats of Yedo Castle. These estates with their beautiful classical Japanese gardens are attractions here and there even today in Tokyo. In my infancy, Count Abe still occupied one of the Upper Mansions and our family lived in its retainers' quarters. Shortly after I was born, my father bought a new house in Kojimachi, one of the best sections of Tokyo, and we all removed to this place.

The city of Tokyo has five million inhabitants. With its enlarged borders recently prescribed by the municipal administration, greater Tokyo includes even wild outlying fields and the spacious beds of the Tama River. However, it is more natural for Tokyo people to think of the city in its old form, an area running about eight miles north and south and the same distance east to west, its southwest border facing the deep archshaped Tokyo Bay on the Pacific.

Tokyo, the eastern capital, was named in the year of the Meiji restoration. Formerly it was called "Yedo" and was the political center of this island empire for three centuries, from the time the Tokugawa shogunate was established and while it dominated the three hundred feudal war lords. Yedo Castle, the present imperial palace surrounded by moats, is situated in the center of Tokyo. Naturally the city has been rich with feudal reminders, of unique and ancient charm, until recently busy westernization has gradually changed the old Japanese town into a modern city. Square, tall concrete buildings and cement-mortared, red brick architecture, with bands of glass windows, for government offices and business places now replace the former daimyos' mansions with sharply-peaked gray tile roofs and with occasional large square windows hung with grass screens, from behind which the gatemen used to watch the people on the street; historical gardens with century-old groves and ponds have been mercilessly destroyed to make way for boulevards. The delicately arched wooden bridges over the stone-walled moats of the shogun's palace and the picturesque canals of Yedo have all been demolished for the building of new bridges in a style of monstrous ugliness, to bear the heavy modern traffic.

The great earthquake and the following conflagrations in Tokyo spurred modernization so fast that almost two-thirds of Tokyo today has completely lost its former beauty.

As I recall the Tokyo of my childhood, my mind dwells on a quiet, charming town, so thoroughly Japanese it was, though my memories go back only three decades. The city is located between two rivers, the Sumida and the Tama. The former runs nearer what was the heart of the city in the ancient Yedo days, and undying romance and pleasure linger on its waters and banks. I used to go to the river bank, Mukojima, in my girlhood to enjoy the cherry blossoms. The avenue of cherry trees continues along the banks far beyond the city confines and it has long been the custom of the people to enjoy gay spring picnics, dancing, singing and playing the samisen (three-stringed guitar) on red blankets spread on the turf under the canopies of bloom and color. When a spring wind carries mild air in early April, all these trees open their buds suddenly. Then Tokyo is, indeed, gay and rich. When I was very young, mother would give a day off to all her maids that they might see the flowers, and the children would go with them for a picnic under the trees. Ueno Park, one of the main amusement resorts in Tokyo, is covered with cherry blossoms in their season. When the aged trees around the red lacquered Kanyeiji Temple blossom effusively the park, with its rolling acres of evergreens, is crowded with merry folk enjoying a carefree frolic. I used to wander among the throngs clinging tightly to my maid's kimono sleeves so that I might not be lost in the crowd, watching brilliant paper balloons, looking at the artificial cherry flowers for ladies' hair offered for sale by peddlers. In later years, while I would still enjoy the flowers, I mingled less with the holiday crowds, viewing instead the mistlike blossoms amid the dark, green pines of the Yeno hills, from a distant point of vantage. From there one could see the cherries fringing the imperial moats along the red brick buildings of the pre-earthquake British Embassy. The trees at that place are old and huge. Laden with pale pink and snowy white blossoms, they made a superb contrast with a wide band of green turf on the far side of the moat. In a quiet promenade over the carpet of pink petals, one would be lost in the enchantment of the scene.

Even after the cherry flowers are gone, blown away like snow, when fresh young leaves have sprouted out on slender hanging willow branches along the banks of the imperial moats, which wind beside the promenade, the flower season continues in Tokyo. White, pink and rose tree-peonies, purple and white bunches of wisteria, red and white camellia, white magnolia and yellow yamabuki decorate the capital, in private gardens, in the parks and in the numerous temple courts. These courts are, in effect, little parks for children to play in and retreats in which old people may rest. Azaleas, white, dark and fair pink, purple, orange, yellow and red, blossom on the grassy slopes along the banks of the outer moats—ever-changing bands of color which flash into view as the electric tram winds in and out of the natural gardens lining the road.

But in the month of June the rainy season comes in Tokyo, calming the excitement of flower-worshippers. The silver threadlike rains wet the houses, trees and streets day after day, cleaning the dusty air of late spring. People go out walking on their two-bladed wooden clogs, five or six inches high, carrying big paper umbrellas, with bamboo frames and handles, which add more grace to women as they walk. But the terrible humidity which accompanies the rain causes dreadful suffering among the poor, who are crowded into the slums along unsanitary canals, under the high bridges at the narrow points along the river, and near the smoking forests of the industrial section.

The melancholy days of Tokyo vanish suddenly with the brightness of summer's arrival. The coming of the summer season in Tokyo was long observed by a festival at the Ryogoku Bridge on the Sumida. All the teahouses and fashionable restaurants on the bank, as well as the roofed boats on the river, were then lighted with colorful paper lanterns. On balconies and roofs wax candles flicker in the evening breeze. Men and women, clad in the thinnest of Yukata for the dark warm summer night, enjoy a magnificent display of fireworks.

The downtown people are more native Yedo-ites—children of the old Yedo traditions—who have lived in this locality for generations, active in every line of trade known to feudal times. They belong to the merchant class, and preserve many of its old characteristics. Big business houses, theaters and tea houses, geisha quarters, the Yoshiwara pleasure enclosure, all are situated within the boundaries of southeast Tokyo.

The uptown district is located in the northwest of the city where the level of the land is much higher and the formation is rolling. Many points of these hills command a view of the city, Tokyo Bay, and even Mount Fuji, miles and miles away. The former samurai class and the present-day upper middle class, mingling with newcomers to the capital and with those who have moved uptown to open small shops, make up the district residents. This section is rich with evergreen plantations, large groves in the imperial palace grounds and other royal palaces. Streets are usually wide enough for two automobiles to pass, exceptions being the grand boulevards in the center around the palaces and along the government buildings, and the straight roads at Nippon Bashi (Nippon Bridge). This was the former starting point of the Tokaido, the main highway of the country, running between Tokyo and Kyoto.

The Kojimachi ward in the center of the city contains the imperial palace, Parliament buildings, court buildings, military and navy offices of the government, Metro Police Station, Municipal Hall, and the headquarters of all big firms. This ward and the Akasaka district, where the subsidiary detached imperial palace is located, with its huge expanse of garden, are the two most sparsely populated sections of the city. In the neighborhood of my father's home, all the residences occupy large tracts of land; from the gate to the house door there is usually a long avenue, and at the back of the house a spacious garden. Each house is surrounded by a six-foot wall of plaster or wood and only the top of the house can be seen from the street. Before the automobile was introduced, when the rikisha was the usual means of conveyance, with a few horse carriages for high nobles, and horse-drawn trams on the main boulevards, there was nothing to cause noise or bustle in the city but the pleasant street cries of natto-bean sellers in the very early morning, clear-voiced poor children or the full-throated exclamations of a woman with a baby on her back. All through the hours of the day the different vendors came and went; their various ways of announcing themselves resounded cheerfully. In the afternoon, when people were preparing supper, the tofu seller's shouts enlivened the street. Modern science has discovered that this bean product—the tofu—is rich in vitamins, and consequently even Westernized Japanese now enjoy tofu among the supper dishes. In the evening, the infrequent shrill piping and melancholy note of blind masseurs accentuated the quiet, while the creaking sound of women's wooden clogs on the frozen street made winter nights seem chillier and lonelier.

Until the summer of my fifteenth year, the residence in Koji-machi was our home. Then this house was torn down and father built a house in European style, designed by a German architect. I love to remember this older Japanese house in Japanese style and its childhood association, although I care very much also for my father's Occidental dwelling which has the air of an ancient European castle.

The Japanese house had a tall black painted wooden gate from which a long narrow path paved with shining white stones led to the house. On both sides of this walk were huge double cherry trees, pines and oaks, casting dark and cool shadows in the summertime. Japanese camellia, jinchoge, the sweet-smelling bay tree, kuchinashi, the Cape jasmine, and white and yellow yamabuki were planted among the big trees, shedding sweet odors in the spring. The plain wooden front gable of the house was barely seen through the thick tree branches. On the south side of the house was the major garden, with a huge pine tree in the center. A big weeping willow hung over the stone well. Old plum trees were there and shrubs planted in abundance but in tasteful groups. Separated from the main garden by low hedges of tea shrubs was a tea garden. The stone under the old maple tree here was especially admired for its unusual celadon hue and peculiar shape. Even tiny moss-covered stones scattered over the ground were prized and cared for, while dead leaves were swept up and taken away every morning by Toku, our gardener by profession, an artist in sentiment. I liked to watch him at the top of a pine tree as he used his scissors so quickly and regularly with a pleasant clicking sound. He gave a good hair trimming to each tree, brushing up the pine needles almost one by one and giving a graceful twist to each maple branch. Often he paused, puffing at his long tobacco pipe and looking up at the tree at which he had been working. I particularly liked this pose. Although he was leisurely in his artistry, he was never self-indulgent. He smoked just one pipeful; then he would knock out the ashes, still smoking hot, into the palm of his hand, scatter them and return to his labors.

"Won't it burn your hand?" I would anxiously ask him.

"No, don't worry, my little lady, Toku's hand is thick like an ironing board." Over and over again he examined the trimming of the trees and foliage. Later he learned to plant Western flowers in the flower beds in our back garden, and he said to me one day:

"My little lady, don't you know that Toku has learned English?"

"What did you learn, Toku?" I asked with curiosity.

"Platanap-Carnation-Strowberri-Churip-Hyashince-Anemone-Glokitaniya—"

"What? It's like Buddha's sutra!" I laughed. But he insisted that it was English. Now he has thrown away his blue happicoats, his vocational symbol, and opened a charming curio shop. My father gave him a little house and this shop for his last years.

Our Japanese home had two stories and was built in the center of the property. The roofs were of dark gray tiles, a giant tile in the shape of the devil's face at each corner to charm away evil spirits. The tone of these tiles was in quiet harmony with the enveloping green trees. The drawing rooms, father's study, mother's sitting room and all the other rooms, including the nursery, student-servant's room, maidservants' room, rikishaman's quarters, lantern room, big bathroom and storage room, were all designed in a zigzag way to break monotony. The floors of sitting rooms and bedrooms were covered with thick green mats bordered with black or brown, six by three feet. These mats were placed tightly side by side in the customary way, the size of a room being known by the number of its mats. Thus a Japanese room is referred to as an eight-mat room or a twelve-mat room, instead of twenty-four by forty-eight or thirty-six by seventy-two feet.

Mother's twelve-mat room was in the middle of the house. On three sides were small closets divided into shelves and drawers where she kept her wardrobe in neat order. These closets were hidden behind beautifully patterned paper sliding screens and one of them contained the family shrine. On memorial days when the members of the family for many ancestral generations were honored, she offered tea, boiled rice, cakes, fruits and flowers at the shrine, all in the diminutive table sets especially made for the Buddhist ceremony. Mother kept cans of cookies and sweets in her room and as children we delighted in these when we took tea with her. The south side of her room faced on the garden and a part of the garden-pondlet stretched beneath the veranda of the room. I remember my younger brother Yoji and I often stretching out our hands to catch the goldfish in the pond or chasing them in the water, wetting our kimonos dreadfully. Mother would gently scold us, saying she felt sorry for the little goldfish's being disturbed like that.

Corridors of plain wood connected our rooms. In the Japanese house they are an important part of the architecture and every morning and evening the maids polish them with a soft cotton cloth, so that they become almost as shiny as a mirror. In one corner of our house was a ceremonial tearoom section artistically furnished, quiet and dark. Father used to talk with his friends there. All the rooms were closed by paper sliding doors or doors of sugi (Japanese cedar), and there was no key for any door except for the heavy plaster ones opening into the "godown." The godown is a peculiar Japanese institution—a place where family treasures are stored. It is a separate building, presumably fireproof, with heavy, white plaster walls and high small windows. When we children were too naughty mother would put us into this dungeonlike place. My second younger brother had more experience than the rest of us in the godown, crying loudly in its gloom.

We all wore kimonos and sat neatly and picturesquely, each on a cushion, on the mat floor. Father wore the kimono at home, but when he went to his office in the morning he donned his made-in-London morning coat or a business suit and a derby hat. As he departed he gave a light nod to the members of the family who came together to the front entrance to bow him off. Then he rode away on his rikisha drawn by Katsu, our family servant. When he came back the rattling of the iron tires of the rikisha against the white stone pavement on the avenue was heard far inside the house; it was the signal for the children to run out, mother and all the maids following, to bow the master in.

Thus I was brought up in a purely Japanese fashion. But Western influences crept into our life little by little, and whenever my father went to Europe on a business trip, he brought home chairs, tables, desks, bureaus, piano and pianola, cinematograph, sewing machines and children's clothes. But father was the only one of us then who actually had seen the Western countries, the rest of the family knowing about them only through the stories and objects he brought back. For this reason our Japanese life could not be changed in its essence, and my little sisters wearing Western dresses were carried on their nurses' backs like little girls dressed in kimonos, and slept just as peacefully after their lullaby, "Nen-nen-yo-o, Okorori-yo."

Memories of the New Year in those days are among the most delightful. Japanese people believe that at the New Year everything must be fresh. Not only the year and the day but man himself must be spiritually renewed. Mother began two weeks ahead to get ready for the New Year, helped by the servants. A grand dusting day inaugurated the preparation. The ceilings, the back of the mats, and every corner of the closets and drawers were cleaned. Big bunches of pine and bamboo boughs were brought to decorate the gate and the same decoration was placed at every entrance of the house, to welcome the good fortune which the coming year was to bring. Mother arranged pine branches and plum flowers in the big bronze vase and put them into the alcove of the room where guests were received. Special foods, enough to last three days for the family and its guests, were carefully prepared in the kitchen. Daintily cut vegetables, cooked chicken, meat and fish were assembled in piles upon piles in square black lacquer-and-gold boxes, strictly prescribed for this occasion.

At the time fixed for the pounding of rice cakes, which came a few days in advance of New Year's, the children got up about four o'clock in the cold winter morning, as soon as they heard the familiar sound in the back yard, under the shining stars. Its sound was like an announcement of festivities. The servants had already steamed rice on the stove temporarily set up in the yard and Katsu and Toku pounded the steamed rice in a big wooden mortar. Then they kneaded it on a board into big square or small round cakes, smiling all the while.

Kimonos and obis, snow-white socks, lacquer clogs, red underwear, silver flowers for the hair with long red tassels were all new for the holiday. Only the brocade sashes might be hangovers. They were handed down from mother to daughter for several generations. So much had to be finished by New Year's Eve that mother and all the servants went to bed very late that night, often after they had heard the first cock's cry proclaiming the New Year's dawn. On the morning of the great day the family got up early to watch the sunrise and to bow in honor of the Sun Goddess. Then all the members gathered together in the grand sitting room and passed around the sake cups, bowing and wishing each other "A Happy New Year!" These sake cups were of lacquer and gold piled one upon the other in three layers and placed on a lacquer stand. Each cup bore the family coat of arms in gold.

My father in his villa overlooking Kamakura beach

My mother

Myself with my brothers and twin sisters, in the clothes my father brought back from London

On the second day of January father invited the staff of his company to his home for a feast. The two big rooms on the upper story were given over to the banquet, and the gentlemen, gay with the New Year wines, laughed and sang. But no lady was included in the party. In those days, ladies paid a New Year's visit to one another after the fifteenth of January, but they were allowed to wish one another "A Happy New Year" at any first meeting throughout the month of January. The New Year meant such a long observance and celebration in those slow, leisurely days! Now that has all been changed.

Mother often got sick during the strenuous New Year's season, but the children had only fun. They played all day long in the garden with battledores and shuttlecocks or a game played with thirty-one syllable poem cards. We often said, "Wish the New Year would stay longer." But among mother's burdens were the presents to be sent out to all our relatives and friends during this season. Moreover, there were the Seventh Day Festival, the Fifteenth Day Festival, and the days for the servants' vacations, to mention only a few matters to which she must attend. We never dined out, for it was considered undignified except when formally invited. Later, when I spent a New Year's Eve in New York, watching the bustle on Broadway, the gay restaurants where men and women dined together cheerfully, I was struck by the sharp contrast between the domestic burdens put on the shoulders of the housewives in Japan and the freedom of women in New York. Though it has been much simplified recently, the Japanese New Year is still the most festive time for the nation and the most torturesome for wives and mothers.

In the list of the social festivities the second in importance is O-bon, the Feast of Lanterns. It turns suddenly warm after our spring-long rainy season is over, but a busy fortnight in the heat comes to every housewife. The middle of the seventh month is set aside for the Bon Festival. During that time families exchange presents again as they do at the New Year's season. On the thirteenth of July the family shrine is cleaned; meals, joss sticks and burning candles are placed before it. According to Buddhist tradition, it is thought that all the departed members of the family come back for the three days of this festival. When there are members who have newly been listed in the book of the dead, the relatives send paper lanterns to the family shrine. At my father's home, when the priests came, we sat in front of the shrine observing the rites. The priest first read a Sanskrit sutra in a loud voice, meanwhile ringing a bell, burning incense and bowing many times. Then he read another sutra and bowed; he repeated this for some time. When the ceremony was over father stood up and stepped to the shrine to burn incense. Then mother followed, and the children in the order of their ages, but when the turn came for my naughty younger brother, his little legs slept entirely and he could hardly crawl to the shrine.

Our family religion was Sodo-Shu,[1] one of the subdivisions of Zenism, a Buddhist faith. Nobody in the family talked about Buddha or worshiped him with any religious sentiment, but we considered the Buddhist temple the proper place to bury our dead. We were brought up indifferent to any creed, merely following the formalities of the family religion in which the Feast of Lanterns played the most important role. Mother never allowed us to leave the city for our summer home until she had taken us to the ancestors' graves during the Feast of Lanterns in the middle of the hot July. Afterward we went to the seashore at Kamakura to stay until cool weather returned to Tokyo.

In the midst of the still-persisting feudal mode of my life, when the family was almost a self-sustaining community, my mother's household duties were overwhelmingly numerous. She was responsible, not only for the cleaning, the washing, the cooking for the large household, for keeping immaculately clean the house with its many rooms and zigzag corridors, and attending

---

[1] Sodo-Shu is introduced as Soto-Shu in the *Pilgrimage of Buddhism*, by J. B. Pratt.

to the thick wooded spacious gardens, but also for the annual supply of bean paste for breakfast soup and the great barrels of pickles for every season and every kind of meal. The cleaning of the house consisted not merely of dusting and polishing, but of repapering the hundreds of screens at least twice a year. Being delicate, these were easily torn, and the children found secret delight in sticking their fingers through them when their parents were not looking. Cats, too, took to the mischief of the children, by scratching and making passages through the screens.

The washing was as complicated as the cleaning of the house, for the winter kimonos, haori-coats, obi-sashes and underwear, all lined and often padded with cotton or raw silk, had to be taken apart, laundered, starched and dried on boards or frames, and put together again. The bed quilts and cushions had to be taken through the same process. Because of the poor heating system, the winter clothing and bedding were large, heavy and numbered many pieces, adding to the burdens of the mother.

Mother had many faithful servants, however, to help her with her numerous household duties. For generations young maids from the same families came to us to learn house management, and stayed with us until they married. Mothers and daughters, sisters or cousins entered our household and worked faithfully, never thinking of changing master or mistress. Indeed, it was a shame for them to do so. O-ko, for instance, was with my mother before I was born and remained with her longer than I did.

III

Childhood

YUKICHI FUKUZAWA, a prominent educator in the early Meiji period and a forerunner of the feminist movement, says in his book on Japanese Women: "It is a shame to treat one's better-half as a tool, giving a prize when a woman gives birth to a son." But sons were exclusively welcomed to the family, especially the first-born.

My father was not so old-fashioned as to give a prize to my mother when my elder brother was born as his heir. He gave his son a name, however, beginning with a character which signifies filial piety, for he considered that to be the first and fundamental moral precept for this child. Receiving the gentlest care befitting the first-born son, my elder brother was shy and quiet in his nature. He never had a quarrel with his brothers and sisters, and behaved with dignity from his early years. But he was afraid to go to the kindergarten when the time came; he wound his arms tightly around a pillar in the house, the farthest from the front door. He was too timid to sing when he was told by the teacher to do so. His resistance was not resentment and his sense of dignity saved him from anger.

My second brother was named with the Chinese character "Ocean" because he was born while father was abroad. He was naughty and intelligent, keeping always at the head of his class from primary school to college. When I was almost five years old, Chiyo, my nurse, told me that twin sisters had been born to the family. I remember peeping in at the wee babies, tiny like my dolls—sleeping in beds covered with red quilts. Mother always dressed them exactly alike. They both had very big, bright eyes. When they were old enough to go to school with me, the teacher asked mother to tie their hair with ribbons of different colors so that she could identify them.

I used to have more boys than girls for companions as I liked to be out-of-doors, playing baseball and tennis, or climbing trees. Bamboo stilt-riding was my favorite pastime. Toku often made bamboo stilts with a pair of long straight stalks, six or sometimes eight feet tall, to which were attached pieces of wood to hold the feet. When I rode these stilts I felt suddenly grown up high and walked like a giraffe or ostrich in a zoo, with long, long steps. Mother, of course, did not approve of this, saying complainingly, "You can't be married if you behave like a boy that way." But I thought Kayo and Kiyo, my gentle twin sisters, could be good brides in my place.

These two girls preferred to stay indoors, playing with dolls, and cooking the New Year's feast for them. They cleverly designed a fashion book in both Japanese and European modes for their little dolls. They made their own dolls and arranged these alongside their manufactured dolls on silk cushions in the nursery.

One day Toku told me that we were to have a big farm in the suburbs of Tokyo and spend our week-ends there. Toku was promoted to the superintendent's post on this new estate. On our first trip to the farm we took the streetcar which carried us to the northwest terminal of the city; there we transferred to another tram which ran along rough suburban roads past rows of small shops and flat houses. The outskirts of Tokyo consist of level land divided into vegetable gardens and forests of chestnuts and other woods, with rolling hills everywhere in the distance. Large open spaces spread out along the Tama River which runs to the sea, fed by many small streams. Its clear water is used by the city dwellers. Every Sunday after riding twenty minutes on the slow electric tram, we got off and took a pleasant walk along the bank of the creek to our farm, carrying white rice, boiled eggs, cold chicken and vegetables arranged in the partitioned lacquer boxes, which were so heavy that we had developed a good appetite by the time we reached the farm.

Covering acres of land, the country place was picturesque, with tall twisted pine woods on the west side, where we would hang hammocks and read story books or take soothing naps. The shrill young cicadas thrilled rather than offended us. Adjacent to the pine woods was a chestnut forest, and a thick grove of tall bamboo, the round straight graduated trunks lifting high, the leaves rustling pleasantly over our heads as they touched and rubbed in the breeze. Often we hunted young bamboo sprouts, digging in the black soft earth around their roots.

A brook ran through the forest where we could catch little fish and where myriads of tadpoles frolicked in the paddy pools along its bank. The rest of the land, on the Musashino Plain, was open under the immense arch of the azure sky. At the center of the property, on the top of a gentle slope, father built an artistic Japanese week-end villa of small five-mat rooms. Tennis courts covered with soft green lawn, flower beds, hot-houses, an orchard and a vegetable garden, were there for us to enjoy. We sated our thirsty throats with strawberries, loquats and persimmons, fresh and abundant. It was real recreation, coming to this farm, and we thanked father who did so much for the happiness of his children.

With the rapid development of the suburbs and the ever-increasing population, this sort of delightful spot in the neighborhood of the city has been consumed by Greater Tokyo. The people have lost the unspoiled fragrance of earth in a breath of air, and the natural aspect of the sun sinking below the horizon, leaving a reflection on the forests as crows go back to their nests in the pine groves. All these lovely places of former days have been altered from green meadow lands into crowded modern real estate. The picturesque old thatched cottages have given way to cheap wooden houses with roofs of galvanized iron and red-brown painted tin, which cram the narrow crooked suburban streets. Foreigners often are puzzled by this aspect of Japan.

Visits to the farm were varied by trips to the beach—to Kamakura, about forty miles from Tokyo. Today Kamakura is a healthful residential spot for suburbanites who commute to the capital. In the summer Tokyo residents move en masse to the Kamakura shore for the sea bathing, riding every day by hundreds of thousands on the government railroad. All the year round it is the Mecca of sightseers. About eight hundred years ago this seashore town was the capital of Japan. Yoritomo established the first feudal government there. The place is well favored by nature, surrounded by wall-like hills opening only on its south side, Yui beach on the Pacific. The climate is mild at all seasons, and the scenery is marvelous.

The giant Buddha meditates at Kamakura, upon his lotus throne set against a background of hills covered with green forests of ancient pines and cherries and plums. They are planted in the Buddha's garden, pouring showers of pink petals and delicious scent over him in the spring. Gently, dreamily, passionlessly, he reposes. The solemnly beautiful face with the half closed eyes has been described by Lafcadio Hearn as typifying all that is tender and calm in the soul of the East. Kamakura is rich with many other historical monuments and centuries-old shrines and temples.

The red lacquered shrine of Hachiman and two most famous temples of the Zen sect, Engakuji and Kenchoji, are surrounded by deep forests of mastlike cryptomeria, whose tall brown trunks, straight and aspiring, lift the visitor's eyes to the sky which fills him with serenity.

In these holy places I loved the religious solemnity of the atmosphere. At the Engakuji and Kenchoji temples one passes through numbers of gates, of stupendous structure, with sweeping curves and huge gabled roofs. Big tablets—written in Chinese ideographs—attract the eye. At Kenchoji temple I used to climb up the dilapidated stone steps, with grass springing in every breach and break, up the shady hillroad to the little temple of the famous bell several hundred years old. The bronze bell itself is nine feet high, its surface covered with text from the Buddhist sutra. It rolls out deep yet musical sounds over the hills—a mournful murmur which, long-continued and echoing back from the hills, led my thoughts far back to the Japan of feudal days when Kamakura was at its peak of glory.

The ancient graves of feudal heroes and their women are arranged in the always-quiet temple courts, their eternal sleep uninterrupted by the soughing pine woods. At the front of the inner temple hall are plain round wooden pillars, cross beams and vast eaves which sustain the ponderous and complicated upper structure. Temple fountains of bronze stand before the doors. From its immense and beautiful lotus-leaf metal, forming a broad shallow basin kept full to the brim by a jet in its center, I was wont to scoop handfuls of crystal water to quench my thirst. These were all dear places of my childhood, and they remain both dear and unchanged.

My grandfather lived at Kamakura after he retired from social activities, and mother sent her six children to this summer place every year from July to September, and sometimes during the short holidays in the spring. In those slow and leisurely days, a trip from Tokyo to Kamakura was a full day's undertaking. A train of several rikishas would carry mother, elder brother, myself, younger brothers and sisters and maids—two youngsters would ride in a rikisha together, and one or two rikishas carrying big trunks of bedding, spare kimonos and accessories, books and toys all wrapped up in the big square green furoshiki (cloth for wrapping) would follow in the rear of the procession. The rikishamen ran with speed on the flat roads

along the moat under the hanging branches of willows or down
hilly roads between the brick government buildings to Hibiya
Park, but they were slow when they climbed hills, making
zigzag curves while the persons who were riding would bend
their bodies forward trying to cause these men less strain.

About forty minutes' ride would bring us to Shimbashi
Station—we can make it in five minutes by motor today—the
terminus of the Tokaido highway. There we bought tickets,
checked the luggage and waited for the railway guard to ring
a hand bell, announcing the train. In the train, mother would
hush the children who, being so excited, were always on the
verge of commotion, for to be on a train was really a rare treat
for us. We never tired of looking out the windows. After ten
or fifteen minutes' ride, we would come so close to the shore of
Tokyo Bay, the water came so near to the track, that the waves
would almost wash over the rails. Not far away several square
islands, built on piles of natural stones and covered with green
turf, could be seen when the sea was calm. These were the
O-daiba, the naval fortifications erected by the Tokugawa government to protect the city from naval invaders. Here the white
sails of cargo and fishing boats would be appearing and hiding
again between the artificial green islands.

Between Tokyo and Kamakura the train would stop at
eleven stations, each time for five to ten minutes, prolonging
the trip on the train to fully three hours. In repeating this slow
journey many times, all the scenery along the route became
thoroughly and affectionately impressed on my mind. When the
railway line ran a little nearer to the wooded hillside along the
Tokaido, the views on both sides were continuations of farms
and rice fields with pine and chestnut trees, bamboo and shrubs
covering the slopes. The farms from Omori to Yokohama
harbor would be covered with the yellow blooms of natane, and
rose renge [1] would thickly carpet the rice fields in the spring. It

---

[1] A kind of grass.

was an immense spread of velvetlike verdure lined with yellow, rose and green patterns luxurious to the eye.

Another delightful panorama from the train window in the spring was the succession of peach orchards. They came in flat masses of trees five or six feet high. As the train sped along, one saw a succession of pink and white blossoms. A peach tree in full bloom near a farmer's cottage contrasted with the rich brown thatched roof and made the blossoms look like a blazing jet of fire.

But in the late summer the view from the train was nothing but green. Green foliage and green fields. Only one-sixth of Japan is arable, which is a great pity from an economic standpoint, but highly advantageous from the standpoint of beauty. The cultivated regions themselves are broken up and broken into by invading mountains and long arms of sea, where crops give way to forests or to fishing villages. One of the charms of the country is the endless, intricate extent and rich variety of its coast line. Japan has no great rivers, such as those running through continental lands, but it is full of mountain streams, cut off into irrigating ditches to supply the paddy fields. The rice fields are built in rectangular plots with narrow lines of black soil for partitions. And in early June, in adjoining fields, the harvesting of the first wheat and the transplanting of the rice begin. This transplanting is terribly hard labor, yet to the onlooker at least it seems appealing: a group of eight or ten young men and maidens in line, the orange or purple obis and red underskirts of the girls, their hair covered with white and blue tengui-towel, impart a touch of gaiety to the picture. Their kimonos tucked up above their rugged knees, all of them advance together in a strong march over the flooded fields. These rice fields of vivid green in the summer and waves of golden brown in the autumn harvest season meet the eye of travelers all through the country where the soil is arable and fit for irrigation.

Around Totsuka, a flat territory of farms, the land is narrow and the landscape more hilly. The rural cottages, dotted here and there along the road or on the hillside, are strangely picturesque in their ancient style, dingy, neutral-tinted, with steeply-sloping roofs of thatch above clay walls and paper shoji screens. Often on the sloping roofs are green patches of some sort of moss, and on the ridges rows of sweet flag bearing pretty purple flowers. I loved those gardens on the roofs of village cottages, and wanted to plant similar ones on my father's villa in Kamakura.

After running through a tunnel, we were at Kamakura Station. On the open ground outside the station a fleet of rikishas was always awaiting the travelers. There would follow then another procession of rikishas—their speed is slower in the country—which would carry us through the narrow streets of Hase, then turn down to the little town on the seashore redolent with the odor of drying seaweed, borne from the shore by the gentle breeze. This harbinger of vacation and the seaside would excite us children and we would jump from the small platform of our rikishas and present ourselves gaily to grandfather impatiently watching for our coming.

My grandfather was a true samurai, very stubborn, unwilling to accept a new social order. We loved him, but with a bit of fearfulness. He suffered from rheumatism, and could not walk without someone to support him. Ordinarily he sat in a big chair with a nurse attending him. When the children made too much noise, grandfather's thunder broke through the whole house and we ran upstairs, our haven of safety.

Our house at Kamakura was situated at the western edge of the town. It was built on the cliff at the foot of the Inamuragasaki promontory, whose green arm stretches far into the bay. The house had an excellent view of the whole town and the broad beach of dun-colored sand which continues on the farther side of the horseshoe arch embracing the bay. The water's ebbing and flowing made a pleasant sound all the day and night, bringing also a delicious occasional breeze into the villa through the opened shoji screens. On a moonlight evening, the long line of beach and the flickering reflections of light on the calm water, seen through twisted old pine trees surrounding the house, made us sentimental. Beyond the straight line of land was another peninsula, then once more a land fading gradually into the farther distance with the chain of dotted lights twinkling and twinkling without sound. In the morning the sea was blue and it was gradually turned into a deep cobalt as the sun mounted high. When the air was clear, far away on the horizon, specked with snowy sails, the silhouette of Oshima —the volcanic island covered with camellia blossoms—appeared like a dream island, like vapor from the summit of the volcano.

We spent most of the daytime bathing. Sometimes we collected different kinds of butterflies and cicadas, or gathered innumerable kinds of dainty pink, purple, gray or white shells—so pearly on Japanese shores—and kept them in caskets as if they were precious jewels. There were a good many of my schoolmates spending the summer here, so the long days were never too long for me. Evenings were spent with grandfather who told us old, old stories of how he fought for his "lord" in the civil war at the time of the Meiji restoration. And it was the fashion at this summer resort to take a stroll after supper. This attempt at "evening cooling," according to the Japanese fashion, was somewhat playful. I shall long remember searching for coolness with my girl friends by sitting on the edge of the fishermen's boats drawn up on the shore, while far away the rim of shore line sparkled with lights, the plaintive tones of bamboo flutes were wafted from village cottages, and the breeze from the ocean toyed with our hair and our blue and white yukata kimono sleeves. Often, strolling along the narrow country streets lined with little shops, we carried paper lanterns marked with our family crests. With their names dyed in big white Chinese ideographs, these shops exhibited fascinating miniature articles against their indigo draperies. Mother permitted us to buy some souvenirs each year before we left Kamakura. How I struggled with indecision amidst these mountains of sea treasures! There were sets of golden screens made out of numerous varieties of pearl-like shells on which was pasted a picture of Mount Fuji or of cherry blossoms; or small chests and boxes suitable for decoration. And jewelry for girls —rings, hairpins, brooches, necklaces, combs, small fans—all so alluring and at fabulously low prices!

When it was getting on toward the end of August, insects began to contribute their sweet music in the grassy thickets along the hillsides. Grandfather could not go out to the hills to hear them as he would have loved so much to do, so it was the task of the grandchildren to bring the insects to him. Wild autumn plants with pink, white and yellow flowers were growing almost high enough to hide us. We took with us to the hill a sheet of grass mat which one of us held horizontally, making a wall in the grass, while another hung a lantern by the mat wall. Then the rest hunted in the grass. The poor insects, disturbed in their musical mood, jumped toward the light and fell against the mat. We caught them and put them into our bamboo cage.

These insects are about one inch long, with gauzelike wings of a beige color. The matsu-mushi (pine insect) has a brown spot on each wing, and a complicated trilling note, while the suzu-mushi (bell insect) has a soft long-drawn monotone. Their orchestral music is as dear to the Japanese as the spring birds' call is to Western people.

Our matsu-mushi and suzu-mushi were hung under the eaves of the veranda outside grandfather's room. "Chin Chin Chin-chiro-rin - - -," the pine insect sang. And the bell insect tuned in with, "Rin-rin-rin-rin - - - " for the night-long concert. In the morning we fed the little musicians with fresh cucumbers and sliced eggplant. How grandfather adored pine insects! I preferred the bell insects. But occasionally when I woke in the night and heard these insects singing in the darkness of the long corridor, an immense loneliness came over me without reason.

When this village began to decorate its front eaves with red paper lanterns, heralding the autumn festivals, we prepared for our return to the city, leaving grandfather behind, lonely except for the bell insects and the pine insects in the cage and the wild crickets which had gathered without an invitation in our garden to join this grand orchestra.

My grandfather passed away peacefully at the age of seventy. In his will he left me a brown crepe furoshiki with white mountain cherry blossoms dyed upon it, a red tsui-shu (carved and red lacquered) jewelry box and a manuscript bound with a purple silk cord, bearing the title *On-na Daigaku* (*Great Learning for Women*) in beautiful Chinese ideographs. I cherished these three things with affectionate and reverent remembrances of grandfather. But later, when I realized what was written in the manuscript, I could not help revolting against the conception of woman disclosed in this book. It was the epitome of all I have had to struggle against—the moral code which has chained Japanese women to the past. It made me see, not myself, but all women of my race, yesterday, today and perhaps tomorrow. What a strange present to give a young girl!

PART TWO
STUDENT DAYS

Myself at the age of fifteen in full Japanese costume

Princess Aya Tokugawa in her ancient court noble's costume of scarlet brocade. The princess married Marquis Yasumasa Matsudaira

IV

Kindergarten and Primary School—Feudal Discipline at the Peeresses' School

*L*IKE Eton College in England, the Peers' School in Japan has its significance in educating the younger generation of aristocrats. As soon as the great wave of political upheaval seemed settled, in 1877 the Emperor Mutsuhito commanded a department of the imperial household to establish the Peers' School, laying stress upon the importance and peculiarity of character building for the class which was to be the leading force in the nation. Thus Gakushuin began its career and today it is still directly attached to the Imperial Household Department, while all the other institutions for learning are controlled by the Department of Education. Ten years after the Peers' School was founded, the Empress Haruko expressed her intention of providing education for the girls of the ruling class. This she carried out in the Peeresses' School, beginning with a kindergarten where small boys and girls played together. The late Emperor Taisho, father of the present Mikado, the Empress Dowager, the present Emperor and Empress all began their studies in this institution, and many young royal princes and princesses are attending it at present. It is almost a rule for the peers to send their sons and daughters here, and a few children from other families of high social standing are also allowed to enter this school.

I started my schooling at the kindergarten of the Peeresses' School, when I was five years old. Little boys and girls of aristocratic birth were brought to this kindergarten carefully protected by their servants, some wrapped in soft silk quilts and riding on the nurses' knees in the rikishas, as if their parents were afraid even a soft wind might kill their little ones.

The noble features and graceful manners of these diminutive lords and princesses showed their aristocratic background of many generations, but healthy and strengthening activities were lacking to them. Miss Yuka Noguchi, the principal of the kindergarten and a Christian, had been appointed to remedy this defect. She was a student of child psychology and well suited for the position. Preaching the Christian gospel to the little aristocrats was quite another matter, however.

When the teachers greeted the children on my first day at the kindergarten, some hid their delicate faces behind the kimono sleeves of their maids and some kept their mouths tightly shut. I remember I was half frightened and half curious about this new world of the school, but as the days passed I became quite cheerful and naughty also. Fifteen or seventeen girls and about the same number of boys were in my class. Nearly a hundred children were there together, divided into three classes. Several assistant teachers helped Miss Noguchi.

The teachers took us to the flower garden or let us play in the sandbox where we built hills and waterfalls. Then we played tug-of-war under the shadowy wisteria trellises. Indoors, we learned paper folding, and how to make flying storks, sailing ships, blooming lotus, walking postmen and many other shapes with colorful rice paper. Also we drew pictures, learned simple embroidery and other handwork. At a given time, we gathered in the big hall where the teacher played the piano while we sang songs and performed simple dances. The favorite song with Japanese children of any class is the "Song of the Temple Doves."

> Hato Poppo! Hato Poppo!
> Poppo, Poppo to Nai-te Asobe!
> Otera-no Yanekara Orite Koi!
> Mameo Yarukara Mina Tabe yo!
> Tabe temo Suguni Kaerazuni,
> Poppo, Poppo to Nai-te Asobe!

Come, little doves, come, little doves!
Sing your song "Hato Poppo!"
Come down from the temple roof!
Here are beans for you, little doves!
Feed yourself with all the beans I have,
But don't leave me soon,
Play with me, little doves, singing, "Hato Poppo!"

The teachers paid special attention to the enunciation and the manner of our conversation; we used the traditional aristocratic vocabulary which is so different from ordinary Japanese that it sounds almost like another tongue.

I spent two years in this kindergarten; then I was old enough to enter the first grade in the primary section of the Peeresses' School. This meant that I and the other little girls were separated from our boy friends, whom we have never had a chance to study with again or even to see. But the thought that such and such men of distinction today were the little boys who often cried in the playroom at the kindergarten, at my side, is some consolation.

I felt quite dignified when I first put on my red hakama-skirt over my kimono, a sign that I was a student in the school proper and no longer an infant in the kindergarten. The Peeresses' School was located on one of the most beautiful sites in Tokyo, occupying the top of a hill covered with cherry blossoms in the season. The old school is gone in part, but there are remnants of it yet across the Benkei Bashi, the ancient wooden bridge, over the outer moat of the imperial palace by Akasaka Mitsuke, and up the slope through the groves of cherry trees. Formerly there was a tall ancient wooden gate with black painted iron fittings. White walls with tiled tops surrounded the school grounds, enclosing a row of stables and large mat rooms for the attendant maids and rikishamen, accommodations peculiar to this school for aristocrats. I walked to school most of the time as it was only fifteen minutes from my home but sometimes Katsu, our family rikishaman, rushed me there in a swift flight. As he was always proud of his unusual speed in pulling his rikisha for my father, he felt a little girl like me too light to notice. Racing very fast, we passed so many other rikishas carrying my friends that I was quite embarrassed. I had to bow to each of them with an expression of apology for my haste.

Our main school building was a red brick two-storied structure in Victorian style—the Victorian style was ravenously copied in the early Meiji period—with the gilded double cherry blossom, the coat of arms of the school, engraved on the front door. A wooden building, also of Western style, which had much wider windows and surrounded a court, supplemented the main building. A botanical garden and a large wisteria garden were off at the rear, while other open spaces between the buildings were planted with huge oaks, ginkgo, cherry and other trees.

Each class in the primary section consisted of thirty-five girls, about half of whom had come up from the kindergarten. In the classroom each girl sat on an individual chair with a square wooden desk before her, while the teacher took a seat on the platform in front of a large blackboard. Those who spent eleven years together in this school, from the kindergarten through the primary and high school course, came to have a feeling of real sisterhood since the Peeresses' School was the only place of learning for the girls of this class. Among my classmates were the present Viscountess Toshi Matsudaira, Marchioness Tame Tokugawa, Marchioness Aya Matsudaira, all of whom are the wives of prominent nobles. There were four princesses, three girls from marquises', four from counts', ten from viscounts', and four from barons' families. Others were the daughters of high officials, prominent businessmen, and other important people in Japan.

Some girls drove to school in their coaches, but many came

by rikisha with the gilt family crest painted on the back and drawn by rikishamen in black satin happi-coats embroidered with the same crest. Girls of the daimyo families arrived with maids in separate rikishas following their mistresses. When such a family had more than one daughter to send to school, each of the girls was followed by her own maid-in-waiting, sometimes even by a household steward, a man in Western frock coat, or in a kimono and hakama.[1] Thus three girls in a family would have seven rikishas in their grand daimyo procession. Maids and rikishamen waited at the school until the classes were over. I do not know what these men did with the long empty hours, but the maids stayed in the quarters assigned to them, sewing colorful silks into kimonos for their mistresses. The school provided them with a special sewing teacher. Many of my friends were brought up to have everything done for them by maids. They never carried their own books but wrapped them with furoshiki and turned them over to their maids. When they had run about in the playground too much and their long hair had become disorderly, they went to their maids to have it fixed and to have their noses powdered. It was considered a disgrace to look after any of one's own affairs.

The girls played together happily in the school garden, but when we did "playing guests" or "playing princess," it was quite a complicated matter. We had a difficult time deciding whom to choose as the honorable one. When a royal princess was with us we all agreed to ask her to be the "princess" in our play, but otherwise this honor became a serious problem. Each little princess and countess claimed the role for her family, and if the seat of the princess was given to a girl whose family history was less important than another's, the latter would think she was disgraced and would say, "I will leave you!" The whole game would be upset by unpleasant feelings.

---

[1] Japanese ceremonial costume for men.

This quarrel among the girls was in fact ridiculous, but a grave matter to the young.

Among the four princesses in my class was Princess Aya, daughter of Prince Iyesato Tokugawa, who would have been the sixteenth shogun to govern the island empire, if the social order had not been changed forty years before. There was also Princess Tame whose family, the Shimazus, is one of the wealthiest in the daimyo class, and, besides, Prince Shimazu's ancestor was in the same rank with Prince Tokugawa's before the Tokugawa shogunate was established three hundred years ago. The imperial family had later conferred great honors on the Shimazus because of their meritorious work in accomplishing the Meiji political restoration, transferring the power from the Tokugawa shogunate to the Emperor. How these little girls of ten tried to decide in their playtime which family was greater, in reference to their historical background!

Girls from the houses of smaller feudal lords would be humble enough to take the part of ladies-in-waiting, or subjects to the great lady, but the daughters of court nobles who were mostly counts or viscounts, if not so wealthy and powerful as the feudal nobles—indeed, some of them were desperately poor, would not dare to take the part of subjects to the girls from the great feudal families, as they believed that their own families made up the most refined circle around the imperial court. They had the habit of looking down even on the daimyo class as one engaged only in barbarous fighting. These feudal traditions affected the innocent minds of these young girls so deeply that they could not think of a person apart from house and rank. But they may be excused when we consider their heritage of three hundred years of tradition, at least.

"Playing princess" involved plenty of bowing on the maids' part. But these little aristocrats, brought up in endless formalities, could not but be ceremonious even in their play. They bowed and waited assiduously on the princess who like a doll quietly stood or sat on the imaginary throne of grass, and they bowed to each other, exchanging polite greetings and cere-monial gifts. Yet sometimes a flash of imagination appeared. Some brave youngster would take the part of a demon and fall upon the frightened ladies, who ran away screaming. A few were truly terrified, but most of the girls had real fun in this hearty shouting and running.

At the start of the Meiji era, all the Japanese were declared by law to be equal and monogamy was fixed as the foundation of the moral code. But when I awakened to social conscious-ness, only three decades had passed since these new laws had been effective and there was almost no understanding of the actual meaning of equality. It took some time for the people to realize the least significance in this new social order, as must be the case in the history of every great social change. Consti-tutionally we were in a grand new era, but privately we lived in essentially the same old feudal way. Even after the honors of peerage were given to the former daimyos and court nobles, most of them continued to behave as they had before and the wave of revolution did not penetrate the walls of their mansions.

Yet all was not serene even so. For instance, the girls whose families were formerly those of feudal lords living according to fixed traditions of behavior had strange and be-wildering problems to meet in many cases. The members called the head of the family "lord" privately, and "count," "marquis," or whatever the title was, publicly. And these lords were legally married to just one woman, but in reality there were many concubines in the house, and though social custom did not frown on concubinage, it raised grave issues for women. The lords usually divided their household into two sections, known as the "outer" and the "inner." The "outer" section was where the offices were, and was formerly situated in the Upper Man-sion. But when the Upper Mansions were confiscated by the imperial government at the beginning of the Meiji restoration, the offices were moved to the Lower Mansion which each daimyo was allowed to retain as his residence. Usually retainers managed these household offices, and formal receptions, family councils and other business affairs were carried on in this part of the house. The "inner" part was the private residence, connected as a rule with the other part by long corridors within the same enclosure. But these two parts of the mansion were separated completely by the "bell door," and only a selected few men were allowed to go beyond it, for the "inner" part was the world of women. When "lord" went out, he was followed by his wife and attendant women to the "bell door" where the silk-tasseled, big, bronze bell was rung and the lord was received by the men from the "outer" section; these, in ceremonial dress, had been waiting there in a pose of utmost obeisance. The ladies in gorgeous brocades and embroidery bowed the lord off and returned to their high-walled rear quarters. Women were never to go beyond that door except on formal occasions when they received permission. The "inner" part consisted of the lord's apartment, the lady's apartments, those for elderly ladies-in-waiting, those for younger ladies-in-waiting, and the rooms for the maids who worked for those ladies-in-waiting.

"O-Kiyo" and "O-Kegare," "the Honorable Pure" and "the Honorable Impure," were the two classifications into which the young women-in-waiting were divided. The former means the virgin maids to the lord or the lady; the latter indicates the girls who, to use the barbaric Japanese phrase, were honorably touched by the lord. These girls were to attend the lord and lady for life, help them in their dressing rooms, clean, dust and do everything for them. But when a child was born to the lord by one of these women, it was formally registered into the household and permitted to call the lord the "Honorable Father the Superior" and the lady "The Honorable Mother the Superior," while the real mother remained in her servile position as a maid-in-waiting throughout her life. Only after death were the mothers of these illegitimate children treated as semi-members of the family. A gravestone was given to each in the family cemetery with the Buddhist posthumous name honorably engraved.

Although the customs have since been bettered, still the Japanese wife's legal position is precarious. The official council, assigned to investigate possible changes in the civil code, is trying to give the married women the right to refuse the registration of an illegitimate child in her domicile, but nobody knows when this law will be enacted and observed.

Girls of this aristocracy married with great pomp, requiring hundreds of thousands of possessions as a bride—but seldom money or land. Along with their trousseaux, they brought to their grooms' homes beautifully dressed elder and younger maids. They brought their gentility and their training into their new abodes. But they never expected to receive their husband's love for long, if at all. These marriages were arranged primarily for political purposes, interweaving families of wealth and power to enhance glory or to reaffirm a steadfast connection. They were never the outcome of mutual love and understanding. The helpless wife left her fate entirely to the political abilities of the elder lady-in-waiting whom she had brought at the head of her train of maids from her father's house, and it was this woman's business to obtain as many opportunities as possible for the wife to visit her lord's apartment. Whether the wife loved her husband or not was of scant importance, but she did have absolute controlling power over the administration in the inner household. Even the lord's most beloved "honorable impure" was under her rule. Naturally the lady's displeasure was chiefly aimed at those

women who were the lord's favorites. Oh! How much agony
and cruel struggle seethe even today behind the magnificent
formalities and the thickly powdered and smiling faces of Japanese wives! I regret to say that we have not yet come far in
the battle to throw off these unreasonable customs of the past.

Girls who have been brought up in the midst of these
struggles often take them as matters which cannot be helped,
but a few like me, whose families have had particularly clear
records, find it impossible to tolerate such unreasonable traditions. Never can I accept the feudal discipline of women
which, strongly surviving, teaches them to repress jealousy to
an extreme degree, jealousy being the worst possible sin for a
woman! The wounded pride and the suppressed passion of
these aristocratic women cannot but be turned into distorted
forms of hypocrisy in the strong, and horrible cruelty in the
weak. It reminds me of the old story of Ishido-maru, whose
father was an honorable samurai, living with his wife and
concubines, all outwardly amicable. One night when he happened to waken he saw both his wife's and his concubine's hair
coiling and changing into serpents, which hissed and bit each
other. The serpents were the embodiment of the two women's
jealousy. The warrior grieved much at this revelation of secret
bitterness. Finally, he shaved his head and became a monk in
the Buddhist monastery of Koya-san near Kyoto, where he
dwelt until the day of his death. His son Ishido-maru, never
having known his father, made a trip to the mountain monastery to see him, but the monk, having vowed to cast off all
ties with this world, would not reveal himself, though the boy
was before him and anxious to meet his father face to face.
Our ancestors wept to hear this story recited to the accompaniment of the biwa harp! But how can I?

The feudal moral code has made Japanese women's inner
struggles severe beyond measure. One of my intimate friends

at the Peeresses' School was Sumi-sama, a charming little princess, whose great-grandfather was a court noble well known for the role he had played during the Meiji restoration in helping the young Mikado to regain his rights. Sumi-sama was just a little younger than I. The long-inherited aristocratic beauty could be seen in her features, in her long, long hair, which she wore hanging down her back, and in her graceful bearing. She was kind and pleasant to everybody, and I truly loved her. When she was in the third grade, and I in the fourth, suddenly a new girl entered my class, who was introduced as the elder sister of my dear Sumi-sama. Sumi-sama never had told me that she had an elder sister, and to my surprise there was only a few months' difference in their ages. The sisters were dressed exactly alike and came to school followed by a common train of attendants. The elder girl was much shorter than Sumi-sama but there was a close facial resemblance. Sumi-sama's attitude toward her sister was cold and distant, although she observed the conventions. This aroused in me a great deal of curiosity about my friend's family. Soon I learned that this newcomer from the house of the prince was a child born to Sumi-sama's father by a so-called member of the "Honorable Impure"; for some reason she had previously been sent to a common school. Recently, however, she had been separated from her own mother, formally registered and gathered into Sumi-sama's select circle, evidently to the latter's distaste. There were many illegitimate little girls among my schoolmates: their life appeared placid on the surface, but their inner life was always touched with tragedy. Sumi-sama's sister was never treated cordially by anyone. After the two girls graduated from the school, Sumi-sama was married to a young nobleman belonging to a great feudal family. Her sister was married to a man whose father was a newly-created baron. Recently the news that Sumi-sama's niece had become a member of the Communist party, which is unlawful in Japan, and had been arrested came as a great shock to all the nobility. But this young aristocrat communist committed suicide soon after she was released by the authorities, leaving her mother in unconsolable sorrow. Others, who know the bondage of feudal customs still encumbering the proud aristocracy, more easily understand the revolt of this young princess which ended so dramatically.

V

High School Years

AT THE age of twelve, I finished the primary course in the Peeresses' School and entered the high school in the same compound, which was supposed to correspond to the boys' middle school. In reality there was a distinct difference between the two in the standard and character of learning. Boys were taught and trained to be "great personalities"; girls were first and foremost taught to become obedient wives, good mothers and loyal guardians of the family system. This discrimination was not calculated to encourage girls to independent thinking. Women were not expected to be pioneers in any enterprise.

The five years' education in the girls' high school was looked upon as the grand finishing course, so that few girls remained at school for postgraduate work. Arithmetic, algebra, Euclid, physics, chemistry, national and foreign geography and history were taught, but we were only allowed to peep into the world of science and did not spend much time or energy on any one of the more approved subjects. Japanese literature, both classical and modern, covered the largest part of class assignments, for as a matter of fact well-educated Japanese citizens had to learn at least four or five thousand Chinese ideographs, most of which are pronounced in three or four different ways and written in at least three styles. A vast amount of attention had to be bestowed on these. Besides this strenuous memory work, penmanship, painting, drawing, music, sewing, embroidery and cooking were taught in both the Western and the Japanese manner. The girls were kept quite busy.

Even penmanship for the Japanese is no trifle. A woman cannot marry into a good family if she reveals a sign of low breeding in her handwriting. And men will experience disadvantages in getting positions unless their handwriting is good. When distinguished men travel and stay overnight in a hotel or a country inn, they are always pestered by the host for specimens of their handwriting. The innkeeper will bring white silk or rice paper and an instrument as big as a club, asking them to write some lucky verses or seasonal sayings—a note of distinction in comparison with the scribbled signs of others in the guest book! Their calligraphies will be mounted and put on the wall in the guests' rooms. Nor does penmanship mean writing with a pen. Japanese writing is done with a brush and actually it is sensitive painting, even when the brush is enormous. The artistic quality of Japanese writing reveals the personality of the writer as much as a painting does that of the artist, so that it cannot be entirely replaced by the convenient typewriter.

At school, therefore, we spent hours and hours bending over our desks and white sheets of rice paper, in our hands big and small brushes which we dipped in India ink, writing Japanese characters, stroke by stroke, trying to present graceful and dignified ideographs. For this work we had one of the greatest teachers of calligraphy in Japan. His name was Gadô Ono: it was then and still is almost a magic word to the Japanese. People would pay fabulous prices for a strip of paper bearing his exquisite brush strokes expressing a thirty-one syllable poem. In the classroom we had the printed models of his calligraphy and carefully imitated each stroke and each shape of a letter. The teacher came round the room, commenting on each girl's work and correcting it with his red brush. No sound except his soft footsteps was heard throughout the hour. The students were intent on learning this sacred art and breathless over the movement of the brush. Not satis-

fied with the classwork, most girls went to the teacher's house
for private tutoring. Being a private pupil of this great master
was one of the clear marks of aristocracy.

It was almost the same with drawing. For this art we used,
besides India ink, a dozen colors and many kinds of brushes;
and along with rice paper, sheets of white silk. We had printed
models of the teacher's drawings and spent many hours trying
to copy, not only the shape but also the brush strokes forming
a bamboo, a chrysanthemum, a plum branch with a nightingale sitting on it, a misty view of Mount Fuji, or a mountain
cascade. Over and over we repeated these subjects, for we
could not get a passing mark until we could draw them in the
proper shape without any mistake in the strokes. In addition
to this, we had to work swiftly, being allowed only a quarter
of an hour or twenty minutes for each assignment.

Another lesson, rather unpopular among the girls, was
ethics. In this class we were taught that loyalty and filial piety
are the chief and fundamental morals, that our conduct should
be directed to expressing our sense of gratitude to the Emperor
as obedient subjects, and to parents and ancestors as faithful
daughters. At the Peeresses' School, the girls recited these
precepts every morning before the lessons, saying, "We girls
in the Peeresses' School shall respect the imperial family, and
try to be model subjects loyal to the Emperor and the Empress . . ."

A Westerner might consider this ritual a religious exercise,
but it was not that. It was a ritual of Shintoism, which is rather
the cult of the state. Religiously, Buddhism has most influenced
the Japanese mind and trained it to believe in "the fugitive
nature of life on the earth." Nothing of either Shintoism or
Buddhism, however, served us as a moral guide in the way
Christianity serves the West. This ethics class at our school was
relied upon for character building. Its substance lay in the
Confucian teachings emphasizing loyalty to the ruler and duty

to parents. We were brought up to think frequently of our obligations to our elders and to the Emperor. We were taught what "we ought to do and to be," but never did we discuss questions of personal freedom and independent thinking or the right to be guided by one's own conscience. A familiar proverb said: "Good medicine is bitter to the mouth: so is good advice to naughty ears." Naturally the girls disliked these preachings, pounding again and again on tired ears.

To reinforce these moral obligations we were given lessons in "manners and etiquette," that we might be disciplined in modesty and reverence. Our school had a separate house, built in pure Japanese style, for instruction in etiquette. It had a mat floor and an alcove in which the essential ornaments were placed in strict accordance with the prescriptions of the Ogasawara School of Etiquette. We took off our shoes before we entered the house and sat rigid on the mats. We learned formality of every possible kind, such as wedding and funeral ceremonies in both Shinto and Buddhist styles, the reception of guests, and entertaining or being entertained at table. The complexity of this instruction was such that we had to practice, for instance, sitting and standing positions, and three forms of bowing: to elders, to equals, and to inferiors. As in everything else in Japanese life, these three different social degrees were taken into account. A most circumscribed way of living!

To entertain and to be entertained at table was an affair of the most agonizing maze of rules. A formal dinner in the Ogasawara style requires the correct use of two or three soup bowls, five to nine dishes, a sake cup, and a rice bowl, all lacquered black outside and red inside, served on three to five different lacquered trays, with ponderous dignity even though the actual food they contain is unsubstantial. Every movement in handling the chopsticks and bowls, in eating and drinking, was prescribed for us, in its proper order too, even to the approximate number of grains for a mouthful of rice! We had to learn how to train the servants: their manner of carrying trays, walking on the mat floor, and sitting to offer sake or rice. In the etiquette practice-hall we girls sat absolutely silent and took part by turn in this ceremonious play, characteristic of endless leisure and calling for limitless patience. And we were as serious as if life consisted solely of formalities which, if carefully preserved, leave nothing more to be desired. Indeed, knowledge itself could be nothing but formality to us who were to take it from the voice of authority as the infallible guide for the movement of the mind. We were never to criticize or doubt it.

Japanese culture has long rested on the silkworm. So great is its importance as a national asset that empresses have patronized it at court and noblewomen still learn to care for the tiny creatures. What in former days was a creative art has become a cult. When the season came for raising silkworms, the girls at our school, therefore, practiced feeding them and watching the entire process of silk production, from digestion to the soft white raw material outcome. All the girls in my class had been wrapped in silk from their birth, but few of them liked to handle the disagreeable worms which created it. I was one of them; I hated worms of any kind. Occasionally some mischievous companions would put wriggling white worms, two or three inches long, into the drawers of my desk! Once a year we were taken to inspect a silk factory where we saw tens of thousands of the silvery cocoons boiled and untwined into silk thread by the clever hands of the factory workers, whose fingers were blistered from working in hot water all day long. None of the small aristocrats in the Peeresses' School in those days ever thought of the problems of working-girls. Instead, we felt deep gratitude to our ancestors and parents for the fact that we were not born into poor families whose daughters were destined to lead a miserable life.

When my classmates got into the high school grades, usually

at the age of twelve, they felt very grown-up and ladylike and began to wear kimonos with long sleeves. Even the dressing of their hair was different now. Girls in the grammar school wore short hair, but when they were ready for the high school they began to let their hair grow so that soon they could wear a high puff in front, with colorful ribbons on top of the puff, letting the rest of their long hair hang down the back tied with white cords. The longer their shining black hair, the prouder the girls were of it, and often it came down to the back of the knees. A long-sleeved purple silk kimono, a red cashmerc skirt that reached the heels and black Western shoes formed the most prevalent style for the students at the Peeresses' School.

The honor was given the students of this school to visit O-hama Detached Palace or Shinjuku Palace for the spring festival of cherry blossoms, and Akasaka Palace at the time of the chrysanthemum party in autumn. O-hama Palace has a beautifully landscaped garden built for Tokugawa shoguns, who enjoyed elaborate picnics here in the days of feudal splendor. The enormous acreage of this place is largely enclosed by thick groves of old pines, but on the south side it is open to the immense view over a steep cliff of piled rocks to the bay of Tokyo. A lake filled with green water occupies the center of the garden, the winding and twisting lines of its edge providing attractive variations in the picture. The hills and grounds are all of smooth, green turf, constantly trimmed by gardeners of the imperial household. Double cherry blossoms, rich varieties of Japanese maples, pine trees, isolated from the groves and reaching out at strange angles with their knotted arms, are part of the display planted according to the artistic taste and rules of Japanese gardening, so that every view of this lake has its particular harmony. The graceful cherry trees heavily laden with pale pink blossoms call attention to their dark gray trunks, lustrous skins between the pinkish mists, reflected on the water.

At the imperial pavilion which rests in the midst of the lake, the junior girls from the school were allowed to open their lunch boxes. The pavilion was approached by a long wooden bridge with low round rails. Carp of golden red, black and white, more than two feet long, gathered with their families under these bridges to be fed. Big flocks of wild geese came here to entertain the imperial hunting party in the winter season.

Akasaka Palace is located close to the Peeresses' School. Its grounds are attached to the residences of some of the royal princes. The scale of its landscape garden is bigger and the hills are more imposing, covered thickly with numerous varieties of green plants. Many of them, the oaks, ginkgos, camphors, cedars and pasanias, are tall and broad, leaving almost no space for a glimpse of the sky. Hundreds of kinds of trees, uneven in height, each different in shape, sometimes with obliquely stretching branches, give an ever-interesting individuality to a lavish Japanese garden. Under the plants grow thick masses of low bamboo shrubs, and beneath them velvet-like green moss of several species clings to the ground. Maples are queen among all garden trees, competing with one another in their personalities. With their minutely cut leaves like old handmade Spanish lace, with rich hues in blossom time, dark brown, yellow brown, pure yellow, red, scarlet, each separate leaf distinct in form, they epitomize the exquisite work of nature. These displays of bewitching foliage on the rolling hills along the calm lake or over the arched bridges, the water reflecting them together with the colorful kimonos and red hakama-skirts of maidens, gracefully join in a composition of indescribable loveliness. Following the narrow passage paved with gray sandy gravel and few easy steps up and down on the hills, we would reach the imperial chrysanthemum show.

The open spaces on the top of several hills were all taken over for the exhibition. The chrysanthemums, being the honorable flower of the imperial crest, are always handled with utmost care and respect. And all varieties of the flower were exhibited in the sheds whose roofs and walls were made of reeds or delicately framed paper screens. The varieties of chrysanthemums, in shape, color, and style of branches and leaves, produced by the imperial gardeners, were simply overwhelming. There was a type, the sixteen petals of which opened out just as in the imperial crest. There were several thousands of yellow, white or delicate rose flowers, four or five inches long, each on a separate stalk, besides masses of small flowers with branches ten feet long or more hanging down with myriads of blossoms like a cascade. Gold or different colored strips of paper, like our poem cards, were hung from the stems each bearing the classical name of the blossom written in beautiful ideographs, as though a flower must not have its artistic prestige overlooked in the presence of august visitors and on the honorable occasion. It is no wonder the girls were subdued by this compelling artistry.

Nevertheless, athletics as well as ethics and art had recently become a part of our curriculum. And members of the court themselves came to see us perform our exercises. Great preparations were made for their arrival. All around the wide playground were hung thick, black and white curtains as in the war camp of a daimyo. There was a temporary pavilion with reed screens and purple crepe draperies, bearing white imperial crests dyed on the front. On the platform floor of this pavilion was spread a scarlet carpet. A square table covered with gorgeous gold and red brocade stood on it, and a chair of black and gold lacquer. This was the temporary throne for her Imperial Majesty Haruko, wife of the great Emperor Meiji. Next to this pavilion was another set slightly lower and containing seats for the royal princesses.

When Her Majesty and her retinue arrived, the Imperial Navy Band greeted them with the National Song. The Empress was led into the grounds by the principal of the school, Madam Shimoda, who was dressed in a heavy black silk kimono with a skirt of the same color. The royal princesses, daughters of the Emperor Meiji, followed Her Majesty. We were deeply stirred by this noble and beautiful imperial procession. The Empress Haruko was the daughter of Prince Ichijo, who came from one of the five major families of court nobles; it used to be an unwritten rule to select empresses from this noble group. The Empress Haruko had been married to the boy Emperor just as he ascended the throne. A typical Japanese beauty of the aristocratic type, she was also a celebrated poetess. She wrote the "Song of the Diamond" for the girls of the Peeresses' School and it is sung by them on every ceremonial occasion.

THE SONG OF THE DIAMOND

> Even the diamond,
>   When left unpolished
> Will not shine,
>   Its light hidden deep:
> So man, too, after
>   Learning only
> Doth show abroad
>   The Way of Truth.
> Like the hand of a clock
>   That turneth
> Day and night,
>   Bend ye on learning,
> Wasting not a second
>   Of the sun's passing;
> Then what can ye not accomplish,
>   Though it be hard?
>
> Water taketh its shape,
>   Still varying,

With the vessel
That it containeth:
So doth man grow
To evil or good,
With the companions
He chooseth.
Seek ye those merely
Who are better,
Wiser than ye,
And together,
Forgetting not the whip
On your mind,
Step diligently along
The Way of Learning.

On the day of this exhibition the Empress Haruko was dressed in a European costume approved by the Emperor Meiji as the court apparel to be worn on all occasions except those connected with the Shinto sacred rites. She looked beautiful to us in this Western costume, her bonnet trimmed with a large white ostrich feather and a veil, her hands sheathed in long white kid gloves. The ladies-in-waiting were dressed in a similar manner, but the four young princesses wore embroidered kimonos in the pure ancient imperial style, the coloring of which was all according to the color regulations instituted about a thousand years ago when Japan produced a highly cultured society centering around the imperial court. The princesses, who were in their teens, wore kimonos of peach, green, scarlet and purple, respectively, with big peonies, storks, bamboo, turtles and holy clouds embroidered on them in gold and rainbow hues. Over the kimonos they wore red or grape-colored hakama-skirts of taffeta of the ancient court style looking like hoopskirts, and they walked in little silk shoes of the old court style. Their hair, dressed in the imperial style, hung down their backs without ornament, but the straight shining mane added to their youthful distinction. Seated in the pavilions, our royal guests watched our athletic exercises from beginning to end: Swedish gymnastics, graceful minuets and square dances with orchestra accompaniment, and maple hunting—a dance with purely Japanese music. About six hundred girls from five to seventeen took part in the events of the day. The senior class conducted a Red Cross drill which was quite militaristic, for it was designed to show their skill in bandaging wounded soldiers and carrying them on litters from the field to the camp.

Even at this athletic meeting—which was in spirit a sort of ceremony in the Japanese mind—the girls wore long-sleeved purple kimonos, red cashmere shirts, and high-heeled shoes. Only when it was absolutely necessary did we tuck up our two and a half foot sleeves with red or white silk bands. But in this fashion we performed the Swedish gymnastics before Her Majesty! Our tucked sleeves were cumbersome, but they were beautiful—streaming and fluttering, with the undersleeves of bright scarlet or pink adding to the color.

The girls felt proud of their opportunity to perform in the presence of Her Imperial Majesty. She was to them a gracious mother, and indeed we called her "The Mother of the Nation." She sat on her throne motionless except for an occasional smile as she watched this ingenuous play. Sometimes she smoked her golden pipe, respectfully offered by a young lady-in-waiting, who filled it each time from a gold lacquered tobacco box. Every time she accepted her pipe, she lifted her veil to smoke it—it held just enough for three short puffs. Looking back through the years, I can see that the Western manners adopted by the progressive young Emperor were not wholly incongruous with the graceful, etiquette-loving nature of Japanese aristocracy.

These athletic meetings, which the Empress honored with her presence, occurred at the time of commencement and at the anniversary celebration of the founding of the school. In commemoration beautifully shaped Japanese cakes in plain wooden boxes were given to each student. For the November celebration the cakes were in the form of maple leaves and chrysanthemums. Or they might depict a stork, turtle, rock or bamboo to signify the Empress's birthday. These cakes were more than welcome. For at least two hours all the girls had had to stand in straight rows on the wide space in front of the school gate, waiting for the imperial procession. It was finally heralded by mounted horse guards who preceded the imperial carriage. Mounted troops of the imperial guards, carrying the scarlet flag of the Empress, enlivened the procession. Its dramatic point was, of course, the magenta-colored carriage in which the Empress sat alone on the back seat, a lady-in-waiting of the highest rank facing Her Majesty, in a bent position, on the front seat, each holding a white lace-trimmed parasol. We were signaled to begin bowing slightly when the imperial flag came in sight, and to continue our bows, making them lower and lower, until Her Majesty had passed before us. The girls longed to see and worship Her Majesty's noble face, but we were not allowed to look up in the imperial presence. The Empress remained an exalted mystery.

The Emperor and the Empress are divinities to the Japanese, and those who had received special favor from the imperial household felt more deeply the divine grace of Their Majesties. Being homogeneous in racial traditions, we are one big family in the island empire with the imperial rulers at the head. How could a girl like myself born in the Meiji era, when the restoration of the Emperor was the main political excitement, and reared under its spell, fail to be moved by the spiritual force which the Emperor symbolized? One day I was talking with a cousin of mine who had been baptized a Christian and educated in a Catholic school. He was a faithful member of his church. We were talking about God. I said that the Emperor was our living God, and he and his ancestors and descendants would be our gods forever. My cousin told me that there was but one God, Jehovah, and that our Emperor was just a living man, although unquestionably he was a great man. "What a heathen you are!" I cried. This argument between a young girl and a young man did not reach any conclusion, ending only in hot tears, for neither could convince the other.

The Great Emperor Mutsuhito, posthumously known as Meiji or Enlightened Ruler, about whom our argument revolved, ascended the throne in 1868 when he was fifteen years old. The great political restoration, which made this possible, he accomplished with the aid of wise counselors, later called "Genro" (Elder Statesmen). These counselors have now passed into the mists of history, save Prince Saionji, grand eighty-one-year-old gentleman who joined this group around the Emperor and who, still living, is today revered by all for his connection with the successful political revolt. It was a difficult undertaking for the young Emperor not only to overthrow the feudal government, which had usurped power from the Mikado and held it for more than eight centuries, but to open "the land of mystery" to the world. Kneeling before the spirits of his ancestors, the young Emperor, one hundred and twenty-third mikado and direct descendant of the Sun Goddess, took the charter oath to act upon these five principles:

(1) To convoke an assembly widely representative and decide all policies according to public opinion.

(2) The upper and the lower classes shall with one heart execute economic policies.

(3) Civil and military officials as well as the common people shall all accomplish their desire, and no one shall be made to feel fatigue.

(4) Harmful customs must be abolished, and hallowed be the universal way of Heaven and Earth.

(5) Knowledge of the entire world shall be sought in order to strengthen the foundations of the imperial throne.

The Emperor Mutsuhito was the finest example of a man not only fitted for the throne but for a great act in history. He was diligent throughout his regime of forty-five years. He never left the capital to avoid the heat or the cold. Nor did he consider personal pleasure in other respects, except a performance of the No drama once in a long while. He loved wrestling while he was a boy, and used to practice it with his playmates, the sons of the court nobles. Of course, his playmates, yielding the honor of victory to the young prince, were always thrown to the ground by the August Child, until he learned one day the truth of the situation: it was bad form to defeat the crown prince. He refused, I am told, ever to wrestle again.

The Emperor warned his people many times that they must refrain from luxury. He set them a good example in this matter and was exceedingly anxious to prevent Western influences from demoralizing our national character. After his death we were allowed to see the furniture and other things he had kept around him, and were amazed at their simplicity.

The Emperor Mutsuhito encouraged education. It was he who set up a universal educational system which has brought to Japan a literacy higher than that of any other country in the world. It was his genuine pleasure to attend the commencement of the Tokyo Imperial University and the military and naval colleges. Silver watches were given to the students at the Imperial University on such occasions, and swords to the young cadets who had studied especially well.

Although the Emperor adopted the most progressive methods of administration to reorganize Japan and start her on her way as a modern civilized country, he was devoted to the old Japanese culture. He was a poet, as his Empress was a poetess. He communicated his gracious thoughts to his people in verse, while his formal edicts were given out in the difficult and dignified Chinese style, not readily understood without explanation by a teacher. But in his poems he expressed himself naturally and intimately! There we learn the human side of the Emperor.

> The old man, cultivating his hillside farm alone,
> Sending his sons to the battlefield!

He gave voice to his sympathy for the old farmer whose sons were recruited for service in the Russo-Japanese War.

Again he wrote:

> Stirring up the charcoal in my fire bucket,
> I think of the cold biting in the huts of the poor.

The imperial poet and poetess always preside over the New Year poetry contests in which the public at large may compete, their compositions being restricted to the conventional verse of thirty-one syllables. Girls in the Peeresses' School compose verse for this occasion, and sometimes theirs are among those selected to be read in the imperial presence. No material prize is given, but to have one's composition read before Their Majesties and to the greatest scholars of the country in the exalted regions of the imperial palace is the highest possible honor for a humble subject of Japan. The newspapers print the poem and the biography of each fortunate winner.

But even an emperor has his limited span of life. I was at Kamakura beach when our family was called back to Tokyo, suddenly, in the midst of the July heat. His Imperial Majesty's go-furei was the cause. This is something difficult to translate accurately, meaning roughly the sickness of the members of the imperial family. Soon after the Emperor had attended commencement at the Imperial University, he felt ill, and doctors—there were about eleven of them—announced the seriousness of his ailment. I remember distinctly how great a shock this was to the nation. The Emperor had never been ill in his life! The doctors issued bulletins several times a day and people waited anxiously for encouraging news. But the news grew worse and worse. All the citizens of Tokyo worried. They suffered because their great father suffered. Streetcars ran slowly, trying not to make a noise. The populace gathered around the palace moats under the green willows or in the huge front grounds. During the ten days that His Majesty was ill, more than ten thousand men and women, old and young, assembled every day, looking anxiously toward the palace beyond the white walls of the ancient castle of Yedo. We could see only the bronze roofs of the palace, the rest being hidden behind the high-walled moats, in the mystery of the pine forests. We, the infants of His Majesty—we spoke of ourselves in this way, prayed to the gods, the ancestors of Japan, to bring back the royal health. Day and night his subjects stayed around his palace praying silently. Ten thousand people gathered without making a sound. The masses whom even thousands of policemen could not hold in silence when they did not want to keep quiet, were here under the hot July sun hushed with one accord in real prayer. Papers reported that many men committed suicide in the hope that their ancestors would accept the offering of a private life as a substitute for that of His Majesty the Emperor Mutsuhito!

At last the great spirit of the Meiji Emperor ascended to heaven, and darkness fell upon the nation. The imperial mourning lasted an entire year, divided into three terms, and the girls in the Peeresses' School wore black kimonos all that time. During this period of mourning we moved quietly, at school, on the street, and even at home. We did not laugh. We played no music. Even marriages were postponed until the year was over.

Nothing could be more impressive than the funeral of the Emperor. All our court ceremonies of a religious nature follow the ancient Shinto ritual. No other nation possesses such an uninterrupted tradition. The funeral ceremony to which I refer was performed strictly after the manner of two thousand years ago, except that its scale was enlarged by the enhanced splendor of the modern nation.

When the Great Emperor's funeral took place, Tokyo and Kyoto were carried back in sentiment and atmosphere to ancient Japan. The tenth of September, forty days after the Emperor had passed away, was decided on as the day of the imperial funeral, and according to regulation it took place at midnight. All the streets along which the funeral cortege was to pass were cleaned beforehand, and kept in the utmost cleanliness and quiet. Electric lights were turned off and pine torchlights substituted. Big bundles of pine torches were burned at the center of each crossing, and square white wooden lanterns were set up along the streets, which were covered with fresh white sand on which no one was allowed to step until the procession had passed. We girls gathered in the school compound before dark and went to the place which had been reserved specially for us along the funeral line, that we might pay our respects to the imperial hearse. At eight in the evening we heard the first gong, in the distance through the darkness, which signaled the start of the Mikado's cortege from the palace. The funeral procession extended more than a mile and numbered about ten thousand attendants, all in ancient silk costumes, varied and magnificent.

The high officials who were given the honor of following the imperial hearse practiced walking long beforehand in their ancient robes, wearing crowns and lacquer shoes. Navy and army officers were in Western uniforms. Flags and streamers of gold and silver brocade reflected the torchlight. The Mikado's coffin was borne on a huge carriage of black and gold lacquer drawn by eight carefully selected and trained oxen. The carriage was made in such a way as to utter mournful creaking sounds when the big wheels turned. Court musicians played plaintive ancient music on bamboo flutes with wailing tones which harmonized well with the general emotional atmosphere. We spectators all bowed low to the coffin, murmuring eternal farewell to our beloved Mikado in our hearts but not with our voices, although quiet weeping was heard here and there. Thus we continued our silent prayer until the second gong told us that the son of the late Mikado—the new Emperor of Japan, who was already at the temporary shrine built on a field just outside the city for the purpose—had received the coffin and was now going to read his words of grief in the presence of his father's spirit. We bowed toward the shrine in what we call the "distant" bowing.

We did not know until early the next morning, when the newspapers informed a sorrow-stricken people, that General Count Maresuke Nogi and his wife, Countess Shizuko Nogi, had committed suicide at their residence, each leaving a poem and words of explanation for their deed.

General Nogi was a popular veteran general at the time. The late Mikado loved him and appreciated his simple straightforward character and his loyalty. Indeed, the Emperor had entrusted him with the very important task of educating the younger generation of peers. So for several years before his sudden death the general had been president of both Peers' and Peeresses' schools. The girls delighted in seeing him on his favorite horse, Kotobuki, in his khaki military uniform with a huge decoration of the Rising Sun on his left breast. His gentle low voice still speaks in my ears when I think about some ceremonial occasion on which he read to us the Mikado's Rescript of Education, before the altar in the school hall where the sacred pictures of the Emperor and Empress were hung. The anniversary of the founding of the empire, on the eleventh of February, and the Emperor's birthday were then and remain the great national holidays, and both were celebrated at school.

On these occasions, the school hall was filled with pupils rang-
ing frcm kindergartners to postgraduate students. We sat
quietly in rows, until the president and the dean came into the
hall leading the young royal princesses who were then attending
the school.

After "The Song of the Diamond" had been sung we
bowed deeply, and while our heads were bent the screens of
the altar were opened to disclose the holy images of the Emperor
and Empress in their ancient robes, with crown and fan. At
this moment General Nogi enacted his role. After bowing
three times to the imperial images, he proceeded in measured
steps to the platform by the side of the altar! There the school
president's secretary held out a square lacquer tray covered with
an imperial-crested piece of purple crepe. This, with the respect
of a Catholic priest invoking the very Host, he delivered into the
general's hand. Every motion of the ritual was carried out as
prescribed. The general took a roll of manuscript from the
tray, held it high, bowed, and then began to read. In slow
cadences he recited the sonorous charter of Japanese education.

Know Ye, Our Subjects: Our Imperial Ancestors have founded our
Empire on a basis broad and everlasting, and have deeply and firmly
implanted virtue. Our subjects, ever united in loyalty and filial piety,
have from generation to generation illustrated the beauty thereof. This
is the glory and fundamental character of our Empire, and herein also
lies the source of our education. Ye, our subjects, be filial to your parents,
affectionate to your brothers and sisters; as husbands and wives, be
harmonious; as friends, true; bear yourselves in modesty and moderation;
extend your benevolence to all; pursue learning and cultivate the arts and
thereby develop intellectual faculties and perfect moral powers; furthermore, advance public good and promote common interest; always respect
the Constitution and observe the laws; should emergency arise, offer
yourselves courageously to the State and thus guard and maintain the
prosperity of our Imperial Throne, coeval with heaven and earth. So
shall ye not only be our good and faithful subjects, but render illustrious
the best traditions of your forefathers. The way here set forth is indeed
the teaching bequeathed by our Imperial Ancestors, to be observed alike

by their descendants and the subjects, infallible for all ages and true in all places. It is our wish to take it to heart in all reverence, in common with you, our subjects, that we may all thus attain to the same virtue.

We were bent at the right angle all this while until the general finished reading the words of God, the Emperor.

Then the national invocation to the Emperor was sung in unison:

> May our Emperor live long,
> Till ten thousand years roll on,
> Till pebbles to great rocks shall grow
> And be with moss o'ergrown.

Before the ceremony was closed the draperies were dropped quietly to veil the holy images again. Then General Nogi gave his own oration, celebrating the occasion and moralizing on it. He was in his black full military uniform, wearing a cap adorned with tall straight white feathers.

After General Nogi's first visit to the Peeresses' School many old customs were ordered changed. The Emperor feared that the Japanese people, having been victorious in the Russo-Japanese War, would lose their good habits of self-denial and frugality, and acquire a taste for comforts and luxuries. The veteran general accordingly stressed the moral virtue of enduring great hardship. We were forbidden to wear silk kimonos at school and the length of the kimono sleeves was shortened to symbolize restraint in luxury. The beautiful square boxes of decorated sweets formerly presented to the girls on each ceremonial occasion were simplified. A girl, whose brother had sent her photograph to a beauty contest conducted by one of the presses and who, fortunately or unfortunately, was given the first prize and announced in the press as its charming winner, was immediately dismissed by General Nogi as if he were turning a disobedient soldier out of his army. He preached to the girls that woman's beauty is not judged by her physical attraction, but must be reckoned in terms of virtue. The girls were thoroughly shocked by this rough treatment from their military president. Soon afterward, however, we learned through the papers that the girl who had been thus dismissed from the school was engaged to the heir of a marquis and marshal, a young captain in the imperial army. And still more surprising was the news that the person who enacted the part of the honorable go-between for this marriage was our austere President Nogi himself! Strict in principle and humane of heart was General Nogi, who stood as the highest exemplar of Bushido.

Concerning General Nogi's suicide, there has been much discussion; there have been many conjectures, as well as wonder and admiration. It may be criticized from various points of view, but to the Japanese it cannot fail to be a national testament to loyalty and nobility of spirit.

It is said that when General Nogi was entrusted with the investment of Port Arthur during the Russo-Japanese War, he committed the error, at least in his own opinion, of directing his attack, not against the key forts in the chain surrounding Port Arthur, but against the citadel itself. In the frightful carnage that followed, he lost tragic numbers of his soldiers, including his two sons—he had only two. Finally reinforced and at the suggestion of another general, he redirected the attack against 203 Metre Hill which dominated the circle of the forts and the harbor itself. By that decision the port was won, and the tide turned completely in favor of the Japanese, shortening the duration of the war. But the dead, the general thought, had died unnecessarily, owing to his mistake. He brooded over it. Amid the triumphal joy of the nation over the outcome of the war he was sad and thoughtful. Remembering another blunder he had made once before in a civil war, he had no strength to face the honors and tokens of gratitude bestowed on him by the Emperor and the nation. He meditated immediate suicide, for it seemed the only way for a samurai to ease his conscience-stricken mind. "Stay with me, general, at least as long as I live, for I need you," the great and gracious Emperor had implored.

The general obeyed the imperial command to the letter. With the passing of his master, however, the loyal servant sat on the mat in his small bare room and ripped open his body. His wife, a wife of a samurai, did likewise.

I sat in my own quiet room where I had placed the general's picture on the table and burned incense, praying to his noble spirit without a spoken word. Then tears burst from my eyes; I cried and cried until father came in and convinced me that a true lady must control the expression of her sorrow. This was in September and I was sixteen on the day of General Nogi's burial.

A great hero he was, but he was more than that to me. He was my dear school principal, so dignified, noble, gentle and fatherly. Soon after his death he was deified and his old residence was made into the Nogi Shrine. He has become a great focus of national worship—a national image!

PART THREE
THE AWAKENING OF YOUTH

VI

The Obedient-Wife-and-Wise-Mother Principle and Artistic Culture

"YOU should not wear your Western clothes any more, Shidzué," said mother one day. "They are proper for a little child in the playground, but they look too childish and undignified for a grown-up girl like you. Don't you realize that you are to prepare to be a good and beautiful bride soon?"

I loved my Western dresses which my father had brought back from London and was allowed to wear them until I was twelve years old for playing out of doors. When I was only nine, however, mother gave me a purple obi-sash that was stiffly padded and lined so that I could never wear it until my maid had tied it in a big bow at my back. I longed for a peach or a red sash without a lining, but mother was definitely determined to train my body to endure all the uncomfortable stiffness of Japanese clothes. She thought that loose Western dresses and free outdoor play would spoil the dainty looks of her daughter and so even Saturday afternoons or Sundays, which were the only days free from school lessons, she insisted on my being suitably dressed and occupying myself with lessons in flower arrangement, and in the tea ceremony.

In spite of the tide of liberalism that had been breaking over Japan with the new social order, influencing literature, men's education and other aspects of culture, women's world remained true to the conception which survived from the feudal age.

"A good wife" and "a wise mother"! How well these words sound! Indeed, there could seem to be no objection to them in any society or age. But when we peel off the skin from this perfect fruit of feudalism, we expose bondage to husbands and subjection to the tyranny of the family system as a whole. Consciously or unconsciously my mother taught her daughter to crush her desires and ambitions, and trained her to be ready to submerge her individuality in her husband's personality and his family's united temper.

Girls were to study first of all how to please their husbands' parents with absolute obedience. Mother never thought it possible that I should become a good companion, discussing social problems or politics with my husband or reading books with him. She was not worried about the plight of women or the state of the nation but thought it of the greatest importance that she should educate me in such a way that I might not be criticized. She did not wish me to be the sort of girl who did not fall in with the ways of her husband's family. Time and again she told me that this was her greatest anxiety about me. And indeed she could not help this attitude. The possibility of divorce was involved. Unwillingness or inability to conform to the ways of her husband's family was enough excuse for any husband or any mother-in-law to send a bride back to her parents disgraced for life as a "divorcée."

In the April of my seventeenth year, the commencement of my class was held at the Peeresses' School. The girls were delighted with the honor of receiving their certificates of graduation in the presence of Her Imperial Majesty the Empress Sadako, the present Empress Dowager. Each name was called by the dean and each of us stepped forward in turn to the front of the gorgeous imperial throne, making three bows to Her Majesty and receiving the certificate handed out by General Viscount Oseki, successor to General Nogi as president of the school. The certificate of thick rice paper, mounted on

silk brocade into which was woven the imperial chrysanthemum and paulownia designs, contained words exquisitely written in a mixture of Chinese and Japanese letters. It took some
time for the fifty-nine girls to receive their certificates indi-
vidually, but the Empress patiently watched them, always with
a gracious smile on her noble face.

After the ceremony was over and all the receptions and
parties were closed, the girls gathered here and there under the
big cherry trees in the schoolgrounds, drenched in the raining
petals and in tears over the sorrow of leaving the school where
they had spent fifteen years, day after day together enjoying
their carefree youth. Their tears were those of girlish senti-
mentality, but also of fearful anticipation of heavy responsibili-
ties soon to be forced upon them.

Marriage for the Japanese girl meant losing individual
freedom. She was allowed a peep into the romantic side of
marriage through classic stories such as *The Tale of Genji*. The
few books selected for us to read treated of the romance of
court life in ancient times. But what the teachers preached in
the classroom about a woman's morals, and the repeated words
from our mothers' lips, made us aware that a step out from
the school gate was a step into the woman's destiny of subjection, where every girl's lot was inevitably cast. Three of my
former classmates were already married, having left school
when they were sixteen. One of them was already a mother.
There were also a few who were engaged to be married very
soon. Those marriages and engagements were arranged by
their families regardless of the girls' individual interests.
Little Princess Tame Shimazu had been engaged to Marquis
Raitei Tokugawa, and her sister had been engaged to the heir
to Prince Tokugawa, since babyhood in the cradle. Romance
may come after an engagement of this kind but never before,
as such girls have no opportunity whatever to know boys other
than their relatives.

On leaving school, my life changed entirely. A few of my classmates remained in school to take the postgraduate course, but the parents of most of us thought too much education spoils a woman's precious virtues—obedience and naïve sweetness— and that awakening one's individual desire is the seed of unhappiness. My parents shared this conventional opinion so I was to keep myself busy with flower arrangement, tea ceremony, cooking and sewing, besides my lessons in English and the piano with foreign tutors. Mother trained me to be capable of every possible kind of domestic work. I got up at five every morning and worked in the gardens, both front and back, helping the servants. I swept the ground with a bamboo broom, printing, as I did so, dainty lines on the soft earth. I trimmed the bushes, branches and leaves of the trees according to the rules for gardening. I watered the garden paths, the rocks which were scattered here and there under the trees and the irregular stepping stones all over the garden. All the rocks and stones had to be washed, and the trees had to be well sprinkled with water. Moss and lichens must shine with a fresh verdure against the early morning sun rays. In the late afternoon this watering was repeated for all the gardens.

Ever since I was very little I had watched my mother arranging flowers to decorate the rooms, but I did not begin my lessons in flower arrangement until I was twelve. Then the flower master whose name was En Ka-an, an old gentleman dressed in a stiff dark kimono, came once a week to instruct me. Bronze vases, porcelain, bamboo or lacquer containers were set on the sheets of gay-colored matting spread on the floor to protect it from being soiled. Then all kinds of seasonal flowers from those on the tree branches to little garden blossoms and moss were carefully laid on the matting. My first lesson was begun in the most formal style with herbaceous peonies to be arranged in a bronze vase. My teacher fixed the flower branches himself first and presented them to me with a reverent bowing.

He then explained the basis of the technique, indicating the three essential points—the Leading Principle (Heaven), the Subordinate Principle (Earth), the Reconciling Principle (Man), adding that any aspects of flower arrangement, formal, semiformal or informal, which did not embody these principles would be barren and dead. Then I was asked to take out all the branches from the vase and rearrange them by myself.

My awkward hands, fitted rather for a tennis racket than flower scissors, tried hard, twisting and twisting to make eleven pieces of peony branches stand as they had stood before. Poor flowers, they began to wither, held so long in my warm hands! The old master sat motionless, uttering no word to help me, but patiently watching my struggle, with a gentle smile.

En Ka-an was the head of the Koryu School. His family had been concerned with this flower philosophy for generation after generation. He was not only a genius in his arrangement of the flowers, but was skilled in collecting the exquisite materials, sending his men to remote mountains and distant fields to secure fresh wild plants or branches of forest trees to add to those cultivated in flower beds and in gardens. The selection of flowers and branches is of the greatest importance in the flower art.

A joy of approaching spring, for example, may be ushered in by an early spray of slender mountain cherry, or a pleasant coolness suggested on a summer day by white cow lilies taken from some old temple pond. It would be a wasteful attempt to learn the philosophy of nature by purchasing dozens of roses or carnations from a glass show window on a crowded street. The flowers raised in hothouses in exactly equal sizes and shades, and even of standard length, appear to say: "The machine age has come in floriculture!"

Putting aside this discussion of art, I come back to the realities of the actual struggle at my peonies. I finally succeeded in making all the branches stand up straight in the vase, but with no taste or grace. Five flowers and two buds were turning their faces this way and that, like untrained boys at school. I bowed to my teacher as I offered my poor arrangement. He bowed also to the vase, saying, "What a beautiful piece of art you have executed!" but in the very next second he had pulled out all the branches and rearranged them, giving a vastly different effect even to the eyes of a young girl. Then he bowed again, repeating: "What a beautiful arrangement!"

I was quite embarrassed when my teacher said "What a fine art!" knowing that my attempts were not at all fine art. But later I learned that this master of the ancient cult always commented on his flowers in the same way. Even at times when I secretly felt that I had done particularly well or terribly badly, his words never varied. Whether my arrangement was a little better or decidedly worse, he always greeted it in the same manner, "What a beautiful . . .", thus hinting at the meaning of "Know thyself!" in any line of learning.

I continued to study this art until I was married and again whenever I lived in Tokyo as there is no limit to what one may learn. Finally the flower instructor's degree was given to me with an esoteric manuscript in which forty-five secrets of handling flowers were written by the master's own hand, and a name—a flower name, so to speak—was also bestowed upon me to be used in the circle of flower artists. So this old master still comes to my mother's house and I escape once in a while from all the arguments and mundane vexations of my hurried modern life into the silent beauty and peace of the flower philosophy.

These complications and arguments from which I need sometimes to flee had come into my life in a strange way. Among my relatives, I was particularly fond of my mother's uncle, who had studied law in Germany and had been in the judicial department of the government for many years. He must have been quite a westernized gentleman when he first came back from abroad, judging by his big Occidental style residence. Like many other Japanese, however, as he grew older he came back to Japanese ways by instinct, tired of the heavy atmosphere of painted rooms with superfluous furniture, pictures and knickknacks, missing the traditional simplicity of the Japanese dwelling.

So he left his active life together with his Western style residence and fled to his "retiring house," built in his garden among the trees. Uncle Moto devoted the rest of his life to the study of the Zen sect of Buddhism. His little four-and-a-half-mat room—his library—was piled high with Buddhist sutras. He loved Dharma and his little sutra chamber was decorated with an image in wood, a carved Dharma, with big eyes and a dark face, wrapped in red cloth. He also loved to make tea, sitting before the iron kettle in an adjoining ceremonial tea-room, the ritualistic atmosphere of which was imparted by dark wood, dark plaster walls, and bamboo latticed windows. Both of these structures were built in such a way as to suggest refined poverty—the spirit of united Zenism and teaism.

One day when this aesthetic uncle came to visit my mother he watched me as I served a cup of green tea to a guest. He liked to tease children and he cried, "What a tall girl you are! Poor girl, you are growing only in your height like a fire alarm thief!" You who have never seen old Japan may not understand what my great-uncle meant by this phrase and so I must explain it.

Before Japan erected skyscrapers in her modernized cities, the towns were flat, being filled with only one- or two-story houses and the tallest object in each ward in the town was a ladder with a big fire alarm bell on the top. My uncle meant to say that I was growing like "Jack and the Beanstalk" and could reach to the top of the ladder from the ground if I wanted to steal the bell. In those days tall girls did not fit the Japanese standard of beauty. So mother and uncle agreed that I needed some special accomplishments to offset my height. Mother therefore accepted uncle's invitation for her daughter to come to him every Sunday afternoon and sit in the four-and-a-half-mat tearoom, to learn how to move gracefully in that space no bigger than a compartment in a Pullman car! Hence my training for the rites of Tea began as if they were a punishment for growing!

I was only fourteen years old then. How I envied my brothers and cousins who went out to play tennis on Sundays, while I was kept in that gloomy diminutive tearoom, sitting beside the old tea master, listening to the water boiling in the iron kettle on a charcoal fire! The music of the teakettle has been perfectly described by Kakuzo Okakura, in *The Book of Tea* ". . . and quiet reigns with nothing to break the silence save the note of the boiling water in an iron kettle. The kettle sings well, for pieces of iron are so arranged in the bottom as to produce a peculiar melody in which one may hear the echoes of a cataract muffled by clouds, of a distant sea breaking among the rocks, a rainstorm sweeping through a bamboo forest, or the soughing of pines on some faraway hill."

However, it was only in later years that I really learned to enjoy the spotless cleanliness, the deep quiet and the music of boiling water in my uncle's room. When I was patiently sitting there at fourteen peeping out into the blue sky from the small window, my heart wandered off to the tennis match while my poor awkward feet slept soundly under my tightly folded knees. Our tea master, Kawabe, an aged gentleman and celebrated teacher in the Omote-Senke School of Tea, sat always next to the low platform—the tokonoma—on which the ceremony is performed. Besides me, there were present also my great-aunt Moto and one of her daughters with her friend, young and naughty like myself.

Aunt Moto had the true tea connoisseur's taste. She arranged flowers on the tokonoma according to the spirit of this rite, for an explanation of which I must quote again from Okakura: "It is essentially a worship of the Imperfect, as it is a tender attempt to accomplish something possible in this impossible thing we know as life."

I remember that Aunt Moto liked to put into the clay vase a twig with only one leaf shaped like a broken paper umbrella. I remember, too, the fact that I paid little attention to what my aunt had tastefully arranged on her tokonoma as a finish to the aesthetic atmosphere of the room, being more interested in the porcelain bowl in which she always served the sweet cakes which belong with ceremonial tea. My irreverent tea-mate and I never failed to take one every time our turn came to swallow the regulation three-and-a-half mouthfuls of the bitter beverage.

I continued to keep up my lessons in the tea ceremony until I was married, repeating the same every Sunday. To comprehend the tedium of this study, a knowledge of its details is necessary. First I had to carry a water pitcher, a small lacquer tea caddy, a bamboo dipper, immaculately white linen napkin and other accessories one by one from the anteroom—the midsuya—to the tearoom; then I had to arrange them on the spotless mats according to fixed rules which, though seemingly complicated, actually signify the least wasteful labor. Then I made a bowl of tea by pouring boiling water on the finely powdered green tea leaves and whipping the mixture with a delicate brush made of split bamboo.

This may sound very simple. But since every object used and every motion of the hand, wrist and body is prescribed, the tea ceremony is a difficult thing to perform ritualistically. It is really an art of the most sophisticated culture, as Okakura shows, and our home and habits, costume and cuisine, porcelain, lacquer, painting, music—our very literature—all have been subject to its influence. No student of Japanese culture could ignore its presence. I am now grateful to my great-uncle and aunt who suggested my learning it thoroughly and who gave me a chance to get a knowledge of these tea rites while I was young. It requires ample leisure to practice until one can master the spirit of this art as well as its mechanics. One must reach the power of intuition toward it just as in the case of flower arrangement.

VII

Mental Awakening

TWO great influences affected my girlhood development. Mother, of course, was the one who trained me day and night with love and care, to become "a good wife and wise mother," and a "lady" too, versed in the Japanese fine arts. But my young uncle, Yusuke Tsurumi, was the one who first developed the intellectual side of my life.

Mother was the eldest of the Tsurumi family among eight brothers and sisters. Her brother Yusuke, who is twelve years older than I, came to live with us after the death of his parents, and at once the new kind of education began for me.

It was the summer of my eleventh year, and mother took us to spend our vacation at Shiobara Hot Spring, instead of going to the Kamakura beach as usual. The family doctor had advised mother that my youngest brother, Hiroo, needed the change on account of his delicate health. We all liked the idea of change ourselves and were excited to be traveling so far for the first time in our lives. Shiobara is famous for its maple blossoms as well as its waters. Today we can reach this charming place in a half day, as the mountains have been modernized with electricity and gasoline, but in those days it was aloof from machines and seemed a long distance from Tokyo.

For this trip, we packed rattan baskets with kimonos, sashes, white two-toed tabi-socks and many pairs of wooden clogs. Mother, my elder brother, two younger brothers, a cousin, Uncle Yusuke, and maids made up the company. We

started by an early train from Uyeno Station by the park from
which many railroad lines start to the northern provinces of
Japan proper. We traveled ninety-two miles straight north
through Musashino Plain, enjoying the everlasting panorama
of distant hills and the succession of peaks which drew an irregular sky line at the rear of the immense green land of rice
fields and mulberry plantations.

When we arrived at Nasu Plain in the afternoon, a cool
mountain breeze was blowing, crossing over miles of a wilderness of pampas grass as if it had come to greet our company.
We hired an old-fashioned horse wagon and traveled ten miles
on a white straight country road across the plain between narrow streams of crystal water, westward to the foot of the Shiobara mountains. It was a surprise for city children to come to a
place where there were few people, to see colts that had been
playing and eating grass along the road or in the bush run to
their mares, astonished by the approach of our wagon.

All the while, Uncle Yusuke never ceased his pleasant conversation, telling us legends—which we enjoyed with fear and
awe—of nine-tailed foxes who appeared in this region, of will-
o'-the-wisps and bewitched travelers, of the evil stone which
killed anybody who touched it.

As we approached the mountain, the driver changed his
horse, to make ready for another four or five miles of hard
climbing. "Kana-kana, Kanakana, Kanakanakana . . ." the
autumn cicadas were singing in the coolness of the mysterious
cryptomeria forest. Our wagon was advancing up and up between the hills into the very bosom of forest-covered mountains
by a series of steep hairpin curves. Then suddenly we emerged
from the cliffs and the Broom River came into sight, like a belt
of deep cobalt blue with little white waves breaking on the surface. It is a rapid stream winding along the bottom of the
narrow valley, gathering waters from more than seventy cas-
cades which pour into it from both sides of the ravine. Along

its banks are some ten large and small villages with hot mineral springs.

The driver's horn echoed in the distant mountains and the stamping of the horse's feet continued like the boom of a drum. We wound along the narrow path in the midst of nature's delicate cabinetwork, uprising peaks on the right and the swift river, with its constant murmuring beneath the cliff, visible suddenly as we advanced, then receding again in the shadow of the green maple bushes, in a game of hide-and-seek. We were thrilled every time our wagon dashed into a dark tunnel of mountain rocks, then emerged again directly in front of a mountain cascade falling down from the edge of a pine-covered peak, as if we were to be dashed into the jade green basin of the waterfall. Uncle Yusuke explained to us that this narrow path of beauty became famous after the celebrated author, Koyo Sanjin, described the charm of the place.

It was after sunset when we ended the day's trip with its excitement and joy. Old-fashioned kerosene lamps lighted the mountain inns along the river. Soft dreamy vapor rose here and there from the widely opened windows of bathhouses as our company arrived safely at one of the inns. It was the first time we had ever stayed in a country resort, and we were much bewildered when the host, hostess, clerks, bath clerks, clog-keeper and numbers of young maids all came to the entrance hall kneeling and bowing to us with words of welcome. This much exaggerated form of bowing him in and out makes the traveler tip heavily on the day of departure; otherwise he would be uncomfortable ever again to cross the threshold of this elaborately repeated etiquette. However, mother found herself over-whelmed by heaps of presents—souvenir towels, wooden clogs, chopsticks, spoons, postcards, all stamped with a maple pattern for remembrance of the place—given in return for the generous tip which she bestowed upon the host. After the excessive greeting ceremony, we were led upstairs to a quiet suite of mat rooms where we washed off our fatigue in the big natural stone bathtub filled with the hot mineral water which spouted between the rocks.

Uncle Yusuke had brought books with him to read during his holiday—books on law, economics and politics which he was studying at the Imperial University. He was extremely diligent with his college work, but he had time for us too. We had such fun with him going down to watch the swift river, climbing up the hills, wandering about in the green forests, or running after wild ponies on the country road. We all loved to hear him tell stories, for he was a genius at the business. Later, he developed into a distinguished lecturer and talked to large audiences in America as well as in Japan. Our affection for Uncle Yusuke knew no bounds because he never let us grow tired during those monotonous days in the mountains. He always had some way to amuse us.

Uncle Yusuke lived with us for seven years after that. It was he who whetted my curiosity and stimulated my ambition to know more. This was exactly what was lacking in my school education, which in those days never aimed at cultivating or enlarging the mind but drove any imagination or curiosity into narrow boundaries of orthodox morality and formality.

Uncle Yusuke did not preach his broader gospel of humanism or liberalism by borrowing maxims from books to make us sleepy. In his conversations, he illustrated his points with human examples gleaned from the histories of East and West. He talked about Alexander the Great, Caesar, Brutus, the Maid of Orleans, Napoleon, and Nelson. His enthusiastic interpretation of these great figures of the West made me a hero-worshiper. But the stories of honorable soldiers in the battle for humanity, such as Florence Nightingale and Abraham Lincoln, moved me even more.

I remember one rainy afternoon, while we were staying in the inn at Shiobara, some lonely traveler was beguiling the time with music, for the low tones of his samisen strings were heard across the corridor—a soft accompaniment to our uncle's story-telling. My brothers and I sat quietly, looking up through the silent silver threadlike rain, at the rocky mountains covered with green foliage. My uncle, who was in the center of our group, was reciting the history of Joan of Arc, "A humble shepherdess, suddenly moved by an inspiration from the God of Heaven to leave her sheep behind and appear in silver armor on a white horse at the head of an army. She led the French soldiers from long unfavorable battling to victory for her fatherland! How-ever, a heroine's life too often concludes with tragedy, and it was so with our heroine, Joan of Arc, who suffered martyrdom like many of our famous Japanese characters." The Maid of Orleans appeared suddenly in our lives and passed away as suddenly, like a falling cherry blossom. Our interest was held to the end as Uncle Yusuke concluded: "So France was rescued by a little girl's heroic action and devotion!" When he finished this long story of Joan of Arc, tears were flooding from my brothers' eyes and mine.

I also loved the story of Abraham Lincoln. His life from log cabin to White House! His act of emancipating slaves in the face of opposing guns and swords! Uncle Yusuke told us about a great book written by a Western woman which helped to promote emancipation, so *Uncle Tom's Cabin* became very dear to me and I felt that "little Eva" was my personal friend.

Such strange Western stories charmed us; but Uncle Yusuke also recited stirring tales of Japanese and Chinese heroes. It is curious how children long to hear the same romances over and over. I never tired of Uncle Tom and in later years when I had chances to travel in America, on crossing the state of Kentucky, as I stood on the bank of the Mississippi River "Tom" came to my mind so poignantly that I was convinced that good works of any literature or art are of universal appeal to children.

My younger brother Yoji used to cling to Uncle Yusuke's

shoulder and urge him to repeat his favorite tale about *Nasu-no-Yoichi,* the Japanese Wilhelm Tell. "Yoichi was the mightiest archer in a Genji war camp," Uncle Yusuke would begin as we followed him along the shadowy mountain path beside the rushing stream. "The enemy, the Heike clan which had been in power for many years, finally lost their battles and were driven to a corner of the Inland Sea, sailing off in a fleet of big boats with young princes and princesses of Heike. Meanwhile as if they were teasing their foes, on the shore, out from the fleet of the Heike, a young maid in scarlet costume appeared on the deck of a boat, anchored at the head of the fleet. She held a tall pole with a fan on the top. It looked as if she were saying, 'Hit us if you can!' Yoichi took the dare." Every time this climax was reached, with staring eyes, we held our breath.

"Urging his horse forward," the wonderful storyteller went on, "from the beach into the shallow water of the sea, he paused a moment to pray to his God of Arrows, 'God, the ancestor of Genji Clan, the God of Victory! Show mercy on me!' Shame would be great if he missed the target. It would not be compensated for even by suicide. After a long prayer to his God, and a secret farewell to his parents, he set his arrow to the aim, while the maid stood with a sweet smile holding high the target, a golden fan with a red rising sun, glittering on the waves, on the distant boat rolling and pitching on the water. Instantly a white arrow whirled through the bright sunshine, hit the fan in the center of the notch, and the fan fluttered down to the water. Cheers arose both from the friends on the shore and the foes on the water!" And we children heaved sighs of relief. No warrior could fail to admire such skill and such daring, and we young people were all the descendants of warriors.

The story of *Shokatsu Komei* was my elder brother's favorite. I, too, loved the Komei who was full of wisdom and was likewise loyal to his Emperor. The tragic end of his life is well known to those who read the Chinese classics, but I shall not repeat it here, for tales of war occupy too much of the thoughts of the Japanese both with respect to their own history and to that of our neighbor country. Uncle Yusuke had to continue day after day telling this story to the very end, though he did it as briefly as possible.

This young uncle of ours had ideals no less than knowledge. He was always at the head of his class. Though he was a true student, he was also humorous and witty. He had a profound admiration for William Jennings Bryan, the great American orator, whom he had heard in Japan. It was his secret pride that he had once shaken hands with Mr. Bryan. My uncle acquired the ambition to become a great statesman as well as an orator. He believed that politics in the land of the Mikado would change from bureaucracy to democracy, provided such as he helped the change along! He had political aspirations. He felt that he could use oratory for his ends. Soon after his graduation he threw away his black university uniform and got a position in the government. His maiden speech was delivered at a public meeting and at once won for him acclaim as a promising orator and a budding statesman.

How I enjoyed watching him pose in front of my father's big dressing mirror, practicing his speeches again and again with grand gestures! In his newly-made suit, with a gay necktie which he had not quite succeeded in learning to fix properly without his niece to help him, and with his hair thick and lustrous standing up stiff like a hedgehog's, he would shout: "I cannot help my tears flooding from my eyes when I think of the most heroic decision of the great Admiral Togo at the famous Battle in the Japan Sea!" He raised his voice then and continued: "The Mikado's land cast her fate on this particular battle in the Japan Sea, lying in wait there for the Baltic Fleet! . . . To glory, or for misery, it rests upon your shoulders! Soldiers, fight well!" Practicing upon Admiral Togo's historical commandment, Uncle Yusuke himself was moved by his own grand speech. He paused to weep.

"Uncle! What a shame to show tears!" I cried, stepping out into the room from my hiding place. "You have often told me that a samurai hero never showed his tears even in the heaviest sorrow! You sentimental samurai!" Then we both laughed together at this seriocomic practice of speechmaking and gesticulating without an audience!

There was no worry about the unemployment of intellectuals in those days, and ambitious boys from the university could make headway in their chosen careers as soon as they graduated. Men of wealth or political power offered their beautiful daughters to them in marriage. Uncle Yusuke married the only daughter of Baron, later Count, Goto, as soon as he left the Imperial University.

"Be ambitious, grow to be an important woman of Japan!" These were the words Uncle Yusuke reiterated while he was in our household. Yet he never forgot to add, "But always with sweet womanliness." Uncle Yusuke's whispers have lingered in my ears all through my later life. Although my interpretation of "great woman" changed as my mind matured, my attitude toward life, "where there is a conviction, there is a way!" never changed and for this I am grateful to my uncle's influence in my girlhood days.

Another person who colored my thinking was Dr. Inazo Nitobe, well-known in the Western world as an interpreter of Bushido. He introduced the samurai spirit of old Japan to the Occident, as Lafcadio Hearn did the general culture of the Japanese. Dr. Nitobe devoted most of his last years to the League of Nations, which he served in an official capacity. Previously he had been sent many times as exchange professor to America and delivered his message of "peace on mutual understanding." I first began to be acquainted with him when he was nominated president of the First College of Tokyo, the boys' school celebrated as the nest of the brightest youth of the country. Dr. Nitobe was the center of admiration for young people at that time, as an educator with a liberal mind, and as the embodiment of Christian humanism.

When Dr. Nitobe took the presidency of this college in Tokyo, Uncle Yusuke had already finished his course there and was a student at the Imperial University, but he was in close contact with Dr. Nitobe, since he attended the lectures on colonial administration which Dr. Nitobe gave at the university. Meanwhile, a group of students, including Uncle Yusuke, formed a society which was a kind of reading club and met once every month with Dr. Nitobe as leader. Meetings were held at the members' houses by turn. The members of this club were utterly charmed by Dr. Nitobe's personality as well as by his comprehensive learning and wide knowledge of the West. They were as devoted to their teacher as samurai had been to their feudal lords. The greatest respect was shown him by his followers, and they literally followed the Chinese precept which commands: "Three steps behind, not to step on the shadow of your teacher on the earth."

One day the club met at my father's house, and Uncle Yusuke gave me permission to sit quietly and listen to their talk. I anxiously watched Dr. Nitobe. With my preconception of the man, he impressed me almost like a living god. Young girls or boys easily worship a big man. Dr. Nitobe was a big man to me, as he was to Uncle Yusuke. Motionless I watched him talking to these men about Goethe, Wordsworth and Tennyson. Of course I could not fully comprehend what they were saying or reading, but such names as Carlyle, Dante, Milton, Kant, Longfellow and Victor Hugo became familiar to my ears, as I often after this sat listening to this great man with his exceptionally thick eyeglasses.

Mother allowed me to wait on table when she served an evening meal to my uncle's guests. It was a high round table covered with a snow-white tablecloth. At ordinary meals we never used cloths, but kept to the bare low table of fine wood. The usual guests were served on individual lacquer trays, but when she entertained this Christian scholar and his group, mother used the white linens which father had brought back from London. Dr. Nitobe did not touch his chopsticks until he finished saying grace; so all the young men around him followed his example. This was quite new and strange to me who never had seen Christians dine before. Bamboo sprouts sliced and boiled with soy bean sauce were served in blue and white Kyoto porcelain and, for these, chopsticks were available. Beside the sprouts were placed huge pieces of beefsteak on white English plates with silver knives and forks as the proper implements. Sake was taboo at this table, for Christians were supposed neither to drink nor to smoke, but fresh strawberries were served with cream and sugar.

This combination of Eastern and Western dishes and modes of eating harmonized with what uncle's guests were discussing, talking and laughing about in Japanese, interspersed with many words in English, French and German—namely, the great universe. When the meal was about to end, Dr. Nitobe took some pieces of o-ko-ko, Japanese pickles made of horseradish, little turnips and various green vegetables which were dipped into the brown rice powder paste and preserved to make a delightful sour taste. This is quite a national dish. I had been told that it was not good manners to eat much o-ko-ko, although I liked it very much. So I thought this big man of my admiration would not touch such vulgar food. "Very delicious!" commented Dr. Nitobe, taking some more. "My wife thinks this o-ko-ko is indigestible and she does not care for its peculiar flavor. So I miss this national dish at home," he explained to my mother. And he continued munching all kinds of pickles, until he finished his meal with a bowl of toasted tea which I had poured for him from a painted clay pot.

Soon I learned from Uncle Yusuke that Mrs. Nitobe was an American of an old and rich Philadelphia family. The disciples of Dr. Nitobe were as devoted to her as they were to her husband. They admired her attitude toward him. It must have been difficult for an American woman to be married to a Japanese whose position was only that of a professor in a local college in northern Japan, and be forced to stay in so remote a place for some time. The living standards of Americans and Japanese are materially different and Mrs. Nitobe endured many hardships. But she never looked down on the Japanese, as many Westerners do, closing their eyes like a blinded carriage horse, unable to see the artistic and spiritual civilization Japan had been developing for thousands of years, dismissing them as an inferior yellow race whose civilization commenced only fifty years or so ago; in other words, when the yellow race met the white race.

I read books given to me by Dr. Nitobe. Among them were two big volumes called *Character Building* and *Path in Life*. I read them over and over like a Christian girl reading her Bible. Thus I was baptized by the spirit of humanism. Uncle Yusuke was my mentor; Dr. Nitobe was my reverend minister.

PART FOUR

STEPS TO THE LIFE OF
RESPONSIBILITIES

VIII

Marriage to a Young Baron

MARRIAGE is a predetermined fate for a Japanese girl. There are parents who betroth their children before they are born. Some babies are engaged as soon as they take their first breath in this world. Within this social scheme some girls grow beautifully; others peep out like white plum blossoms buried under the snow of winter, nobly but painfully accepting their lot without any hope of joy.

It is an unwritten code that a Japanese woman shall have only one man in marriage in her lifetime. Should she be left a widow when young, it is her duty to burn incense before her husband's spiritual presence in the family shrine and before his gravestone until the forty-ninth day, and after that once a month; also she is supposed to look after her husband's "left token"—that is, their children—as her only happiness, never caring for any other thing throughout her remaining years.

To break the marriage tie on her own initiative is unthinkable for any well-bred Japanese woman. To have it broken by her husband is a tragedy. The grief of "a broken mirror" completely overshadows a divorced woman's life, and she and her family have to accept the cold scorn of society. A girl is taught to submerge herself in her husband's family, accepting her husband's ways with absolute willingness; but the husband and his family can divorce her for any simple reason. "This woman does not meet the way of my family" is sufficient to get rid of her. Consequently a divorce certificate is often called "the three and a half line note"—so short and simple is it!

Feudal Japan made harsh discriminations between the classes and the sexes, and even murders were justified when the samurai considered an action or remark insulting to their dignity. Today Japanese law solemnly declares that man and woman, high and low, rich and poor, are equal in its eyes. Human life and rights are strictly protected by its authority since the great Mikado of the Meiji era inaugurated a new culture. But when we come to the matter of customs rather than statutes, woman is still kept in an inferior position.

What parents would find satisfaction in leading their daughters to a sacred wedding carriage if they thought they were to be treated like children or insane people? My mother did not realize that her dignity was cheated by the discrepancy between our book of civil law and our practices in private, nor did I ever in my youth think for a minute that a definite line divided a woman's rights before and after her marriage. But I discovered in time that she marries to lose her privileges as a person. She can divorce her husband only when he has left her alone with ill intent and without economic support, whereas the husband can divorce his wife if he so much as suspects she has insulted him or his honorable elders. Usually divorce cases are not brought to the courts, but quietly accepted by the weaker sex with a little promised alimony which she may or may not be able to collect.

Without bothering their heads over the legal side of marriage, girls and boys grow up and wed according to the law of "Izumo God," the god who makes the sex matches for the Yamato race. It is only a recent phenomenon that we have so-called "old maids" as a by-product of the higher education of girls. Having no historic term to cover this case, the Japanese have had to coin a new English term, "old miss," which is now widely used to mean the unmarried woman of, say, over twenty-five. Nor did Japanese men experience bachelorhood until

Western industrialism brought a high cost of living to this Island Empire, delaying matrimony.

On a bright spring day in my seventeenth year, I had finished my morning duties in the house and was sitting alone on the silk cushion by the balcony window, looking down on the fresh young leaves of the weeping willow in the garden, whose slim green branches were swaying to and fro in the soft breeze. At such times romantic sentiments without any reason occupy a young maiden's heart. Suddenly the back screen slipped open and a servant told me that I was called to my father's room. Cheerfully as usual I appeared in his presence; mother was also there. I bowed lightly to them and asked: "Is there anything you would like me to do, honorable father?"

He replied, "I have something to tell you, Shidzué. Sit down, please." My father said this in an affectionate but solemn tone. I sat down on one of the big English chairs, feeling that something very important was at hand. "You have finished your schooling now," he continued. "So your mother and I are thinking about your future, wishing to make you happy by arranging a suitable marriage for you!"

The word "marriage" shocked me. A young girl brought up in the atmosphere of the old Confucian doctrine which declares, "Male and female children shall not be together after the age of seven," naturally held men in considerable awe.

I was brought up with my brothers, of course, but I never thought of them as of a different sex. Now girlish shyness overcame me so that I could not raise my face. I sat with my head low and my eyes fixed on the edge of the Turkish carpet. Father went on to say that a marriage was proposed by Baron Keikichi Ishimoto, the son of Baron and Lieutenant General Shinroku Ishimoto whose services in the Mikado's army during the Russo-Japanese War had been rewarded with a title, many decorations and great honors. Lieutenant General Ishimoto was dead. He had passed away two years before while in Prince Saionji's cabinet as the Minister of War. The services for the third anniversary of his death had just been held by his widow and his six sons and daughter. The young Baron Ishimoto was now a student in the Imperial University of Tokyo and would finish the mining engineering course there in the coming summer. A position had been promised him by the Mitsui Mining Company, the largest of the kind in the country, and he was to enter upon his duties as soon as he graduated from the university. Dr. Wataru Watanabe, the head of the Engineering Department of the university, as well as close friends of my father, had given the most favorable recommendations for the young baron as one of the brightest and most serious-minded students in the senior class. Father closed his exposition of the suitor's merits by saying, "Think it over quietly, for your parents desire your happiness. But they are not forcing you against your will."

I did not answer, but burst into tears and covered my face with the long sleeves of my wisteria kimono. "Do you hate to marry, Shidzué?" father inquired gently, patting my shaking shoulders. "No, father, I . . . I just feel like crying." Father and mother did not seem quite to understand what caused their daughter to behave like this, for I was normally an exuberant child. They left me alone and I continued to wet my kimono sleeves.

A proposal by a young man of a prominent family did sound agreeable, but how could a young girl of seventeen, who had not quite outgrown her world of dreams, arrive at a decision on such an important matter in her life? One thing, however, was clear to my mind. "An ambitious statesman" was my ideal for a husband. I did not like the idea of marrying an engineer. Another anxiety was felt on account of father's description of the baron's character; he sounded so serious that I feared he would be as upright and sober as a "bronze Buddha." I preferred a character, human and even a little faulty. But these were not the reasons which led me to weep. My tears came from sweet regret at the dropping of curtains over my girlhood so soon. Girls like freedom to meditate and dream without obligations. To be confronted with such a responsibility just three weeks after my actual graduation from high school! Why not wait a year or two? Happy girlhood never comes back! That was my sorrow.

On the same evening Uncle Yusuke, who had just been married and had established a new home, was asked to come and talk about this family affair with me. Training in our home forbade children to contradict their parents in any matter; so we young people never discussed, never argued about things in their presence. But to talk to Uncle Yusuke was quite different. I could argue, if I wanted to. I asked for his opinion about the problem of my marriage, trusting him to give a good judgment based on his liberal way of thinking.

"What a lucky child you are! You would be the most fortunate woman in Japan if you were to marry the young baron!" I was quite amazed. "Why is that, uncle?" I asked. "How could you see through my future like a prophet?" My uncle did not hesitate. "Because," he said, "Baron Ishimoto is one of the brightest disciples of Dr. Nitobe and I have known him quite a while." Then he told me more about this young man, relieving my anxieties, and his eloquence persuaded me even to begin to like the baron. Uncle Yusuke's explanation of why the young suitor had selected engineering for his profession moved me more than anything else.

Although Baron Keikichi Ishimoto was born in a family of wealth and honor, he was a humble student of Christian humanism. He was very gifted and was one of the honor students granted the privilege of studying without having to pay university dues. With his mother's consent, however, he always gave away his privilege to some other youth whose family was in need of such consideration. As for his Christianity, it was not met with the same domestic sympathy, his parents considering the religion merely a foreign fad. This young man secretly attended Christian meetings to hear the gospel preached. One day he listened to Colonel Gumpei Yamamuro, the present Lieutenant General Yamamuro, of the Salvation Army, talk on "Christian soldiers." The Colonel's fiery words, "Be a corner stone of society," impressed him strongly, and he made up his mind that he would not seek for fame, or money, but be "the man who supports the floor," to use the Japanese phrase. He wanted to be a social reformer, and play the role of friend of laborers. Thus he chose to be a mining engineer, a profession which would keep him in close touch with the humblest kind of workers and their problems. "He is not going to be a mere machinelike man, but a courageous soldier for his cause. Don't you think he is a wonderful young fellow, Shidzué?" Uncle Yusuke finished his long oration on the baron. I had no idea about "laborers" but Uncle Yusuke's remarks satisfied me.

A day was set for the bride-to-be to see her bridegroom-to-be. Three black lacquered rikishas carried father, mother and me to the house of the "go-between" who had arranged for this marriage. It was a bright early May day, the sky was blue and the breeze was soft. An hour's trip through and across the narrow, crooked streets of Tokyo carried us to the Koishikawa district where Mr. Matsuda lived. When the tires of our rikisha sounded on the gravel of the garden in front of the Matsuda mansion, Mrs. Matsuda came out to greet us. She told us that the other family was already there, waiting for us. As I entered this home, my eyes fell on a set of old Tosa screens representing, against a background of dull gold, some court nobles at their banquet. These stood in the front room. All the sliding screens being open, soft voices could be heard from the inner room beyond.

I hesitated a moment, as my heart beat a little faster. Somewhere a voice whispered, "You are to see the very next minute the only man in your life." I do not know how my mother felt. She touched lightly my comb inlaid with lustrous mother-of-pearl, and arranged my green obi-sash embroidered with white peonies. Then I stepped into Mr. Matsuda's big thirty-mat reception room, with its vista of a thick-wooded garden beyond. And I found there three people sitting on heavy Chinese silk cushions—two elderly ladies and a handsome young man, tall and thin, in the black and gold-buttoned uniform worn by students of the Imperial University. It made him look young but dignified.

Before we took our seats on the cushions by the tokonoma we were introduced to each other formally by Mr. and Mrs. Matsuda and polite bowing was exchanged many times. "I am a humble girl, but I shall be glad if you recognize me hereafter," were the words I repeated with deep bows. The young baron was smiling as he talked to his mother. I cast many a shy glance at him stealthily but critically. Neither of us talked much but sat quietly hearing what the elders had to say.

"Do I like him? Does he like me?" I repeated in my mind while a grand dinner was being served on the big lacquer trays. It was a formal dinner with three trays for each person, containing delicacies of the sea and the mountains in handsome lacquer bowls and Kyoto porcelain. But I could little enjoy this feast, on account of my repeated silent queries: "Do I like him? Does he like me?" In time I found myself reassuring myself: "Yes, my first impression of him is favorable and I hope he is pleased with me!"

I do not know what other girls do and think on such an occasion. It is considered proper even today in Japan for an honorable marriage to be arranged by this formal process. Some people are anxious to introduce the Western love match to our society, but they have not yet succeeded. Some young people think they have fallen in love at first sight and others only develop mutual love and understanding after they marry. I still cannot give my opinion as to whether this arrangement by parents is a better custom and one to be preserved or whether the Occidental love match should be encouraged. Marriage is destiny, after all.

After this "seeing each other" prelude was over, both sides were to give their answers to the middleman. Mine was "Yes" and my parents were relieved. So a family council was solemnly called. Father, being the head of the Hirota family, of course had the right to give the decision on an affair of this kind, but it was customary to get the approval of other members of the family. And the great-uncle, uncles, aunts and cousins all agreed to this betrothal of the eldest daughter of the Hirota family to Baron Ishimoto. Mr. and Mrs. Matsuda brought the answer of the other side, equally positive and favorable. Thus we two young people were finally engaged.

At the end of May, a lucky day was selected on the Moon calendar and set for an announcement of the engagement. The exchange of betrothal presents was the principal ceremony for this day. At that time custom still prescribed on the girl's side the gift of sendai-hira, a stiff silk for a skirt to be worn by the man over his ceremonial kimono, but this has been widely displaced today by some woolen material for a man's Western swallow-tail coat. My gift of cloth was sent from my father to his prospective son-in-law and a wide piece of brocade for the bride's ceremonial obi-sash was presented according to the old rule by Baron Ishimoto to me. The seven materials for good luck which were to accompany the exchanging of the cloth and the Kyoto brocade were arranged on spotlessly clean wooden trays according to conventions. These comprised a pair of thick white paper fans, meaning more prosperity in the future, a bunch of dry seaweed (Laminaria) called "kombu" which in Japanese has the same sound as the word meaning child-bearing; a bunch of fine white dry noodles which from their resemblance to white hair symbolize the permanence of the marriage; and two other objects of similar significance. They were beautifully decorated with artificial pine branches on which were fastened flying storks and mother storks in their nests, all made of silk. These pines and storks also symbolized long life and prolific glory to the family. In addition there was a tray holding a list of the names of the members of my future husband's family including uncles, aunts and cousins— sixty in all. The same was handed from my family to his and hereafter both families were to be as relatives.

The betrothal ceremony started early in the morning. A household manager of each family departed with presents for the other at the same hour in a rikisha and it was arranged that they should meet in the middle of the street, exchanging mutual congratulations from their carriages. Mr. Akikusa, a bald-headed man in a black silk ceremonial kimono embroidered with white family crests, arrived at our home from Baron Keikichi Ishimoto's with the customary presents which were ceremoniously accepted by my father and arranged in front of the gold screen in our large white reception room. Father opened the spotless plain wooden box, and took out a brocade obi embroidered with pines and chrysanthemums in gorgeous colors. I was quite happy and thanked Mr. and Mrs. Matsuda who visited both families by turn that day to congratulate everyone. A red-rice, whole-seafood and bean feast was served at the family table in the middle of the day. Brothers, sisters and all the servants came to say "O-medeto" to me, except my little brother Hiroo who said to me, "I don't want to give my dear sister to anybody; I feel sorry to see my sister going away." A sweet and sad expression came over his face. He was nine years old at the time.

Formal calls now had to be exchanged by both families. It

was early June. The rainy season had not started yet, the sky was blue and trees were turning dark green. We received an invitation to dinner from the Ishimoto family, and we were asked to arrive a little early in order to see the garden.

Of course I was thrilled to be taken to see for the first time my fiancé's residence. Baron Ishimoto's house, built in the old Kyoto palace style, stood in the Koishikawa district. The big square wooden gate had heavy swinging doors with iron fittings and a roof covered with dark gray tiles. Soft gray gravel covered the drive beyond the gate, and tall ginkgo trees with their fan-shaped leaves stood on both sides like giant sentinels. In front of the entrance hall were camellia plants and dark brown Japanese maples.

The house itself was divided into two wings: one Japanese and one foreign. It is fashionable among wealthy Japanese to build both Western and native quarters although the Occidental copy is not always successful. First we were led into the foreign wing, where the baron and his mother, his aunt and the rest of his family received us warmly. As father and the baron, the heads of the two families, exchanged greetings, my father said: "Mysterious fate has connected both families. We are all humble people, but I am honored to present my daughter to you that you may treat her with favor." The baron replied: "We are humble people also and mysterious fate brought us here to accept your honorable daughter as a bride in our family." I was formally *being given* to Baron Ishimoto's *family*. The idea of giving a daughter to a family and not to a man is much more distinctly expressed in the case of the marriage of the eldest son than of a younger one. The eldest is regarded as the symbol of family pride, while younger sons are treated as persons less important to the family. I bowed and repeated the same words of humble greeting, oh, how many times—perhaps ten times—as I was introduced to each of my five future brothers-in-law and one sister-in-law and even to the head of the maids who was over seventy-five years old and had served this family for more than thirty years! She bowed to me folding her small body double, her formal Japanese coiled hair becoming especially conspicuous in the act.

Then we moved slowly out to the garden. First father's black shoes, mother's low and soft mat-covered paulownia clogs and my blue silk sandals beat a soft tread around the house from the front entrance to the big natural footstone leading down from the house. A servant in a blue-black silk coat announced that everything was ready in the garden. We took no initiative ourselves. That is not done in aristocratic circles. We waited to be ushered down the slope along the stone steps into the garden several acres in size at the foot of the slope on which the house stood. A hill covered with a chestnut forest formed the center of the garden. Through the woods ran a brook softly murmuring on its course toward an artificial lake at the foot of the hill. Narrow wooden or rattan bridges crossed the meandering stream. The water of the large pond was green and natural stones of various shapes and sizes were set all around its edges. Lotus, cow lilies, reeds and iris were blooming in rich profusion. A wisteria trellis built on the bank cast shadows from the purple flowers hanging in bunches some four or five feet long. In the shadows bees were humming peacefully. The wide gentle slope on the top of which stood the house and along which the garden path led down to the pond was entirely covered with azaleas in full blossom. Peach, white, pink, lilac, orange, dark rose, there they clustered and the splendid sight was inspiring. We took a brief rest in the grass-thatched arbor at one side of the spacious ground sloping up to the hills of azaleas.

My future mother-in-law was not happy until she had shown us all parts of the garden, even her flower and vegetable beds. I followed her everywhere. I was dressed then in a pale crepe kimono with a wide sash of silver texture embroidered with camellias, my sleeves hanging almost to the ground. The design on my kimono of some sweet China pink, blooming by the water and painted on the silk, was thoroughly approved. The baron's mother told me that she loved to see her daughter-in-law in beautiful kimonos as she had six sons and only one daughter of her own to delight her eyes in that way.

I did not speak a word to my fiancé while we were walking in the garden, but was always careful to follow his mother closely. Finally we were taken into the cryptomeria woods, where a diminutive shrine to Inari (a popular Fox God) set on top of some stone steps was opened to the guests. Old red paper lanterns were hung on both sides of the small altar, in the center of which a sacred bell was suspended, breaking the quietness of the woods when it was shaken by occasional worshipers.

A formal dinner concluded this ceremony. When my rikisha descended the hill as we were hurrying home, I heard frogs croaking in the dark swamp. I looked up at the sky and saw that stars were twinkling high above, and the evening breeze which toyed with my hair was cool upon my hot body and soul! I had learned nothing from this visit about the man I was to marry. But I knew his background.

A formal return call took place a week later, the Ishimoto family being entertained by mine in the most elaborate Western manner. French food was carefully prepared and served by stewards in full dress. Silver and porcelain brought back from Europe by father graced the feast. Father in his turn took our guests to every part of his castlelike home equipped with modern conveniences. He even took them to his favorite retreat—the bar downstairs where he kept old Scotch whiskies, French wines and other Western liquors. He showed them how to play shuffleboard and other games in the basement. But my fiancé's mother did not seem quite to understand the beauty of Western rooms in the Louis Quatorze style or a chamber furnished with a north-European stove. Unused to chairs, she must have found them ridiculous. My mother told me to play on the piano for my fiancé, and I selected a Beethoven composition. I had been trained to appreciate the conveniences and the accomplishments of the West as well as the arts of my native land, for my parents wanted me to be able to adjust myself to the ways of a husband, whatever they might be. And I had such facility in adapting myself to the Western manner of living that it was actually painful for me, after I was married, to go back to the pure Japanese house and live with an old mother-in-law in true native fashion.

This she held to rigorously, however, and she was a woman of strong character. She had helped her husband win glory and wealth, she had brought up her seven children with strict discipline and she had worked hard to keep her domestic affairs in order. She cooked well; she sewed swiftly. In later years when she felt that she had done all that she should do as a good wife and wise mother, she had begun to devote more time to her own pleasure such as writing thirty-one syllable poems and learning "Utai" (the singing part of the No play). She liked to have parties at home, inviting her friends to see her azaleas or to hear the cuckoos in her garden. Often she went to see the No drama and to the Kabuki theater. Being a widow, complete mistress of her own home, and moreover, the practical head of the family, she was at liberty to live her life as she pleased. And her choice was the traditional Japanese way.

She had very little sympathy with objects or ideas that came out of the West. Westerners were to her "red-haired barbarians." Her adherence to custom had prevented her son's visiting his fiancée freely, for she thought it beneath his dignity to visit a woman often. To talk over the telephone or to write to each other unnecessarily was in her mind a sort of promiscuous conduct in violation of her moral standard and not to be countenanced even after our engagement. She wanted to pound into her future daughter-in-law's brain the Confucian doctrine of female inferiority.

Whether in the East or in the West, however, nobody could ever succeed in building a fence between two people who love each other. Confucianism could not quite separate me from my betrothed. One day before we were married my parents sent a note to Baron Ishimoto asking him to come to tea and supper, as we were about to leave the city for a summer vacation and he also was going away to take up his new post in western Japan. I was excited from early morning until his arrival, as I helped mother arrange fresh flowers in the drawing room and dining room. Mother had told me what time my fiancé would appear. The bell rang exactly at the stated moment, and before the maid came to attend to the door, I had opened it instantly, for I had been waiting secretly nearby. Blushing, I slipped him quickly a long letter written in India ink on fine Japanese paper and wrapped in a pale blue silk fukusa. The smuggling of a love letter quite succeeded! His answer came in the same manner whenever he visited my family but he had to invent all sorts of excuses in order to get his mother's permission to see me. In spite of the admonition of Confucianism, the sprout of affection grew smoothly, and after he left Tokyo for the mining field we were allowed to write to each other freely.

My stepping out for the last time from the school gate under the falling petals of cherry blossoms, my being engaged under the rippling bunches of wisteria flowers, and plans for my marriage in the snowy Christmas season kept my mother extremely busy. She lost weight conspicuously. Her devotion, her strength, her care seemed to be concentrated upon her eldest daughter during these days. It was the time for her to put a finishing touch on her maternity—to teach her daughter to behave gracefully and nobly, not to be blamed as a young baroness and daughter-in-law to the widow of a great public man. Mother regretted that the opportunity for her to give final training and advice to her daughter was so limited. From morning till night she paid particular attention to every action or remark of mine. She even came to my bed every night to see whether I behaved well while I was asleep. To sleep properly on the wooden pillow without ever letting the head fall from it is still a strict requirement for a daughter of a samurai.

Another anxiety of my mother was to prepare a complete trousseau for the bride. Father was generous about the expense of furnishing a splendid outfit, befitting the baron's rank. In my trousseau accordingly there were two divisions. One had to do with furniture, including large chests for bedding, and chests of drawers for kimonos, all made of old paulownia wood unpainted but polished to show its natural grain. The other consisted of bedding and clothes. There were several sets of bedding to be used at different seasons and on different occasions, such for example as for a wedding, for guests, and for ordinary use. Kimonos and obis were prepared for the four seasons, with appropriate underwear and wrappers. Jewels, silver and even paper of all kinds and for different purposes figured in my equipment. The whole heap of possessions was carried by four two-ton motor trucks to the baron's mansion five days before our wedding. In later years when I traveled in China and happened to attend a grand wedding in a wealthy family, I discovered that the Japanese trousseau was far more complicated than the Chinese.

These tremendous masses of furniture and clothing were, of course, not planned with regard to the actual circumstances of married life, but to indicate the rank of the bridegroom's family, and especially to please the mother-in-law, who already had every essential and luxuries as well. My possessions could only double the beautiful but useless heaps of stuff in her own dwelling and serve as an added nuisance. The poor bride could not remember all she had brought to her husband's home and was overwhelmed by the task of trying to keep her things in order. But perhaps the trousseau gratified someone. It was exhibited to relatives and friends of the bride before it was carried to the bridegroom's house. There it was exhibited again to the husband's family and to his relatives and friends. The great amount of work connected with all this business almost killed the young bride.

My mountainous trousseau was itemized to the smallest detail in catalogue form, even including my high school diploma, which was presented from my father to my husband's family. This gesture meant that these objects were not the bride's personal possessions but were to become the property of the groom's family, like the bride herself. I still keep the catalogue which I translate here:

Wedding robe of white satin brocade covered with embroidery in a pattern of flying phoenix and paulownia blossoms.

CEREMONIAL KIMONOS, PADDED AND LINED FOR WINTER USE

Number

1. White plain silk with streaming sleeves (2 layers) (to be worn at wedding ceremony under the robe)........................ 1
2. Plain silk with streaming sleeves [1] in cinnabar (to be worn soon after the wedding ceremony)............................ 1
3. Black crepe with streaming sleeves with figures of white storks and pine trees (to be worn for the first half of the wedding reception) 1
4. Crepe with streaming sleeves in celadon with figures of cherry blossoms, and a lacquer carriage of court nobles (to be worn for the latter half of the wedding reception)...................... 1
5. Crepe with streaming sleeves in indigo with figures of chrysanthemums, a boat and waves (to be worn when calling on the relatives after the wedding)................................. 1
6. Black crepe with sleeves of ordinary length [2] with figures of young

[1] Three feet eight inches.
[2] Two feet three inches.

Number

pine trees (to be worn on ceremonial occasions after the wedding is completed).. 1

7. Crepe with sleeves of ordinary length in lavender with figures of court lady's fans (2 layers) (to be worn for parties)......... 1
8. White plain silk for underlayers.......................... 2
9. Crepe brocade with sleeves of ordinary length in grape color without figures (to be worn for the memorial services of the dead) 1
10. Underlayer in pale celadon for the above..................... 1
11. Purple crepe brocade with sleeves of ordinary length (2 layers) with figures from the "Tale of Genji" (to be worn for parties)... 1
12. Omeshi crepe, with chrysanthemum figures embroidered (2 layers) (to be worn for formal calling)..........................

CEREMONIAL KIMONOS LINED FOR SPRING AND AUTUMN USE

1. Black crepe with sleeves of ordinary length with figures of phoenix, pines, bamboos, and plum blossoms (to be worn on spring and autumn ceremonial occasions).......................... 1
2. White plain silk underlayer for the above.................... 1
3. Lavender crepe with sleeves of ordinary length with figures of cherry blossoms and tambourines (2 layers) (to be worn for parties) 1
4. Pale blue brocaded silk with sleeves of ordinary length (to be worn for the memorial services of the dead).................. 1
5. Underlayer of cream color for the above..................... 1
6. Indigo crepe brocade with embroidered willow branches and a barge (to be worn for formal calling)........................ 1

SKIRT

Grape-colored taffeta (to be worn in the Imperial presence at the alumnae gatherings at the Peeresses' School)................. 1

CEREMONIAL KIMONOS FOR SUMMER USE

1. Black gauze silk with sleeves of ordinary length with figures of willow branches and a stream (to be worn when invited to wedding ceremonies)....................................... 1
2. White gauze underlayer for the above....................... 1

3. Blue-streaked gauze silk with sleeves of ordinary length with figures of seven autumn flowers (to be worn for parties) 1
4. White silk underlayer for the above 1
5. Pale blue crepe gauze with sleeves of ordinary length with figures of hagi flowers drawn in India ink (to be worn for parties) 1
6. White silk underlayer for the above 1
7. Pale blue crepe with streaming sleeves with figures of China pinks along a stream (to be worn for parties) 1
8. White silk underlayer for the above 1
9. Maroon crepe with sleeves of ordinary length without figures (to be worn for memorial services of the dead) 1
10. Brocaded mauve gauze with sleeves of ordinary length without figures (to be worn for memorial services of the dead) 1
11. Wisteria colored brocaded chiffon with embroidered rain and cherry petals (to be worn for formal calling) 1

CEREMONIAL OBIS, ONE-PIECE, FOR WINTER, SPRING AND AUTUMN USE

1. White satin [1] covered with embroidery to go with white wedding robe
2. Karanishiki brocade with figures of pine branches and chrysanthemums (to go with the black winter ceremonial kimono with streaming sleeves)
3. Gold Karanishiki brocade, with flowers woven in Sodatsu design (to go with celadon ceremonial kimono)
4. Itonishiki brocade with figures of autumn leaves in various colors (to go with any autumn ceremonial kimono)
5. Beige Itonishiki brocade with figures of lady's fans (to go with the phoenix ceremonial kimono)
6. Gold Itonishiki brocade with figures of chrysanthemums and paulownias (to go with indigo blue ceremonial kimono)
7. Tan shuchin brocade with figures of flower circles (to go with formal calling kimonos)
8. Navy blue shuchin brocade with figures of fans (to go with semiceremonial kimonos)
9. Tan shuchin brocade with Egyptian figures (to go with semiceremonial kimonos)

[1] A one-piece obi is four and half yards long, about a foot wide, made out of one big piece of cloth folded double lengthwise and always reserved for ceremonial use.

10. Green plain silk with embroidered peonies (to go with semiformal kimonos)

CEREMONIAL OBIS, ONE-PIECE, FOR SUMMER USE

1. White Shioze silk embroidered with figures of daimyo's maple festival (to go with blue summer ceremonial kimono)
2. White brocaded gauze with figures of flowers
3. Silver brocaded gauze with figures of Japanese harebells (to go with any summer ceremonial kimono)
4. Pewter thread brocade with figures of maple leaves (to go with hagi-figured ceremonial kimono)
5. White linen with checkered figures (to go with midsummer ceremonial kimono)
6. White Itonishiki with quail-colored stripes (to go with semiceremonial kimono)
7. White Itonishiki brocade with figures of autumn leaves (to go with semiceremonial kimono)
8. Silver brocade with camellias (to go with ceremonial blue kimono)

OTHER KIMONOS PADDED AND LINED, LINED OR SINGLE FOR VARIOUS SEASONS AND OCCASIONS

	Number
1. Plain omeshi crepe with embroidered family crests	1
2. Striped crepe	7
3. Figured crepe	2
4. Tied-and-dyed crepe	1
5. Shima mud-dyed brown and white pongee	1
6. Various figured pongee silk	10
7. Figured muslin	2
8. Figured or brocaded silk underlayers	8
9. Plain omeshi crepe with embroidered family crests	1
10. Striped crepe	5
11. Brocaded crepe	1
12. Oshima mud-dyed brown and white pongee	1
13. Various figured pongee	9
14. Brocade crepe	2
15. Striped crepe	4
16. Striped gauze silk	5
17. Echigo linen	1

Number

18. Creped serge.. 2
19. Serge 5
20. Flannel 6
21. Muslin 3
22. Figured linen.. 2
23. Figured pongee.. 7
24. Satsuma white and black cotton........................... 1
25. Indigo cotton with white figures......................... 8
26. White cotton with indigo figures......................... 22

Total 117

OTHER OBIS

1. Itonishiki brocade lined with crepe....................... 4
2. Plain silk lined with crepe............................... 5
3. Muslin one-piece.. 1
4. Various lined obis.. 4
5. Streaked gauze silk lined with plain silk................ 7

HAORI-COATS

1. Indigo brocade gauze, for summer.......................... 1
2. Brocade crepe lined with family crests.................... 7
   in navy blue
       violet
       maroon
       grape
       grape with stripes
       green with scattered figures
       purple brocade omeshi crepe
3. Striped omeshi crepe...................................... 1
4. Brocade crepe padded...................................... 1
5. Striped crepe padded...................................... 1
6. Omeshi crepe padded....................................... 1
7. Various figured pongee lined.............................. 6
8. Various figured pongee padded............................. 8

OVERCOATS

1. Brocade crepe.. 1
2. Brocade gauze for summer................................... 1

Number

3. Brocade crepe for spring... 3
4. Brocade crepe padded for winter............................. 1
5. Alpaca woolen raincoat.. 1
6. Serge raincoat.. 2

NAGAJIBAN (PETTICOAT KIMONOS) FOR ALL SEASONS

1. White brocade crepe with streaming sleeves.................. 1
2. White and red figured with streaming sleeves................ 1
3. Scarlet brocade crepe with streaming sleeves................ 1
4. White brocade crepe with sleeves of ordinary length........ 1
5. Red with figures.. 1
6. Scarlet brocade crepe with embroidery....................... 1
7. Tied and dyed brocade crepe................................. 1
8. Muslin figured.. 5
9. Pink streaked gauze crepe with streaming sleeves........... 1
10. Pink brocade crepe... 1
11. White streaked gauze... 1
12. Figured crepe... 1
13. Various gauze with figures................................... 4
14. White linen with embroidery................................. 1
15. Omi-linen.. 2
16. Figured crepe... 1
17. Muslin figured.. 3

Total 27

UNDERWEAR

Flannel sets... 6
White cotton sets... 20

TABI (Socks)

White silk socks.....................................(Pairs) 24
White calico socks..................................(Pairs) 30

APRONS

Striped cotton overall.. 1
White calico apron... 2

MISCELLANEOUS

	Number
Colored cloth pieces:	
Embroidered	36
With dyed figures or painted	23
Total	59
Brocade crepe sashes for tucking up kimono	5
Scarlet brocade crepe sash for night kimono	1
Obi clasps with silk strings	15
Small sashes for tying up obi	11
Gloves (Pairs)	7
Sable muff and boa	1
Shawls and scarfs	6
Obi frame	2
Linen handkerchief (Dozens)	8
Brocade hand bag	2
Leather hand bag	4
Purse	3
Ceremonial silk bag for carrying paper handkerchief	1
Mirror case	2
Perfume bottle	3
Fan	3
Silk for lining and underkimono (Rolls)[1]	15

FUROSHIKI CLOTHS

Tan Shioze silk ceremonial fukusa, lined with scarlet and embroidered with figures of lucky plants, family crests and tassels in gold	2
Ceremonial fukusa	6
Tea ceremony fukusa	1
Silk furoshiki	4
Muslin furoshiki	6
Green with white figured furoshiki in various sizes	10

JEWELRY

Gold watch	2
Silver watch	1
Chain	4

[1] One roll is 13 yards long and 1 foot 2 inches wide.

Platinum with pearls
Platinum with diamonds and pearls
Platinum and gold with stones
Gold

	Number
Ring	4

Platinum with seven diamonds
Platinum with six diamonds and a sapphire
Gold with 11 diamonds and a ruby
Gold with 3 diamonds and 2 emeralds

Obi clasps...	6

Pearls, diamonds, and emeralds clustered
Gold tambourine with pearls and diamonds
Jade carving with diamonds
Jade carving
Silver and copper carving
Silver carving

Brooches	2

Gold with pearls and emeralds
Gold carving with pearls

HAIR ORNAMENTS

Tortoiseshell:

Plain	2
Carved	7
Gold and mother-of-pearl inlaid............................	2
Carved and pearl inlaid for Western hairdressing............	1
Carved for Western hairdressing...........................	2
Coral ball..	1
Jade ball..	1
Silver carved ball..	4

Combs:

Gold and mother-of-pearl inlaid...........................	3
Tortoiseshell, pearl inlaid, coral inlaid......................	3

Beads:

Coral	1
Jade	1
Silk piece...	6
Artificial flowers for Western hairdressing......................	4

CLOGS AND SANDALS

Pairs

Black lacquered clogs...	2
Plain wooden clogs..	2
Plain wooden mat-covered clogs.................................	2
Black lacquered high clogs for rains............................	2
White silk sandals..	1
Silk or velvet covered ordinary sandals.........................	3

PARASOLS AND UMBRELLAS

Number

Embroidered tan parasol..	1
Embroidered white linen..	1
Black silk parasol with handle of silver carving.................	1
Indigo silk parasol..	1
Paper umbrella...	2

BEDDING AND CUSHIONS

Arabesque figured on blue silk for guest use...............	(Sets)[1]	2
Flower figured pongee set for ordinary use.................	(Sets)	2
Streaked gauze silk summer quilts for guest use...........	(Piece)	2
Linen crepe summer quilts for ordinary use...............	(Piece)	2
Flower figured muslin.....................................	(Set)	1
White blankets..		2
Steamer blankets..		2
Linen sheets and pillow cases.............................	(Doz.)	1
Black and gold lacquered wooden pillow....................		2
Pillows for ordinary use..................................		2
White and blue linen mosquito net.........................		2

(one for eight-mat room, one for twelve-mat room)

Dark brown heavy silk cushion for winter guests............	(set)[2]	1
Blue and white streaked gauze summer cushion for guests......	(Set)	1
Brocade silk cushions for couple use.....................	(Pair)	1
Muslin cushion for couple use...........................	(Pair)	1
Bedding and cushions for maid...........................	(Set)	1

[1] One set of bedding consists of two lower quilts and two upper quilts.

[2] One set of cushions consists of five pieces.

FURNITURE

	Number
Kakemono (picture scroll for Doll Festival use)	2
Chest of drawers	6
Big chest for bedding	3
Cabinet	2
Bureau with mirror	1
Full-sized mirror with stand	1
Chest for woolens and furs	1
Needlework chest	1
Chest for shoes and clogs	1
Clothes horse	1
Towel horse	1
Dinner table	1
Writing table	1
Bookcase	1
Books (Boxes)	3
Fire brazier (Pairs)	3
Writing set for India ink and rice paper	3
Flower vases	6
Flower vase stands	4
Flower arrangement utensils (Set)	1
Tobacco set (Set)	1
Cigarette set (Set)	1

MISCELLANEOUS ARTICLES

	Number
Wardrobe trunk	1
Suitcases	2
Rattan suitcases	3
Velvet traveling bags	2
Toilet cases	4
Portable toilet set	1
Razors	3
Various sewing articles (Box)	1
Various laundry utensils (Box)	1
Japanese paper (Box)	1
Toys, color piece, purse, belts, etc. (Box)	1
(for gifts to servants on various occasions)	
Boxes of formal gifts (various silk rolls) to be presented to the elders and close relatives of husband's family (Box)	20

Diploma of Peeresses' School.

A key case to be handed to the formal receiver of the trousseau.

A case of crystal seals of the bride.

UTENSILS (JAPANESE)

	Number
Lacquered dinner trays of various kinds	27
Lacquered or carved wooden trays	15
China plates and rice bowls	29
Picnic lunch plate (Set)	1
Gold and lacquered New Year's Feast set	1
Lacquered soup bowls	10
Tea set of Satsuma porcelain (Pieces)	10
Silver tea set for green tea (Pieces)	10
Teakettles (silver and iron)	2
Tea trays (Sets)	3
Basins	3

UTENSILS (WESTERN)

Tea sets	2
Coffee sets	1
Silver teaspoons (Doz.)	2
Fruit set	1
Silver fruit knives and forks (Doz.)	1
Knives and forks for dinner (Set)	1
Dinner spoons (Set)	1
Dinner plates	36
Linen tablecloths and napkins (Doz.)	1
Electric cooker	1
Picnic lunch basket	1
Cooking utensils (Boxes)	2

Of these heaps of things, most articles were made to order. Greatest care was taken with the ceremonial kimonos, thirty in number. First mother called the clerk from the ceremonial kimono department of the Mitsukoshi shop, who had always come to our house to solicit orders. They talked over colors and designs, so that each color and each design would symbolize the particular occasion on which a garment was to be worn and would never be repeated. The artists at the store worked out the designs on white silk material; then the painting and embroidering department, after many careful experiments, carried out the schemes. Finally the sewing department fashioned the cloth into flowing robes with red lining and they were sent to our house neatly folded in white paper boxes.

For all this labor and for the exquisite materials used, the price for the embroidered wedding robe alone came to about Y700 ($350) and each of the ceremonial kimonos with streaming sleeves cost from Y300 ($150) to Y500 ($250).

For other kimonos, haori-coats, and petticoat kimonos, mother went to various silk shops to choose materials. To get two hundred of them in half a year must have been a tremendous task. It was the same with the obis. The jewelry and silver were mostly ordered by father from Mappin Well in London and the hair ornaments of numerous carved and inlaid pins and combs, all representing happy figures, were ordered from the White Peony Company, the most select shop of the kind in Tokyo.

The furniture, such as the chests of drawers, cabinets, bureaus, desks and flower vase stands of paulownia or chestnut had to be made to match one another; they had oxidized silver fittings bearing the family crest. The lacquer utensils also had to match in color, design and shape.

The entire cost of my trousseau must have been over Y20,000 ($10,000), which may seem an inexcusable sum to spend on a young girl's mere clothes and their accessories. But this was almost all I was to take to my husband's family, for a Japanese bride was not supposed to bring any money or real estate; if she needed pocket money she was obliged to sell her gorgeous clothes or ornaments. She had to keep her things carefully so that they might last all her life, for she could not hope to have any new clothes unless her husband or her mother-in-law happened to be interested in dressing her up in a style more modern than that of her wedding trousseau.

Wedding presents, as the West knows them, hardly made up any part of my trousseau, as such gifts in Japan are mostly limited to white and red silk cloth and dried katso fish. Porcelain, which is easily broken, tea things used for condolence presents, and handkerchiefs, the name of which sounds unlucky to Japanese ears, are strictly taboo on this occasion. But silk cloth was given—in rolls of white and red decorated with artificial pine, bamboo, and plum branches and storks and turtles. Sometimes these rolls were shaped into various lucky figures such as the big tai-fish, rising sun, pine tree, or plum blossoms, all made out of one long piece of silk tied with silk thread and gold and silver strings. Since the gifts came from families and not from my personal friends and were more symbolical than useful or amusing, there were comparatively few things I really could enjoy.

December 23, 1914, was set for my wedding day. I got up at dawn for meditation. Then I wrote in my diary my last thought as a virgin and a member of the Hirota family. It was snowing softly outside and I felt the snow was purifying me for my sacred day. After a light breakfast, the process of "making up the bride" began. First, at six o'clock the hairdresser came with her assistant. My hair was coiled up in the shimada fashion, the proper coiffure for a bride, after being oiled and perfumed until it looked like lustrous black satin. The double knot high in the center with big puffs all around made my face look small indeed and accentuated the line of the neck, in approved style. Five pieces of light amber-colored tortoiseshell in exquisite carving decorated my hair.

"Beautiful, Shidzué-Sama!" said O-ko, a middle-aged maid who came to my family before I was born and was going to wait on me in my new home after I was married. "It looks almost as if dew were dropping down from your hair, such watery luster!" she repeated. But to me it felt heavy like the iron helmet of a samurai.

I took a hot Japanese bath to steam the hair and also to make my skin ready for thick powdering and painting. Another professional woman made up my face, neck and hands, etiquette demanding that a bride be painted like an ivory image.

A pure white habutai-silk kimono with full-length sleeves that touched the floor, a white satin obi with flowers embroidered in gold and silver, a heavy white robe with phoenix and paulownia blossoms embroidered in gorgeous color to wear over the white silk kimono, composed my wedding costume. This pure white ceremonial apparel—the same in color that is worn at a funeral—signifies that a bride is a person dead to her family circle.

I took the seat of honor for the farewell dinner, among all the members of my family. It was a Japanese meal. Sake was served at the table, and used to toast the family on the approaching marriage within its ranks.

Solemnity governed the whole affair. Everybody kept utterly silent until father spoke quietly and gently the words of farewell to his daughter, his final admonition. He said gravely:

"Father bird and mother bird love to have their young birds with them forever, but when the young birds grow fully, they fledge out leaving their nest and parent birds behind. This is the day for my beloved daughter, Shidzué, to use her own wings. She will meet bright sunshine under the blue sky as she flies, but some day her wings may have to fight with mean rain or cross wind. It is life as it is. Conduct yourself honorably, Shidzué, and be happy in your new nest."

An eighteen-year-old bride accepted this admonition only with tears, unable to speak a word.

Mother did not comment, but looked serious and pale in

her black ceremonial robe. Everybody began to take up chopsticks and eat without speaking. Suddenly Mrs. Matsuda, who with Mr. Matsuda had participated in earlier rites, began to weep; she even took her handkerchief from her sleeve and wept bitterly. How could I control myself from bursting into tears too? I sobbed like a child. Mother said quietly to me that I had no time for crying today because the moment had come to depart. Yes, I must start now to leave my dear family, and put my carefree girlhood behind me. O-ko at once became energetic with her powder puff, fixing the bride's make-up again and again, so easily was it spoiled by falling tears. Sisters, brothers, servants and all the other people of the household stood in the front court, as my carriage drove out from the gate leaving two parallel gray tracks on the ground which was covered with soft snowflakes.

A sacred fire was lighted and sacred salt was scattered around the front entrance of our house by Toku, the old gardener of the family, a rite which signifies "Thou shalt *never come back again.*"

I was saying to myself over and over: "The marriage vow shall not be broken in any circumstances. I shall not go home whatever the struggle I must face in the future. Have I to die in difficulties I shall do so alone." The thought of such a filial break pressed heavily on the mind of the one who was leaving her family and upon the hearts of those who were sending her away. Bondage to the old family system tightened tenfold and even twice tenfold the ties of the young woman with her own kin. Even the passionate love of her husband was felt to be like moonlight on a cloudy night to be covered up easily by the strong power of dark mischief. So the stern but pathetic determination of a Japanese bride often hides the happiness of a wedding day behind a storm of tears.

The wedding itself was performed in the grand reception room of the Ishimoto residence and was conducted by Baron

Yujiro Nakamura and his wife, who now took the place of Mr. and Mrs. Kosei Matsuda as the second go-between. The "Three-three-and-nine-times exchanging sake cup ceremony" united two souls and I became the wife of Baron Keikichi Ishimoto. The sake cup, used but once for the ceremony and broken immediately when it was over, was made of white clay according to the Shinto tradition. The sake was served by the conventional butterfly-boy and butterfly-girl, roles played by the little children of Mr. and Mrs. Matsuda. The ceremony ended in the Utai music rendered by Mr. Matsuda,—a passage from the No play *Takasago* based on the legend of an old couple turning into pine trees after having enjoyed a long life of mutual help and love. This is the proper close for every Japanese wedding. A most solemn ceremony in which every one looks as grave as possible was at last ended—to my great relief.

The bride was then taken into her new dressing room, and her white robe changed into a long-sleeved cinnabar kimono. Thus the maiden who had left her own home in a funeral shroud was restored to life in her husband's family. The ceremony of uniting the parents and their new-begotten child and that of sanctioning the new sisterhood and the new brotherhood took place next. It likewise consisted of passing round the sake cup. The bridegroom was dressed in a black habutai-silk ceremonial kimono with its five big white crests of Count Sakai, the former daimyo of the Ishimoto family—the robe having been "honorably given" by the late daimyo to Baron Ishimoto's grandfather.

For this ritual the newly married couple knelt side by side on cushions like a prince and princess of the Doll Festival, their backs to the center of the tokonoma on which were hung a pair of kakemono of white storks painted by Kiitsu Hogan, one of the great artists of the eighteenth century. An enormous branch of a moss-covered pine tree with a little bunch of white daisies entwining themselves around it was arranged before the kakemono: the pine signifying masculine beauty and glory; the sweet white flowers the womanly virtues of obedience and modesty.

There followed the couple's first eating ceremony, a meal pompously served on gold and lacquer trays according to the command of tradition: "You shall eat together." But I could hardly touch the gay display of food.

The wedding of a rich Japanese girl makes her a complete "robe hanger." A professional dressing woman ran after me all day long, often changing my costume to harmonize with successive ceremonies. All the accessories had to be changed for each costume and tying up the obi is necessary each time—a wonderful art but an incessant torture to its victim. The bride had to endure this with patience, and be careful not to faint even when the long thick textile being wound around her choked her very breath.

My cinnabar robe was changed for a black streaming-sleeved ceremonial kimono painted with white flying storks, after I had received congratulations at a dinner prepared in Western style. At this dinner there were nearly three hundred guests, relatives and friends of the two families. My mother-in-law did not object to having this party given at a hotel, because she knew that it was impossible to have one on such a scale in the Japanese manner, without spending far more time and labor upon it. Nevertheless, some customary Japanese rites were observed and in the middle of the dinner the bride left the hall, to appear again in another handsome ceremonial kimono of celadon color embroidered and painted with a gay ox-drawn carriage covered with cherry blossoms.

As the evening drew to a close the bride and bridegroom were taken from the hotel to the bridegroom's home by the first go-between, leaving the guests behind. Another, and the last, changing of costumes for the final ceremony of the day was made. A set of screens painted with gay flowers of every season surrounded the wedding bed laid on the new green mat floor and covered with soft silk quilts. Mrs. Matsuda alone attended this last rite—"entering the bridal bed"—and left us within the screen with the congratulation "Omedeto-gozai-masu!"

IX

Life of a Bride in a Big Family System

MY FIRST bridal night was cut short by my maid O-ko who waked me at five in the morning. It was dark and cold. I had to dress before my mother-in-law left her bed, and she had a habit of retiring late and of waking up early. It was the duty of a bride to please first her mother-in-law and serve her husband next. My mother-in-law did not treat me like a young girl as my parents did. She looked on me as a full-grown woman. Perhaps this was natural since my husband was much older than I and I must correspond with his age. Besides, I had to behave with an elder sisterly dignity toward my brothers-in-law some of whom were several years older than I.

I took my first breakfast in the midst of the entire family. My mother-in-law and my husband sat on silk cushions, but I, with the rest of the family, sat directly on the mat without a cushion. I had three sets (one consisting of five pieces) of cushions for the guests and three pairs for my own use in my trousseau, yet I had to sit on the cold mat, shivering, to show my humble attitude toward my elders. After the meal, my mother-in-law admitted that I was still too young to take on my shoulders the whole responsibility for the house, but she would show me the ways of the Ishimoto family and I must learn them as quickly as possible. She did not lay down any definite rules or principles. She wanted me to learn by observation. She did not fail to remark, however, that I had to serve my husband with respect as he was the head of the family since the death of his father. I must wait on him when he dressed and bow to him when he went out and again bow him in at the entrance hall when he returned. Of course the same formalities were to be observed toward my mother-in-law herself.

Every act of mine must be approved beforehand by these two. When I wished to go out of the house I was to get their consent to leave. As for what I was to wear I had to bring two or three kimonos and obis to my mother-in-law's room, asking which kimono and obi it pleased her to have me don. My poor mother-in-law must have had great difficulty in selecting one kimono out of my hundreds. The task of being a mother-in-law is indeed never an easy one. She has to be a perfect example to her daughter-in-law. She cannot sit lazily in the presence of her son's wife. She has to refrain from spending too much time for her own pleasure because she admonishes the younger woman to think only of family interests. She must, in short, practice what she preaches.

When my mother-in-law had company of her own, it was the duty of her obedient daughter-in-law to attend the guests and entertain them. The same code held in the case of a party for the husband, he being the master of the family. When there were to be guests in the house, preparations had to be started early. The decoration of the rooms was the most important part. After the maids had cleaned and dusted the reception quarters, my mother-in-law taught me how to place the ornaments and the painting scrolls on the alcove or on the ornamental shelves. My husband's family possessed more than a thousand scroll pictures, painted screens and other antiques, all the work of well-known artists, which were carefully kept as the family treasures in the godown. The Japanese regard the hanging of pictures to cover the whole space of a wall as poor taste; decorations are changed according to the season or the occasion. They do not believe that beauty is achieved by rushing. It is a strenuous undertaking to carry long heavy scrolls of painting and other ornaments with care from the godown, and to return those which had previously been on display. My mother-in-law asked me to alter the entire scheme of pictures and ornaments every week for every one of the eleven alcoved rooms. This meant arduous thought as well as labor for sensitive judgment and a keen knowledge of Japanese art were involved.

However, I owe my mother-in-law much, as she gave me a thorough training in our traditional art decoration. Eventually she often trusted the entire choice of scrolls and other ornaments to me. She taught me, for instance, that I should not repeat any scene or object in my plan of decoration. To illustrate, one autumn for a moon-viewing party I selected a set of maple blossom paintings and a pair of Japanese deer, executed by the master hand of Korin, and let the silver moon cast its shadow on the green mat floor of the room. On the lacquered ornamental shelves with their design of dew-strewn autumn plants inlaid with mother-of-pearl, I placed an incense burner of clay pottery in the shape of an insect container. I hung a picture of a full moon on the Musashino Valley at the alcove in the back room where the moon would not shine. My mother-in-law was very much pleased with the scheme and its effect. She felt that I had learned the art of decoration well enough to take my place as her understudy.

There is no privacy in a Japanese house, for the rooms are not locked and usually the sliding doors which separate the rooms are kept open even on cold winter days. So my husband and I behaved like strangers to each other while we lived in the midst of watching eyes. It was a life in which individuality was completely killed in order to create harmony for the family.

I have many friends who have married into big households who keep themselves busy night and day, working for harmony in the husband's family. One of my friends lived in a separate

*Baron Keikichi Ishimoto and myself before going
to our wedding reception*

My father's family with my husband and myself shortly after our marriage

house from her parents-in-law, but in the same compound. She visited them three times a day, so that her days were so filled up with visiting that she could do very little else. Another girl who was famous as a beauty in our class fixed her hair in the old-fashioned way after she married and wore homely old kimonos which spoiled her charm. And this, she told me, was dictated by the taste of her mother-in-law.

My next lesson as a daughter-in-law after that of interior decoration was learning how to take care of the family shrine. Baya, the old family maid of seventy-five years, came to teach me this. The shrine represented a Buddhist temple in diminutive size with wood carving of exquisite workmanship. A little golden image of Buddha was set in the center and the mortuary tablet of my father-in-law and the other ancestral tablets were set on both sides of the red lacquered altar with its golden pillars. Baya showed me how to clean each of these precious things, together with the entire altar, using a tiny brush and soft cloth, and how to arrange flowers in a pair of little brass vases in front of the altar. I loved to handle these tiny art objects; I felt as if I were playing at the Doll Festival. But of course I had to do all this strictly according to the ways of the Ishimoto family. I burned incense in the bronze burner and placed a few joss sticks in the pale green porcelain stand. Candles were burned inside the temple.

Baya was a daughter of a retainer of the Tokugawa shogun and a living memorial of feudal days. She came to my husband's family as his nurse when he was a baby and subsequently looked after his five brothers and a sister. Her wrinkled smiling little face helped me to learn household customs about which I sometimes hesitated to ask her mistress.

On the afternoon of the day following my wedding, dressed in a purple semiformal kimono bearing my own crest, I went to my father-in-law's grave and burned incense there—a visit to be repeated with flowers and incense by the bride at least five times a year. This was the first time I went out with my husband alone; indeed he still seemed to me a half-stranger. However, there was a little chance for us to talk to each other with no disturbance on this visit to the honorable grave.

From the second to the fifth day after the wedding, my mother-in-law took the newly married couple to visit relatives and important friends of the family. This was an essential duty for a new wife to perform. It was not just a simple calling and a sipping of tea; it was a solemn calling accompanied by the giving of handsome presents.

I had known something about this present-exchanging business as I had watched what my own mother used to do, but hereafter I was to perform this task as a means of helping my mother-in-law. Twice a year, in July for the Bon festival and at the year's end, we had to send gifts carefully chosen to meet the need and taste of each person among the relatives and household friends. Also, a happi-coat with the family name and crest on it was presented to each of the artisans, carpenters, plasterers, matmakers, brickmakers and gardeners who had for many years been in the habit of working for the family; rolls of kimono materials were given to the maids and to former maids who had left the household and married. Whenever a baby was born to any of the relatives, household workmen or former servants, we sent clothes for the newborn, followed by gifts for the baby's first festival—the festival of the dolls in the case of a girl and of the sweet flags in the case of a boy.

Still more important was the obligation to attend funerals. When somebody dies among the relatives or friends, a visit must take place immediately to speak words of grief and offer a present of condolence; then one must go again to attend "through night service"; and again for the funeral. After the funeral there come the memorial services: the tenth, twentieth, thirtieth, fortieth, fiftieth and hundredth day service in the

Shinto ritual; besides the seventh, fourteenth, twenty-first, twenty-eighth, thirty-fifth, forty-ninth and hundredth day service in the Buddhist ritual. Then the anniversaries—the first, the third, the fifth or the seventh year to the tenth or the thirteenth, seventeenth or twentieth to the fiftieth and one hundredth year service according to the family religion—should be observed, especially by the wife of the deceased, before the dutiful descendants are quite released from the centenary task of watching over the souls of departed ancestors.

Westerners may understand why Japanese women do not take an interest in club life when they realize that these women, of necessity, see one another on these obligatory family occasions. This kind of household business keeps women of the upper class well occupied. I made a list of my husband's relatives and other people connected with the household, trying not to forget the details of their positions, so that I might make no blunder, fatal to a Japanese wife, in my performance of social obligations.

The seventh day of my new life was the day for me to pay my first visit with my husband to my own family. My parents lived only three miles away but I felt as if I had moved a hundred or a thousand miles. Freedom was not given the bride to visit her own people or even to telephone to them at will. How I longed to see my parents and all my beloved people again! My mind was filled with so many exciting impressions and new experiences which I longed to report. But the garment I was to wear had to be the first consideration. My mother-in-law presented me with a jade-green kimono stamped with the five crests of the Ishimoto family for this visit. Its design was taken from the Utai music, the subject being "Suehiro" which means "glories until the end." Several fans dyed in different shades of beige were floating on a stream represented in "Kanze water" fashion, a classical touch. Custom calls for the bride to be dressed so in a new ceremonial kimono with her husband's crests to proclaim the fact that she has become a member of his family. Mother-in-law also gave me a gold ring with a big diamond, saying: "This is my personal present to my daughter-in-law. This jewel was given me by your late honorable father-in-law as a souvenir from his trip to Europe. I hope you will cherish this in memory of your parents-in-law, and hand it down when you have a son to be married." Adorned with this brilliant ring and "suehiro-fan" kimono, I called upon my family.

As water in a stone urn in the garden freezes on a cold winter day but melts suddenly when spring sunshine comes back, so the thin ice which had covered up my timid heart, by the freezing rigidity of my position in the new home, dissolved easily at the sight of the warm familiar faces of those who impatiently awaited and welcomed me on my first visit home. Sisters and brothers clung to me and attacked me with a bombardment of talk. Mother said that she was pleased to know her daughter was behaving gracefully and nobly. Later, mother told Uncle Yusuke that she thought a daughter was a vapor-like substance in the family, disappearing after long care and discipline, leaving her mother with a sense of something lost forever. It would be disgraceful to confess, but I, the girl-wife, felt more comfortable in the old nest with my parents than in the exalted post of baroness, and I had to be fairly pushed into the rikisha which was to carry me off to it.

Appreciating the strain of learning so many new duties so quickly, my mother-in-law sent the newlyweds to spend the New Year holidays in the country. Thus I counted several days of a honeymoon among my bridal experiences in the old family system. We went into the quiet Hakone Mountains and enjoyed bathing in the hot spring. This was my first chance to talk intimately with my husband and to rest.

Though he looked young, Baron Ishimoto was ten years

older than I and had a wide knowledge of both East and West. He had written his graduation thesis in English and in German. He read the Chinese classics as easily as his own language. So he would have to be very patient to educate his child-wife to his level in such matters. He talked to me about his interest in social problems and his humanistic ideals. The theme of this conversation was hard for me to comprehend thoroughly, but I never tired of listening to him. We were quite happy together.

PART FIVE

DOMESTICITY IN THE MINING FIELD

X

Life on $25 a Month

A YOUNG aristocrat, full of enthusiasm and idealistic dreams, and his newly-married wife, a daughter of a rising bourgeois who had been "put away in a case" to use the Japanese expression, with very limited experience of her own and almost no knowledge of the outer world, began their experimental life, not in the baron's splendid residence in Tokyo, but in the Miike Coal Mining Field in Western Japan, far away from classical and complicated social conventions.

It was one afternoon in late January, 1915, that our long journey from Tokyo ended after we had traveled seven hundred miles along the seacoast of Japan. We had enjoyed wonderful views of the Tokaido, passing along the foot of dazzling, white Mount Fuji, towering high into the clear winter sky with lower mountain ranges rolling beneath like blue and white waves. Then we went on to the Sanyodo, along the Inland Sea. Its dark blue water was dotted with numberless small floating islands, and white sailboats came close to the train window. We arrived at Shimonoseki, at the western edge of Japan, crossed the narrow strait by boat, and continued for another half-day by railroad through Kyushu. In the center of this Kyushu district the Miiki mines are situated, occupying a large territory in the Fukuoka and Kumamoto prefectures with the town of Omuta as the hub of its universe.

This large mining industry belongs to the Mitsuis, the richest family and biggest capitalists in Japan today. The local headquarters of the Mitsui Mining Company, the large chemical factories for the by-products of coal, and the big powerhouse stand out as the monuments of Omuta. The western side of the town faces Ariake Bay, famous for its "unknown fires" which twinkle in the far distance on the waters in autumn. The cause of this phenomenon is still undiscovered despite the progress of science. It is conjectured to be the work of some sort of phosphorescent cell. The Mitsui Company built Miike harbor, and large quantities as well as the best qualities of coal in Japan are transported from there, thousands of tons of it every day.

The coal beds run in a diagonal slope with many branches and at various levels. Black coal is exposed even on the surface and then it runs into the ground deeper and deeper until it lies beneath sea level, under the harbor. The mines of Miike as a whole are divided into five subdivisions deploying downward from one or two huge shafts. Kattachi, one of the district centers and the farthest from the harbor, was the point where my husband was posted as a deputy mining engineer.

For the first time in my life I came to a place far from Tokyo, a place of strange activities, of black smoke and dust. With my maid I stepped out from the train, following my husband who was greeted by some of his coworkers. I almost lost my nerve at the mean and ugly sight of the industrial town with its forestlike everlastingly smoking chimneys, with its provincial-looking population, with the unfamiliar sound of the Kyushu dialect. One of the men of the company who came to meet us at the station informed us that the house allotted to us by the company was not quite ready and so we must stay a few days in the town of Omuta. He took us to a small inn. The next morning my husband left me at four-thirty, saying that after his long vacation he must get to work immediately. He had to walk about four miles from Omuta to the Kattachi pit and had to be there before six o'clock to give orders to the workers.

This hurrying off to a pit was the first great surprise to the young wife who had not quite awakened from her dreamy honeymoon! To my mind, a gentleman worked at his office desk. I had thought of manual labor as the concern of quite another class; so when I discovered that my honorable husband did not conduct his business at a desk, but actually performed physical labor, I was greatly shocked. The problems of laborers which I had heard discussed by men sitting on comfortable sofas in my father's parlor had seemed problems conceived in the sphere of imagination, but those I now encountered face to face were hard and concrete.

We started for our home among the miners on a sunny winter day. Three rikishas left the inn in Omuta, carrying the young couple and the maid along the narrow country roads. On neither side of the road was there a single thing to rejoice the eyes. The high red brick walls of Miike Prison were on the right and tall smoking factory chimneys dotted the hillsides covered with lean and dusky mulberry plantations and barley fields. Country children, astonished expressions on their dirty faces, their little mouths wide open and their noses terribly wet, looked up at the unfamiliar sight of city people riding by in rikishas.

As it had been my firm determination ever since I had first been engaged that I would meet any kind of hardship even "to jump into fire or water" for the sake of my respectful husband as a good wife should do, I did not expect to live always in luxurious surroundings. I was deeply interested in helping my husband carry out his humanistic ideals, which had become mine too. Yet, as a Japanese proverb says, "A blind man is never afraid of snakes," and I, naturally, had been blind to the true meaning of misery, dirt and poverty. My imagination had not gone beyond the boundaries of my personal experiences and my mind had been trained only toward love, beauty, poetry and the womanly virtues. I did not realize what a task I had undertaken.

At the foot of the gigantic iron cranes among the coal wagons our rikishas suddenly stopped and my husband told me that this was the spot where we were to make our "home, sweet home." I questioned myself again and again. "Sweet home? Isn't he teasing me? How could one live in a place like this among dust and the noise of engines?" At this my long dream was broken and I had to realize that it was indeed Kattachi where my husband and I were to live from now on. A poor and shabby village it was. The land about it was hilly and consisted of red clay mud. On one of the bare red hills where the coal shaft went down deep stood a tall wide chimney, fearful black smoke rising from it against the sky. The square wooden barracklike buildings with black corrugated iron roofs were constantly noisy with active engines and sliding belts to shift coal forward. On both sides girls were at work, sorting coal lumps by size. Black fragments of coal were scattered everywhere.

On the other side of this mill, near the shaft, two big public baths, one for men and the other for women workers, threw out great clouds of steam. Crowds of men and women, scant clothes around their bodies, were walking around these bathhouses.

I could see nothing to create industrial glory in this place, but only rows of miners' barns stretching along the narrow stony road which led through a spare village in the valley and then up the bare hills. Many somewhat better-looking residences for the higher officials of the company were built on the side of the hill looking down on the smoke community. I was soon to behold our own dwelling. My husband took me farther along this road, helping my steps since it was easy to stumble on the stones, until we reached a house unspeakably shabby, on the right side halfway up the hill.

The company's allotted residence sounded great, but it was in reality a house formerly belonging to a village farmer, and had been purchased by the company. I thought it could hardly be called "a house," it looked more like a small hut. The houses for lower employees of the company were scattered at the bottom of the hill on both sides of the narrow passage which led from the pit to the upper resident houses on the hilltop. Our "hut" faced this passage, other three sides being surrounded by the huts of a similar kind occupied by the laborers who were not the real miners but working in the pit carrying coal from the miners' hands to the coal wagons. The army of the real miners lived close to us in separate groups.

Entering this old hut I saw four mat rooms with a narrow attic to which we could climb by a ladder. The roof was thatched with brown straw. Modern civilization had been introduced even into this old hut, and we could get dim electric lights in the evening. But there were no bathing accommodations; people who lived in these company houses usually went to the public bath. With all my high resolves I never could endure this strain, and later we treated ourselves to a private bath as the one permitted luxury.

Matsu, my maid who had been with me for several years, remained faithful enough to her honorable mistress to come even to this hut. She helped me scrub the dirty pillars and floors and to make the house clean enough to live in. Even with this faithful assistance it took days upon days. Rats ran about freely regardless of the social rank of the new occupants. When it rained, buckets, washtubs and bath towels of every kind were quickly assembled to catch the water which dropped wherever it pleased through the leaky roof, upon our heads, into my closets where I kept the bed quilts and even on my beautifully polished chest of drawers brought from Tokyo. Luckily I had packed only the worst possible kimonos chosen from my gay trousseau. Most of my clothes had been left in Tokyo, deposited in the care of my mother-in-law who willingly accepted what must have been a heavy responsibility as it is a general rule for a mother-in-law to take charge of a daughter-in-law's trousseau during her absence.

Thunderstorms were terrible in this district and lightning often killed men and women working on the farms or by their huts. How many days Matsu and I, frightened by fearful storms, stayed for hours under the mosquito net—the big Japanese net of grass linen which is believed to be electricity proof!

But nature offered some consolation as well as terror. One hillside not far away was covered with lovely wild plants and I could gather flowers and tree branches to arrange in the vase on the alcove of our humble drawing room. To this etiquette I was loyal and I remembered also my wifely code of bowing when my husband went out to his work at a quarter to six in the morning and came back at six in the evening, though it seemed rather out of harmony with this residence of ours.

The manual workers were employed under a twelve-hour day system, but in reality they were at their places nearly fourteen hours. Naturally the higher employees had to be at the mine nearly the same length of time to superintend them. Thus our new life opened in an atmosphere of extreme simplicity and hard toil. Yet there was much enthusiasm for it.

Life in this mining industry, where everybody is engaged in productive work of national importance, is actually more strenuous than life in the army. There was no holiday on this industrial battlefield, none whatever! Chinese soldiers get furloughs in the midst of their fighting during civil wars. The miners had to work as long as engines were active. No Sundays, no New Year's vacation; the tall chimneys smoked constantly even on the Emperor's Birthday! Like others my husband worked regularly twelve hours a day or the same length of time at night. When his shift alternated every two weeks, he had to work twenty-four hours at a stretch.

His breakfast consisted of a bowl of steamed rice, one of hot bean soup and some boiled eggs. It was prepared at five every morning by Matsu who silently struggled in her narrow kitchen to produce these dishes in a very primitive oven, frequently rubbing her eyes which smarted from the smoke that had no outlet since there was no chimney in the kitchen.

As our day began, my husband placed on our low eating table a small squatting image of the "Peasants' God" made of bronze, which held on its knees a big grass hat that looked like a round tray. After saying grace in the Christian manner, he would pick up from his porcelain rice bowl with his ivory chopsticks a few grains of white rice and offer them on the god's tray. It was an expression of thanks to the people who worked hard to raise the rice, our national food. This image had been sent to us by Dr. Inazo Nitobe, widely known as Doctor of Law but little known as Doctor of Agricultural Science. Such he was, however. While my husband ate alone I would read the Holy Bible to him. I had only learned to read the Bible since I was married, so I did not know much about the gospels of Christ. I could not help feeling uneasy lest I should be praying to some unknown god or gods irreverently. For instance, my husband offered his accustomed prayer; "Hallowed be Thy name, Thy Kingdom come..." Whereas I prayed simply, "Have mercy on him, protect him from all mishaps while he is in the dark pit!"

The lives of engineers were as unprotected as those of the manual laborers on this battlefield of the coal industry. For emergencies my husband always carried a little bottle of perfume in his pocket and an oblong brass plate, on which his name was carved. When men were killed under rocks falling from the roof of the pit, it was hard to know who was who; hence this brass name plate identifying the bearer was very necessary in this profession. The bottle of perfume was my husband's own fancy, like the samurai's artistic way of filling the inside of his war helmet, the kabuto, with incense vapor when death was expected in battle.

My beloved samurai in the modern warfare of the mining industry did not take to the field in gorgeous armor, but in a plain kimono, a cap and wooden clogs, carrying a pair of grass sandals, called waraji, and a paper lantern. Leaving his home and wife while the waning moon in the morning sky cast its shadow on the rough road, he descended from the entrance of the mining pit by the cage. There taking off his kimono, he put on his overalls and slipped the grass sandals on his bare feet which were swollen and often bled from walking in the dirty water. He walked miles and miles along the narrow passages, bending his body almost double, superintending his workers at the coal beds which are usually low and narrow in Japan. When the noon whistle blew, there came half an hour's interval, and he would open his lunch box in the darkness and stuffy air to fill his hungry stomach with the baked fish and rice which I had prepared. In the evening he came back thoroughly tired. His fatigue was too pitiful to see when he returned in the morning after a night's shift and particularly after twenty-four hours of labor.

Was one rewarded sufficiently for such toil, and the constant danger of poison gas, a flood or falling rocks? At the end of every month my honorable husband brought home in an envelope his precious $21.50 (Y43 at standard exchange rate) and handed it to me. The total salary which the Mitsui Company paid to a deputy engineer was $25 a month, but a part of it was reserved in the company's treasury, making our actual income less than that. The rent for our hut was free and we could get fuel, rice and other daily provisions at moderate prices from the consumers' league in the company. So we did not starve. Nevertheless, it was no easy matter to make ends meet and we had to practice every possible kind of thrift.

My mother-in-law generously offered help from her household budget, but my husband did not believe in our enjoying

General view of Mitsui's Miike Colliery in Kyushu

My husband and myself on the porch of our house in the colliery with my brother, Yoji Hirota

A paper carp flying on the flagpole celebrates the birth of our first son (an old Japanese custom still prevailing)

extra privileges while the other employees had to live entirely on their wages and salaries. I kept a record of how I spent the fruits of my husband's labor, a page of which I reprint here.

KATTACHI MINING PIT, NOVEMBER, 1915

FOOD

Rice	$1.25
Oats to mix with rice	.25
Soy bean sauce, salt, sugar, vinegar, etc.	.63
Fish and other seafood	1.15
Meats*	.07
Vegetables	.83
Eggs	.35
Milk	.58
Total	$5.11

* Meat was too expensive for us and we scarcely even smelt it.

INCIDENTALS

Charity to village Salvation Army	$ .50
Postage stamps	1.14
Rikisha three half-trips to town	.45
Party entertainments	.75
Presents exchanged	.88
60 pairs of grass sandals	.40
Tea in the pit	.30
Laundry	1.23
Newspaper	.50
Periodicals	.55
A chair, mousetrap, lanterns, etc.	2.80
Salary to a maid	2.00
Village tax	3.50
Total	$15.00
Gross Total	$20.11

$21.50—$20.11=$1.39

The joy of life may be obtained anywhere, even in a hut. Material abundance is never absolutely necessary for happiness! Occasionally we had a chance to enjoy the sunshine for which my husband hungered. The company did not set any definite holidays for its employees. They had to take a day off however when their strength was exhausted and my husband took his about twice a month. Sunlight is supposed to be equally distributed by the god of nature, but there is at least one exception. Those who work underground for long hours seldom have a chance to see the sun. The miners needed fresh air and so did my engineer. When he took a holiday he absorbed as much fresh air and sunlight as he could. We would walk miles and miles through green wheat fields, breathing in the fresh fragrance of the black earth. We climbed hills to hunt for wild azaleas. We lay down in the daisy fields in the sunshine as in a deep bath. During the heat of summer, we took our lunch boxes into a pine grove and after we had eaten, with the cicadas singing round us, we slept.

Our life in the Miike mines lasted from the beginning of 1915 to the autumn of 1917—until our family doctor advised my husband to take a long rest on account of his failing health caused by hard labor. During these near-three years I had several appalling experiences.

One day a man who had been a mine "boss" called on my husband at our house to ask for a special favor for the sake of his own interests, promising a small commission in return. My husband refused to co-operate. The same man called again the next evening with a dagger in his pocket and threatened the young engineer of the company.

My husband told this man that he would not engage in any unfair practice in any circumstances. He also told him that we had practiced jujitsu for many years in Tokyo—this was true of my husband, but not of me—so that neither of us was afraid of his dull dagger. The rascal, intimidated, went away without harming us. But a few days later, we were awakened by a sudden fire alarm and saw a house, about five minutes' distance from ours, on fire. It was a quiet night with no wind. The flame shot up straight, burnt one house down and stopped. In the morning the wife of the engineer living in that house was found dead in the ruins. Her husband had been down in the pit for his night shift during the fire. The village policeman examined the woman's body carefully, and discovered that she had been killed by a dagger and that someone had set fire to the house to pretend she had died that way. Suspicion was directed to the rascal who had threatened us, but he was nowhere to be found. The poor man whose wife was taken away by such cruelty left this place of woe soon afterward and my husband had to take his place at night. I, with my maid Matsu, was utterly frightened living in such an unprotected house; indeed, we scarcely slept at all.

Another terrifying experience was a gas explosion in the mine. All the factory whistles blew long, almost like panting demons. "Emergency!" "Fire!" People ran toward the entrance of the pit. Some of the wives and children of the miners were already weeping and screaming there when I arrived. I did not cry, of course, but could not stand quietly; so I walked around the house and up and down the front passage. The six o'clock whistle had blown a long time before, but my husband had not come home. In the evening a woman laborer came to me to collect an extra lunch box to be sent down. Impatiently I asked the woman if she knew anything about my husband.

"No, madame, nobody knows who is living or who was killed in the confusion of poison gas!" she said. "I have only the order to collect all the lunch boxes in the village. That's all, madame!"

She left me in a hurry. The night seemed endless. Neither Matsu nor I went to bed. I was brought up on the principle that "a good wife" should not lie down while her husband is at his work. Yet when dawn approached, I seemed to have fallen asleep unconsciously, worn out by the shock and the worry, and I dreamed that God appeared to me in a white robe saying, "I have called your good husband." I awakened covered with perspiration. The next day in the late forenoon the lunch box came back from the pit empty and with a slip inside on which was written: "I am safe. Don't worry, dear Shidzué!"

The following morning my husband returned completely worn out and coughing badly. He slept like a log.

I could gladly have stood the hard life there among the ignorant and exploited miners, if I could only have helped my husband in his study of social problems. But there seemed no way to co-operate at first and the low level of the culture of the engineers and other employees and their wives, who were mostly natives of this southern end of Japan, was too much for me to bear immediately. As they were my husband's co-workers, I had to meet them on equal terms. On any occasion of happiness or sorrow in a family within this circle all the wives worked together to get a grand feast ready for men to eat and women to serve, all making merry and talking on vulgar subjects over their winecups. I worked among the women according to the social rules of the place. They lived almost always half naked in this hot region and when I paid a call I was often shocked to be greeted by the wife of the house dressed only with a piece of white cotton around her waist.

I was also often frightened by a visit from a mine contractor. His kind came into the mining field to drive a bargain over some construction around or in the pit and looked to the engineers for special favors. They almost always came to our house during my husband's absence and asked me to persuade him to aid them, offering me presents for my pains. I always refused the gifts but sometimes they ran away leaving them at my door. The gift was often a basket of stale bananas or a box of musty confections. On my husband's return he always told me to take them back to the callers and the next day my poor maid might have to make a long trip on foot to a neighboring village to return the unwelcome gift.

While I was in the mining regions I often wondered how my aristocratic mother-in-law was ever persuaded to let her eldest son, who was the head of a great family, go so far away to live in such a dreadful place. She had objected to the plan at first, I was told; but on my husband's insistence that it was wise, she yielded. Custom required that the head of the family should be obeyed even by his mother. Since the daughter-in-law had filial obligations, it was my duty to write my mother-in-law a long letter once a week telling everything that had happened in our simple house, most of which was merely a full account of the week's cooking, washing and sewing. Also I had to write every now and then to my husband's other relatives and always at the New Year and at the Feast of Lanterns at midyear formally asking after their health. I sent ceremonious greetings to each of them. My letters were mostly conventional and never revealed in any detail the horrible life of the miners which was what I was most interested in for the sake of my husband, but which could never be understood by the people living in ease in Tokyo. Indeed, even I, myself, had been slow to understand and reluctant to share their woes.

During these years, my husband's salary was raised twice, $5 at a time, according to Western reckoning. In the autumn of 1916, he was posted at Manda pit—much bigger and deeper than the former mine. While we were at Manda our first son, Arata, was born, and a cloth carp banner of five feet was proudly raised on the pole in the corner of our small yard in the country fashion, to celebrate the boys' festival.

XI

Are Miners Human Beings?

*M*Y INTERESTS, which had been at first strictly limited within the scope of domesticity, began to be enlarged little by little during my three years' stay at the mines. This outcome was due to my effort to know more about the subjects in which my husband was most interested.

I began to look at the people around me in a new way and tried to see their lives and problems more sympathetically. One day while I was at Kattachi I asked my husband to take me down into the pit, descending seven hundred feet into the ground. This old-fashioned mine had only one elevator which was used for carrying up and down both coal and human beings. The cage had just a platform to stand on; no wall or rails around it. So when this elevator started downward, it ran so fast that I felt as if I were in an instant thrown and dashed against the hell in the bottom of the earth. Pitch darkness, heat and moisture reigned in this subterranean world. As I groped along the passage guided by my husband and a little dim mining lamp, the ceiling came down lower and lower. I had to bend double and pay constant attention to my steps on the rocky path slippery with puddles of water. Rumbling coal trucks dashed through this dark narrow passage constantly but without any warning of approach—a very dangerous proceeding. I saw—I smelled rather—the rows of stables in the darkness. The horses were worn and feeble, their energy lost by their long stay underground. They were used to pull coal wagons in some parts where the path was wide and the roof was high enough for animals to pass back and forth.

As I went farther and farther, the roof of the pit dropped to less than four feet high. Naked men sat on their knees digging coal with their picks. I felt that I could not go any farther, but my husband told me that the miners worked in places narrower and lower than this and that women had to creep into these passages like wiggling worms to pull baskets of coal out to the place where the wagons stood. Perhaps I did not spend more than an hour in the pit, but I felt that I could not stay a minute longer. I looked at my husband, wondering how in the world he dared to select this profession voluntarily! Yet he seemed to me utterly absorbed in it. He treated the miners in the most democratic manner, a reflection of his Christian humanism. With his sensitive heart and his sympathy for and deep insight into the conditions of the Japanese miners, he seemed to me a true hero, or "a prince in disguise" whom, though I could not quite understand him, I was perfectly happy to follow with absolute trust.

About fifty thousand miners and their families were attempting to survive in this Miike mining district. It may be unavoidable in any civilized country that the life of miners is exposed to more danger than that of any other kind of laborers, but Japanese miners are especially subject to risks and these are largely due to poor accommodations in the pit and to the narrow width of the coal beds.

I was told that when the people in England discussed the nationalization of coal mines in 1919 before Judge Sankey's Commission, under Lloyd George's regime, Robert Smillie, the labor representative said: "The capitalists do not agree to the nationalization of the coal mines, because they are afraid to lose their own profits, but have they ever realized that even one scoop of coal which is carelessly thrown into the stove is obtained by the miners' life and blood? If our capitalists do protect their own profit, laborers have to protect their very existence!" The fact is that the actual loss of miners per one million tons of coal mined in England is about ten persons, while in Japan thirty human lives are actually sacrificed for every million tons. Moreover, the rate of injury by accident in this industry is as high as two and a half to every three miners. If we add the cases of disease directly caused by poor sanitary conditions in the mines and wretched living accommodations, the percentage is even greater.[1]

While we were in Manda or Kattachi pit, no day passed without its accident. Every three or four days I heard the news of a miner's death and occasionally that of an engineer, mostly the result of their being crushed by falling rocks. While carrying coal in baskets from pit to wagons, the girls were often crushed by the sudden overturn of the heavy coal trucks, caught under the big wagons. This happened too often because of careless excessive speed.

I used to stand at the front of our house at Kattachi of an evening when the five o'clock whistle blew and the shifting to the night work began, waiting anxiously for my husband's safe return, while I watched men and women plodding uphill to their homes and downhill to their work, each with a lunch box and pickaxe.

> "Up safely?"
> "With the mercy of the gods!"

They exchanged greetings in this fashion. They were very superstitious, fearing almost any phenomenon as a fatal omen.

> Don't become the sweetheart of a miner, my girl,
> When a gas explosion comes in just one moment,
> Then good-bye, forever, to your man!

They chant songs of sorrow. Nevertheless, widows with chil-

---

[1] The figures of injury and disease for Japanese miners are drawn from the census in 1930 taken by the Department of Commerce and Industry.

dren soon marry other men of the same trade, as there is no choice but to continue sharing this human tragedy.

A strange logic of social life can be seen in the rewards of miners, whose labor is strenuous, whose life is threatened by constant danger and disease. They are paid very little compared with less arduous labor in Japan. During our stay at the mines, I often saw a squad of prisoners from Miike Prison in their ugly red uniforms, with heavy chains on their hips, sent down to the mining pit to work as forced laborers. Often miners had to compete for pay with these groups of chained prisoners. Other wage competitors are the women and children of their own families who are given various tasks because they are so much cheaper.

It was only recently that Japan adopted prohibitive measures against the employment of women miners and against midnight labor in general for women, both regarded as evils in Western countries long ago. While I was at the Miike mines, wives and daughters of miners went down in a half-naked condition, mingling with the naked men laborers. They followed the men and carried out the coal as the men loosened it with their picks. It was ridiculous to expect morality in such circumstances. Women who worked in the darkness had a pale complexion like the skin of a silkworm; they spoke and acted shamelessly, the last sign of feminine dignity sloughing off. Often pregnant women, working until the last moment, gave birth to children in the dark pit.

It would be hard to tell the difference between the life of pigs and the life of these miners. Certainly the human beings were living like animals in barns. There barns were built on the bare hill in rows, barrack fashion, out of poor rough boards roofed with thin sheets of zinc. One barrack was usually divided so as to house from five to seven families. Each one of these booths was about twelve feet square, separated from the adjoining booth by thin boards. The average size of one family was five or six members, and there was only one lavatory for a whole row of barracks. There was neither gas nor water service. It might be bearable in winter to live in a booth crowded with five or six people, but how could one stand the summer heat of South Japan in such conditions?

I felt especially sorry for those who worked at night and had no place to rest their tired bodies by day against another night's work. They just lay down on their mats, while the women were chattering in groups washing and cooking, and the children making noises everywhere. My husband often told me that when their bodies were weary the men became more careless and hardly had energy enough to avoid injury even when they were aware of danger. The people who lived in these barns were strictly watched and loyalty to their employers was enforced. It was impossible for them to run away; nor could labor organizers get among the miners, for labor unions were severely banned in the coal field. Even today the miners are unorganized and exhibit only meek feudalistic submission. However, perhaps owing to their meekness, the Japanese miners are fortunate enough to be protected as citizens and they have never been attacked by machine guns as has happened in some so-called civilized countries!

The miners I knew were usually desperate. They saw no hope in the future, and sought merely momentary pleasures. Men and their wives quarreled a great deal. Men beat women and children. The quarrels were more frequent on their wage-paying days which came twice a month. Many men literally drank nearly all their pay before they brought any pennies to their families. But it would be rash to blame them! Who would dare preach family obligations to men who got only $20 for a month's work? The average wage for men in those days was about forty yen ($20), and twenty-four yen ($12) was the maximum pay for women for their monthly labor. Now this pay has been raised a little. The low rate of workers' wages was not only due to the low social status of laborers, but must be largely attributed to the lack of efficiency in their working power. They could go to their work only sixteen days a month on the average, for their physical strength was unequal to greater strain, owing to conditions in the pits and to the low quality of their food and housing. The women usually went down with their husbands, sometimes taking their babies on their backs as there were no nursery provisions. As soon as children were old enough, both boys and girls went to work, competing for wages with adults. But there was no other way for the population to keep alive unless it could manage to control the overflooded market of cheap labor by exercising birth control.

I often wondered whether the Japanese capitalists were true to their consciences in saying that the beautiful family system in Japan made men, women and children work harmoniously and pleasantly at their tasks, when they claimed Japanese exemption for women, on such grounds, in the international labor regulations drawn up at the Labor Conference in Geneva.

Where is the harmony in fact? Where is the joy of labor in truth? Women who were already fully tired from their long day's labor in the mines returned home to carry pails of water from a distant well to their kitchens. They cooked, washed and nursed like other women whose energies are spent only on such domestic tasks. Naturally they were abnormally nervous and exhausted. They often beat their impatiently hungry children who could not wait for their mothers to cook the meals. Nothing could be compared to the sight of these crowded nests of ignorance, poverty and misery. It is the very picture of Hades! Children were born without love and reared without proper care, receiving even little affection from their parents. Westerners often say that Japan is a paradise for children. I wish this were true, but my impression of the children in mining camps is so vivid that I can never forget the horror of the dirty little creatures who haunted the garbage box at my door. My heart ached when I saw babies coughing badly and left without medical attention till they died. I shuddered to see youngsters screaming and running away from home pursued by peevish mothers with big pieces of firewood in their hands.

"Why must women work outside the home like men?"

"Why must the mother breed and nurse while she works for wages?"

As I watched the lives of these laborers and their women and children, these questions rose in my mind, but I myself did not realize then that they were the seeds that were to grow and revolutionize my own life.

PART SIX

*MY PREPARATION TO BE
SELF-SUPPORTING*

XII

The Influence of the Russian Revolution in Japan

"THE Japanese are omnivorous readers."

This is what people who travel in Japan often say when they see so many bookshops in Tokyo, sometimes occupying entirely a large quarter of the city. Other cities in Japan are not far behind the capital in this respect. Shops for both new and secondhand books are like drugstores in American cities and cafés in France. The great numbers of the bookshops may not mean that the Japanese digest well what they have eaten to feed their great appetite for knowledge, but certainly they read well and they are earnest seekers after new knowledge.

Books, magazines and papers often enjoy an enormous circulation in this country. *Asahi* and *Mainichi,* the two major newspapers of Japan, have circulations not far behind those of the great Western papers. Even more surprising to foreigners are the huge and conspicuous advertisements of books and contents of magazines that occupy the whole front pages of these papers. During the year 1925 Japan was listed as the country publishing more books than any other except Germany. Books are cheap, moreover, and, actually, the reading population is exceedingly large. As for favorites, those dealing with nationalistic or war topics now top all the rest although only recently cheap editions of Marxian essays and the literature of that affiliation were most popular. The vogue for Marxist literature was preceded by enthusiasm for liberalistic writings translated from or influenced by European literatures. Translations from the works of Turgenev, Dostoevski, Gorky, Tolstoy and other Russians long held sway among young intellectuals. Indeed, Tolstoy's *Resurrection* became so popular that it was dramatized by a Japanese playwright and Madame Sumako Matsui, the greatest Japanese actress of the modern age, played the heroine's part. A popular song composed for the play became so well known that even the country children hummed the tune: "Cachusha Kawa-i-ya, Wakare-no-tsurasa, Semete Awayuki Toke-numani, Kamini Inorio Lala, Kake-mashoka . . ."

> Cashusha dear,
> O the sorrow of our parting!
> Short be the exile
> Even like the dying snow.
> So to merciful Father
> Let us pray. . . .

Until the great currents of Russian thought penetrated Japan, Russia had been known to most Japanese only as the defeated power struck down in the Russo-Japanese conflict. To some it seemed an uncanny country with its huge territories neighboring ours, a fact which constantly provoked delicate political relations between the two countries. But perhaps the literature of no other foreign country has ever been more welcomed by the Japanese than that of Russia after the war. The gloomy stories of peasant life and of struggles under the despotic rule of the Czar won such sympathy in Japan that the study of Russia became like a fever among the Japanese intelligentsia in this post-war period. Then when the Russian Revolution took place in 1917, shaking the world's civilizations to their foundations, creating confusion, hatred and praise, interest in Russia almost completely dominated the minds of Japanese intellectuals.

While the Japanese were busy reading the Russian revolutionary literature, social unrest at home began to draw more and more of our attention. The social movement of other years which had taken the form of free and democratic thinking

My husband's mother and brother with us and our son at Kyushu

In the garden at Marquis Kido's mansion. All the ladies were my classmates at the Peeresses' School

against a background of feudalistic survivals had almost completely lost its hold on the people as a result of the persecution
by the Meiji bureaucratic government.   But it began to revive
gradually after the World War, when an unexpected prosperity
and a sudden expansion of Japanese industry brought about
a great dislocation in the relative prices of commodities.   Class
differentiations grew sharper and want kept pace with wealth.

These domestic conditions plus the stimuli of the Russian
revolution brought about rice riots in Japan in August, 1918.
The trouble was started by a group of fishermen's wives in
Toyama, a prefecture in middle-north Japan.   They had been
suffering from the quickly rising cost of living and especially
from the unreasonable jump in the price of rice.   Led by these
women, the mob attacked rice shops.   Quite instinctively and
without any previous planning or agitation, the resentment of
hard-pressed women with hungry children to feed had been a
great factor in the history of every revolution.   And as soon as
this small local incident was reported in the papers, rioting
spread like wildfire.   Similar revolts but on a bigger scale occurred all over the country, until finally Tokyo itself was caught
in the raging flame.

The dissatisfaction of laborers and farmers, whom conditions had pressed down to the level of slaves and whose very
lives were threatened by low wages and the high cost of living,
exploded everywhere after a match was struck by the first rice
riot.   At that time my husband and I were living at Kamakura
by the beach for, as I have said, we were forced to leave the
mining field on account of his physical breakdown.

Driving to Tokyo one day during that August in my
father's Chalmers, I had to go far off the normal route for the
sake of safety.   I was going to Uyeno Station to meet my mother
who had taken my baby to the summer resort of Karuizawa and
was now bringing him home to me.   Along the main road a
huge crowd of excited people were throwing stones at every

automobile that happened to pass, to express their antagonism toward the well-to-do. In those days taxis and other cheap cars were few in Japan, and our imported motorcars were all luxurious ones, seeming to the poor symbols of wealth, exploitation and selfishness.

The Mitsui Company had offered my husband a position in its Tokyo chemical laboratory to study coal washing. He had accepted and at that time he went to this laboratory every day from Kamakura. All his free time was devoted to studying labor problems and their relation to the national wealth. Since he approached the problems on the basis of his actual research work at the Miike mines, the capitalistic organization of society became more and more questionable in his mind, and he began to desire to go abroad to learn more about the issues involved as they were unfolding in Western countries.

In the meanwhile my mother-in-law became very sick and we were called back to the Tokyo residence to look after her. She had been much pleased with the fact that a grandson and heir had been born to the family, and now that her daughter-in-law was expecting the second child soon, she was quite satisfied and passed away quietly.

Our second son was born in the grand house of Baron Ishimoto, an interesting contrast to the birthplace of his brother in the small cabinlike room at the mines. My husband named our second son Tamio, using the first of the Chinese characters standing for Democracy, as he wished his son to grow up in a democratic way.

My husband was not a bit satisfied with his career in the chemical laboratory. He thought the work too easy. He reminded me of an untamed horse, chafing with nerves. He wanted to go back to the mining field to expose his precious life again to the dangers of accident and disease. But instead, as soon as his strength returned, he decided to go abroad to study and he began to prepare for the trip, while I was quite absorbed in maternal love and the care of my two babies. At the mines, the moment I knew I was to be a mother, I began to practice spiritual prenatal care, to read good books and to think about aesthetic surroundings. After the children were born I nursed them both, weighed them from time to time and kept a diary of their growth as Western mothers do. While I spent my days utterly submerged in motherhood, my husband's plan to travel abroad matured, and it was decided that he was to visit America, Mexico and Europe for the observation of industrial as well as general social conditions. The scheme was arranged half officially in the interests of the company and half privately for his own enlightenment.

Knowing well enough his great interest in social problems, I yet could not avoid a certain feeling of anxiety about this trip. I firmly believed in his love for me, but I had a premonition that some unknown power was luring my husband from me, and his going abroad might, I thought, be the first break. My reason approved of his journey to the Occidental countries, but my heart always tried to hold him back. My husband, on the contrary, enthusiastically progressive, told me that he had no desire to make a great gap in the knowledge of husband and wife and wanted me to join him as soon as the nursing period for the second baby was over. So he sailed from Yokohama for Seattle on February 13, 1919.

The postcards and letters he sent from the new places were always interesting to me. He wrote that the English which he had acquired in Japan was quite different from that spoken in America. When he tried to express his opinion to an American he was told that it sounded as though he were reading an essay. He was finding it difficult to pick up collo-quialisms after learning only book English, through Shake-speare, Carlyle and other classical writers. Finally he wrote: "Don't come abroad if you seek pleasure and new fashions in clothes or are planning to spend your time only at the theaters or motoring like other 'bourgeoises mesdames'." But, he added, "Come to me if you will educate yourself, to feed yourself with knowledge of the world, to prepare yourself to swim abreast the world's new tide."

This sermonizing may be somewhat excused since my understanding of social problems and my attitude toward life itself remained on a low and childish level compared with my husband's; since in Japan, as you have seen by my own story, girls spend so much time in being trained in domestic affairs and artistic culture and marry so very young, whereas boys go to colleges and universities and spend all their time studying sciences and sociology and marry much later as a rule. At any rate, the only way for me to catch up to my husband's level was to study constantly, paying careful attention to what was happening in the world, besides doing the daily round of housework and nursing the babies. It was only during these days that I awakened to see myself as an individual and to try to understand my relation to society. I began to take an interest in my own growth while I was absorbed in watching the growth of my babies.

I was often haunted with a prophetic fear that something would happen in the end which would take my husband away from his family, from the life of peace and love we had known together. This psychic intuition acted so strongly on my resolve, that I followed him across the wide ocean although the separation from my children was hard to bear. I wrote in my diary about my struggle in leaving my sons behind:

July 14th, 1919.

The train by which my two babies were going away to Kamakura with their nurses was to start at 3:40. I was standing on the platform of the Tokyo station and looking at the two little faces cunningly peeping at me through the frame of the train window. The smaller one looked like a chick just emerging from his shell in his baby clothes of cream color, lovingly smiling, showing his two pearl-like front teeth. The other face was a little larger with apple-like cheeks looking handsome under shiny black hair, his black eyes so wide open and staring into his mother's face, half puzzled as if to say, "Why don't you come with us?" The train glided out of the station with these two loving little faces framed in one of its windows. Their mother came back home alone carrying the precious picture in her mind, the picture of the "children's faces through mother's eyes," so innocent, so loving, not to be painted even by a great artist.

Coming back to my lonely home, I sat on the cushion in front of my low writing table, still carrying this picture of the two little faces in my mind. I touched my eye with my finger. A few drops fell on my knees. Oh! how could I leave these darlings behind for two years? How could I miss even a day of watching over them as they grew, as they added cunning words to their vocabulary, as they learned more about the art of self-expression? It's a pity to leave them behind. They will miss mother's warm breast. I hate to leave them, it is hard, very hard, to go away.

I much prefer to stay with my darlings but I believe firmly that it is my duty to endure this trial of separation in order to study more while I am young so that some day in the future I can carry out a mother's duties to them in manifold measure.

XIII

My First Trip to the United States

*I*T WAS a great event for the family to send my father and
me off at the Yokohama pier on August 15, 1919. After
hundreds and thousands of bowings, the S.S. *Siberia Maru*
sailed to sea leaving colorful serpentines and flowers and home
people behind.

I looked forward with great excitement and expectation to
seeing the unknown land of the West, and I looked back at my
homeland thinking of my babies and my people. But I was
cheerful and even gay. I had nothing to worry about, my
first voyage taking place under the protection of my father
who, having been abroad many times and being accustomed to
traveling, insisted on accompanying his daughter, whom he had
"brought up in the box," across the Pacific Ocean. He made
this his pleasure trip to America to hand his daughter over
safely to her husband.

It was early morning when we approached the Golden
Gate, outside of the harbor of San Francisco. Through the dim
light of half-dawn the city with the twinkling window lights
looked like a fairyland or like white castles of sugar with silver
filings which I used to see with childish admiration in the show
windows of Western confectionery shops in Tokyo. "Oh,
father, America is here!" I exclaimed with joy. Then I continued to stand for a long time trying to stamp these beautiful
first impressions of a Western town on my memory.

It was the realization of a dream to me, almost religious.
To the Japanese people, planting their feet on the distant Western shore is like a pilgrimage to the land of Buddha in ancient
times. Our ancestors never thought, in those bygone days of

pilgrimage, of crossing an ocean without first exchanging cups of water with their relatives as a sign that this departure was possibly an eternal farewell. So it was natural for me to be ecstatic when I first caught sight of America. I pinched my hand with my own fingers and "Hurt! so this is not a dream!" I said to myself. Father laughed at my childish delight, while he looked after my passport and the trunks.

The soft morning breeze caressed my hair as I gaily turned toward the floating land on the dark green water. September 1, 1919, was the mark of my maturity—the day I first stepped on the great continent of North America full of hope and enthusiasm. I felt serene joy like a bird's in the spring sky, but with this happiness went a serious determination to make this trip fully successful from an educational standpoint.

After the six months' separation, to discover my husband among the Americans at the pier and to find him looking so well was a deep satisfaction. I did not miss the flush of strong will power in his bright eyes, which revealed his state of mind before he spoke a word to me. His lordly manner, and his smartness in getting along in American ways, helped me to find my bearings while I was so overwhelmed by the rush and bigness of the American city, that I could only timidly exclaim: "What tall men!" "What big cars!" "What big horses!" "What wide streets!" Finally my husband said to me: "Don't say any more about the bigness of American things, for you won't see anything but what is big in this country."

We took a room in a hotel in Berkeley where I spent my first night in the West. The city as well as all the hotels were crowded for President Wilson had arrived to inspect the United States Navy in San Francisco Bay. My days were spent in excitement and joy over the reunion with my husband, over interesting places to visit, and over the enjoyment of the California fruits and abundant ice cream.

My husband talked to my father about what had impressed

him in American civilization, and about what he thought of Japan compared with this Western country. He was still the idealist anxious for the improvement of labor conditions at home. Father listened to him quietly and refrained from argument. He looked upon his son-in-law with a kind fatherly eye as if he were wishing him not to go too far with his adventures for the sake of the happiness of his family. These two men had both selected engineering for their professions. But one strictly limited his interest to the sphere of mechanical power, and the other proposed to utilize its productive power in the interest of general human happiness. I recognized a thousand mile gap between the father and the son-in-law, and I thought that in that distance lay the progress of the younger generation.

On the tenth day of September I arrived in New York. It was natural for a young woman to expect something wonderful and beautiful when she arrived at this center of the modern material civilization. Handsome hotels with the most up-to-date accommodations, attractive stores in shopping quarters, and fashionable restaurants with tempting foods—I had expected such things to color my New York life. But this was not to be my lot.

The place to which my husband had arranged to take his young wife was a shabby little boarding house in upper Manhattan Avenue. When the baron took me there in the late evening in a taxicab from the Pennsylvania Station, a woman, about sixty years old, appeared at the door in a queer-looking white nightgown. Her pale face, which looked to me as if she had never seen sunlight, and her thin light hair standing up in the gloomy gaslight made her appear like the wicked witch in a fairytale my mother used to read to me from English books in my childhood. "Ha ha! This must be a ghost house in America!" My imagination instantly went far back to the memories of my early life. The woman spoke in English, but with a strong accent which I could not understand at all, and

I could only catch the word "Sure! sure!" often repeated in her conversation with my husband.

My first night's sleep in New York was disturbed by strange bugs marching around my sheets and pillows. It was a great surprise for me to encounter "Nanking bugs" as we call them in Japan, for we are told that these bugs were the undesirable souvenirs brought back by the Japanese soldiers from Manchuria after the Sino-Japanese War. I had the honor of beholding them for the first time in the great city of New York, far away from the old Chinese city of Nanking!

In the morning in the daylight, I found that the furniture in our room was dirty and cheap. My husband's notion of how we ought to live extended to our meals. He showed me how to get a potful of hot coffee and a few pieces of corn muffin from a Sixth Avenue restaurant. For the first time in my life I took a meal in such a manner, and fared miserably. Even in the simple existence at the mines the atmosphere was different.

Why should we select such a dirty place to live in? I had plenty of money in my bank accounts. I was miserable and unhappy. My father was staying at a hotel in Washington Square. Uncle Yusuke was also in New York and several of our Japanese friends. None of them had the adventurous spirit of my honorable husband, nor chose to explore the slums in New York and to fight with bugs. Uncle Yusuke told me in a joking way that the baron had become a "Bolshevik." "That's that!" I exclaimed to myself. "Aha! He has finally become a real one!" This simple joke of my uncles was enough to explain our strange way of living and our angle of vision in the Occident.

A week after our arrival in New York, my husband took me to see Miss Caroline Dow, the general secretary and dean of the Y.W.C.A. Training School. He helped me to explain to her that I wished to enter the school, get professional training and at the same time learn English in a short time. He also added that I wished to be a self-supporting woman as I did not believe in an easy life based on inherited fortune. So Miss Dow introduced me to the Ballard School at the Y.W.C.A. Building on Lexington Avenue. I registered for the secretarial course, which began October first. The work was so absorbing that I forgot all about my miserable room at the boarding house and became quite enthusiastic about my school life in America.

From the kindergarten to the final graduation, my past education was limited to the Peeresses' School with its feudalistic air; so my experience in an American school training young women for trades and professions was novel in the extreme. I was surprised to find lessons started off without any ceremony. Teachers and students acted in a democratic and simple manner, which was quite unusual to me who had been brought up among formalities. I was the only foreign student in the class and teachers and students took a great interest in this Oriental girl who knew very little English, but who was bold enough to attend a class where native Americans came to study shorthand, most of them having finished high school.

Miss Louise Beiderhase was the teacher of stenography. She gave me a front seat and I concentrated all my attention on her instruction. She was the best possible type of teacher with a strict, precise and energetic attitude toward her class. She knew how to make the snakelike shorthand a live thing in a girl's mind. She impressed me as a woman of strong character. I shall never forget her. Every day from nine to three I worked in this school. I spent two hours in a typewriting course under Miss Boyd who, pointing to a chart on the blackboard, would shout "ASDF—LKJ" keeping time with a stick in her hand while some forty girls pressed keyboards at her dictation. This was easy work for a person like myself who could play the piano, but some of the girls struggled desperately with their unwieldy fingers. For a month or two I could not speak a word at school. I was timid and did not dare to talk in the class, but I studied hard both there and at home. I spent four or five hours on my homework every day. At the end of the third month I began to understand most of what the teachers said. Miss Beiderhase watched me carefully, curious about the progress of a foreign student learning English and stenography at the same time.

Although I had a strong determination for self-discipline and tried not to complain in any circumstances in which I was caught by lot, I simply could not endure the boarding room in "Bolshevik style" very much longer, and at the end of the first month I got my husband's consent to move to a little better place. He did not agree to my consulting anybody about this matter but suggested that I act independently. An independent action is quite contrary to my feudal training. At home I had to consult the elders even about washing my hair, but in America my husband tried to train me to act on my own initiative. So I put a little advertisement in a New York paper which read as follows:

A Japanese woman wants a room in an American family.

A few days later I received about a dozen offerings and I went out to see them. I found a clean small room far uptown at the junction of 157th Street and Broadway. The landlady was a Southerner and both she and her husband were cultured middle-class Americans. They had never taken a roomer before but the fact that I was Japanese lured them into the adventure.

My husband was called off to Washington and left me alone to execute the moving business all by myself. Independent action was not at all easy as yet. I missed my numerous servants who gracefully bowed and waited on me whenever I needed them. I went out into the street and called an expressman. I prepared my short English sentences in my mind before I spoke to him; and my moving affair was carried out safely. I had arranged to pay $65 a month for the room and breakfast.

As soon as I settled into this new room, I locked my door

carefully and tried to sleep, but could not. I was frightened by strange emotions which kept me awake. I walked to the door again and again to see whether it was really locked. I felt that only this frail piece of board was the fortress which protected me from the outside world and from strange people. During my life of twenty-three years I had never lived alone like this but usually in a big family. I missed my parents who would never have left me in such a manner without a chaperon. I recalled the Chinese moral of the lioness pushing her cubs over the top of a steep cliff to the bottom of the ravine to see whether they were strong enough to live in the jungle. My husband had thrown me out in the wilderness of human life where I was unable to rely upon anybody else but had to stand up firmly on my own feet. He arranged affairs so that I should not see any Japanese people while I was learning English. For months I never heard or spoke a word of my native language and this close attention brought remarkable progress in my English within a short period.

While I lived alone, ate alone and studied alone day after day, my husband wrote me from Washington that he planned to go to Europe after Christmas. I comprehended somewhat, at least, his passionate zest for social experience and his ideals to which I paid deep respect, but when I thought of my domestic life, dark premonitions threw a shadow on the future. I was not told much about his European plan, but I knew of the baron's interest in New Russia and said to myself that his trip to Europe was like the one on which "Abraham went out without knowing where he should go." His firm determination to do something extraordinary could be read in his lines.

"This trip may be my eternal farewell to you; if so, be brave always and grow to be a faithful worker for the betterment of the Japanese women's lot." He later wrote: "I will watch your growth as that of a representative woman of Japan. If the women of a nation stay on a low level, there is no progress in that nation as a whole. I am interested in what my friend said to me about the downfall of the great Roman Empire, because my friend attributed it to the Roman women who stopped growing physically and intellectually. If the women of Japan remain on the same level as they are today and don't work to improve their intellect and their physique, there won't be any glory to the future of Japan!" I pondered on these words of my husband's and accepted them, but how could I accept this proposal of separation? I again and again asked him to take me with him even to the limit of the earth.

"I will endure any hardship with you, as I vowed to myself when I was engaged to you," I promised. "Are you going to miss your only chance to study?" he asked me. "Is it your idea to cling to me all the rest of your life? Don't you want to make yourself useful to society?" I could not answer him, but his attitude confirmed my determination to remain in the United States until I had finished my course at school. I must study, I must be a self-supporting woman, I repeated to myself, and I did not ask him any more to take me to Europe with him.

Baron Ishimoto came back to New York from Washington and spent the Christmas vacation with me. He was scheduled to sail for Stockholm on January 3rd. The day for his departure came so quickly.

It was a bright but cold morning. I went out with my husband as far as the corner of the street and said good-bye to him there with a desperate effort to control myself from bursting into a flood of tears. I had been preparing myself to behave bravely as the daughter of a samurai should do, and so I did it fairly well; but as I ran back to my room, I felt as if I had lost everything in the world. I cried and cried to my heart's content. The landlady, Mrs. Nelson, who had been cleaning her breakfast plates, came up to my room to find me on the bed and embarrassed me by saying, "Sweet child! I know you don't like to let him go."

She left her work unfinished in the kitchen, put on her coat and hat and put on mine for me. Then she took me off to a Hoboken pier to see my husband again. I found him among the Swedish passengers and said good-bye over and over until the whistle blew. It was a fearfully cold winter day. My tears and my snivel froze; feet, hands and cheeks were aching in the bitter wind. Mrs. Nelson took me back home and fed me with hot chicken soup. She was kind and attentive, but my lonely soul was inconsolable. When school reopened after the vacation, I somewhat forgot myself and began to study hard once more. I must study, I must be a self-supporting woman. This I held constantly in my mind.

The winter in New York was severe. Heavy snowing often stopped the traffic on the street and laborers toiled to move the solid snowbanks. I caught cold and had to stay in bed for several days. This nourished the misery of terrible homesickness. There was nothing to soothe my lonely heart; nothing in my small square room in Mrs. Nelson's apartment, facing the white walls and with the white ceiling on my head all day long. I longed for my mother's tender voice and the warm inquiries about my health, for soft boiled rice, coddled eggs, and sweet plums on trays. While I was in bed I read the autobiography named *One of Them,* written by a Russian girl, Elizabeth Hasanovitz. This girl, leaving her poverty-stricken family, came to the United States as an immigrant and worked in an American shop for trifling wages. One time she, too, was sick and lay in her cold little bed without friends or family about her, only an empty purse under her pillow for company. She wrote about the miserable life of a factory girl who had to struggle against greedy bosses and icy-hearted employers. After reading it, I said to myself, "What is the matter with me? Born to abundance and choosing this lonely place only at my own will to make myself stronger! Stand up bravely!" I did not catch cold nor was I attacked by illness after that.

It happened during those days that my God of Fortune brought me an opportunity to meet Margaret Sanger, one of the greatest women of the world today. My husband had previously introduced me to Agnes Smedley who had been a coworker with Mrs. Sanger in her early birth control agitation. She took me to see Margaret Sanger in whom I had been deeply interested. Our meeting was on the afternoon of January 17, 1920, Mrs. Sanger having arranged a tea party for me to meet her and a few friends. Her work, her fascinating career in fighting for her cause, had made me picture her in my mind as a big woman of manly proportions. Quite contrary to my imagination, when she received me at the door of her studio, I saw a delicate little figure with charm of a thoroughly feminine type. Still her strong will power was evident in her bright shining eyes. And her thick shining hair gave a touch of eternal youth to her appearance. I felt instantly her magnetism and my respect for her deepened as she talked about her difficulties. Listening to her account of the birth control movement, the memory of the overcrowded miners' huts in Western Japan came back so vividly that the idea of my true mission in life flashed over me. "Yes, Mrs. Sanger's fight has to be fought in my country too! I will carry the banner for Birth Control in Japan!" However, I knew myself better than anybody else. I knew that I did not have Margaret Sanger's courage. I must cultivate courage in my character. Courage would come from knowledge and conviction.

While I was studying, I paid no attention to current events in the world at large, but concentrated on my work. Many Japanese of my own class lived in New York in comfortable apartments enjoying drives, theaters and golf matches, and fashionable dresses, but I maintained my simple life in the Nelsons' apartment. As I loved music, I went to the Metropolitan Opera House once in a while, taking a seat on the top floor from which I looked down on the luxurious boxes and orchestra seats packed with people in evening clothes, wearing diamonds and carrying ostrich fans. Enrico Caruso, the most popular tenor, looked like an ant on the stage though his world-famous voice was well heard even close to the roof where I sat.

When spring came back to New York, and green leaves began to enrich the trees in Central Park and Riverside Drive, I added more and more to my vocabulary of English, and commenced to transcribe shorthand letters on the typewriting machine. I could understand and speak English well enough to make friends among Americans at the end of the school term. Miss Ballard, the chairman of the school, and Miss Beiderhase, my teacher, were pleased to find that their foreign student had made such progress during that short period of time. Though I finished the course, I was unable to remain until commencement day. I was actually going to join my husband in Europe! Before I left, however, the school kindly arranged a little gathering in my honor and a certificate was presented to me decorated with white flowers. It stated as follows:

THE BALLARD SCHOOL
For Practical Education
CENTRAL BRANCH

YOUNG WOMEN'S CHRISTIAN ASSOCIATION OF THE CITY OF NEW YORK

This is to certify that Shidzué Ishimoto has satisfactorily completed the prescribed work as indicated:

Subject	No. hours	Grade	Teacher
Stenography	320	A	A. Louise Beiderhase (Signature)
Bookkeeping	20	A	A. Louise Beiderhase (Signature)
Secretarial duties........	40	A	A. Louise Beiderhase (Signature)
Typewriting	320	A	Mabel Boyd (Signature)

(Signed by) G. B. BALLARD, *Chairman.*

May 28, 1920. *(Signed by)* JEANNETTE HAMILL, *Director.*

Miss Anna Birdsall, hostess secretary of the Y.W.C.A. in Tokyo, and myself in Dr. Inazo Nitobe's garden

Mrs. Margaret Sanger and myself at the time of her visit in 1922

There is nothing to make a person happier than the consciousness of having accomplished something one has set out to do, even though it be such a trifle as to finish one's embroidery in a frame or to pick fresh tomatoes from the back yard after toiling in the soil with one's own hands to grow them.

To me, the winning of this certificate seemed like gaining an invaluable treasure. I had struggled through the long winter battling with loneliness. An inner voice whispered triumphantly: "Now you can be a self-supporting woman, whenever you wish to." My classmates at the school acquired positions in various business firms, some for $18 and some for $25 a week at the start of their careers as private secretaries, while I began to pack my trunks for the trip to Europe.

XIV

My Husband's Disillusionment over Christian Humanism

"MY TRIP to the United States of America is, I should say, more for my enlightenment than for sightseeing merely," Baron Ishimoto wrote in his notebook of random thoughts. "It is an occasion of consecutive spiritual awakenings for me, if I explain it in the term of Zenism—discovering a truth about life yesterday, and today getting another gleam of wisdom. This period of self-analysis is as revealing as my first reading of the Holy Bible."

This short description of my husband's mental state indicates directly and frankly the turn in his life which the visit to the United States had brought about. Christian humanism had been building up his character. His belief in the Christian religion had sprung from the influence of Mr. Kanzo Uchimura, a prominent Christian leader in Japan, and from the liberalism of Dr. Inazo Nitobe. My husband combined Christian humanism and modern liberalism beautifully in his character and action. It was this intellectual idealism which led him to select mining as his profession in order to gain contact with laborers. And his direct experience with physical labor and his familiarity with mining as a whole raised doubts in his mind about the excellence of the capitalistic system of industry. He carried his questions in his mind across the Pacific Ocean to the American continent. His purpose in coming to the United States was to study capitalism more widely and seek answers to his philosophical problems. He hoped to reach conviction by this large experience just as in his early youth he had overcome many of his doubts by reading the Bible and becoming a disciple of Christ.

While he was in America he acted as though he had completely forgotten he was an engineer connected with the Mitsui Company, the big capitalist concern. Soon after he reached the West, he was sent to Mexico to inspect the metal mines in that country. While he was there he happened to meet some American socialists who had crossed the border to agitate in Mexico. He met and talked with still more radical men. He discloses the effect of his association with them in his notebook: "I visited William Haywood at the headquarters of the I.W.W. Haywood started his career as a metal miner. His gigantic constitution, his impressive one-eye, and his charming personality, remind me of our Great Saigo Nanshu." (Saigo was one of the great men who at the time of the Meiji restoration contributed much to the Emperor's cause. Later a group of his former followers who opposed the policies of the central government, organized a revolt. Convinced of their sincerity of purpose, Saigo left his position of glory and honor in the government to join their uprising, was defeated, as he had expected to be, and committed suicide. Nevertheless, a monument to him was erected in Uyeno Park in the center of Tokyo, to commemorate his earlier generosity and loyalty.)

My husband's notebook continued: "Haywood said, 'Workers should be united. Not only within one nation, but the workers of the world must unite. Industry must be democratized,—not only within one nation but the industries of the world must be democratized by the people.' I agree with his idea of the 'Industrial Workers of the World.'" He also added in his notes that William Haywood was far different from the pedantic socialists we often found in cities, talking wildly but never working with sincerity for the attainment of their goal.

The interviews and discussions in Mexico intensified my

husband's unrest. Later in New York he became acquainted with Sen Katayama, the forerunner of the Japanese socialists, who was invited afterwards to Soviet Russia and honored there until his death. At the time of which I speak Sen Katayama was in New York consoling himself for persecution in his native land by writing a history of the Japanese labor movement. When my husband planned to get into Soviet Russia, Mr. Katayama gave him letters of introduction to Lenin, Trotsky and other comrades. Moving steadily to the left, my husband's Christian humanism paled in the face of his radical economic convictions. However, his fundamental belief in Jesus Christ remained even if he did doubt the efficacy of Christianity in furthering social reform.

He wrote again: ". . . The decline of Christianity today may be explained by the fact that it does not touch the point of common interest of humankind. If I may be permitted to express the doctrine of Jesus Christ in one word, it will be 'charity.' The doctrine of Shinran [one of the saints in Japanese Buddhism] is the same 'charity.' Yet the forces which affect us are 'charity,' 'hunger' and 'beauty,' man's response to them being based on his ego.

"We pursue 'beauty,' we go to one who gives 'charity' and we seek one who 'heals hunger.' I recall the wonderful work of Jesus Christ who fed thousands of hungry people in the wilderness.

"Charity and Beauty are one, Religion interprets beauty as 'charity' and art interprets charity as 'beauty.' If there were no chapter in the Bible about the feeding of thousands in the wilderness, or the chapter of Moses receiving manna in the barren field, the Bible would be nothing. . . .

"It is Moses and St. Francis who demonstrated 'charity' to us. It is Rodin and Whitman who show us 'beauty.' And it is Karl Marx and the working people of today who emphasize the need of bread. People who concern themselves with religion today, do not comprehend the true 'charity'; thus the glory of religion has receded naturally."

It was a natural outcome of Baron Ishimoto's growing social ideas that he should live and take me to live in that slum-like place, on my arrival six months after his in New York. When I arrived his first comments on the city of New York were like this:

"The vast population is not the pride of the city of New York. The skyscrapers are not the greatness of New York. It cannot be found in the prosperity of commerce. The pride of New York is found, I should say, in Rodin's original sculpture which the City of New York possesses and whose number is incomparably greater than that of any other big city of the world." I did not understand at first what he meant, but later when he took me to the Metropolitan Museum of Art, I understood. As we reached the statue "Le Penseur" he stopped for a while and said, "I find something prophetic in this work of art. The future human society must be the world in which the man of labor and the man of thought coincide." I realized that his philosophy was changing.

My husband's enthusiasm as a social reformer was evident in his effort during the First Labor Conference in Washington in the autumn of 1919. He helped in every way he could the Japanese labor delegate, Mr. U. Masumoto, and his advisers Messrs. Oshima and Domaye, who were all industrial laborers and had difficulties in the foreign land owing to their lack of knowledge of English. He stayed in Washington during the entire time of the Conference at his own expense to render this aid, although he knew that these delegates were selected officially by the government, ignoring the will of labor organizations, and that the method of selection had met strong criticism at home among the laborers themselves. My husband knew the circumstances of their appointment and he did not approve of the process. But coming to a faraway country, if they could not accomplish anything, the baron felt that the shame would be a heavy burden to all the laborers of Japan. Therefore, he dared to offer his services and give them valuable suggestions, notably about the eight-hour day system of labor. During his activities at the Washington Labor Conference, the manager of the Mitsui Bussan Company gently warned my husband that his support of the laborers would militate against future promotion in the dominion of Mitsui capitalism. The manager was informed that the baron acted in accordance with what he believed. My husband said, "If I don't declare the truth, a stone will declare it."

He had made up his mind, during these days, that he would resign from his position in the Mitsui Company and would work for the happiness of mankind in general. He jotted down in his notebook, his thoughts on this matter: "O God; let your faithful servant work for the happiness of the common people of my country. . . . My service in helping the delegates at the Washington Labor Conference is a mere trifle, but I have studied labor problems for ten years, and am now of the firm conviction that the social position of the laboring class must be elevated. . . . I shall not worry about my personal relations with the Mitsui Company or with my people; I shall fight for the laborers!" He then turned to me, and explained, "If everybody else fails to understand my struggles, you will understand them, Shidzué!" This he said to me before he left New York for Washington to attend the Conference.

Resolving to act and acting may be two very different things, however. He suffered in thinking over his position in relation to his family. He could not deny that he was the son of a former Minister of War and the present master of an honorable titled family. All the other members of his family were in high social positions. His brothers held official posts in the government or were in military service. How could he cut himself off from his contacts with the people of his class?

What would happen to his beloved wife if a revolution took place in her husband's life?

"O God, bless my soul, make me thy faithful servant to work for the happiness of the common people! Give me courage to open a path through the road of thorns!" Thus he prayed. When, struggling desperately, he realized the difficulties connected with shaking off the traditional fetters of the old feudal family system, he even felt a temptation to retire into a remote mountain and live his life alone and quietly. Sometimes he wished that he had died while he was a carefree boy unaware of the bitterness which life can hold.

These turns of inner conflict indicate that Baron Ishimoto has a good and honest nature. When moments calling for action presented themselves, his sentimental indecision was swept away and his heart and soul were filled with an indomitable spirit.

While he was in Washington helping the labor delegates, he determined to visit Soviet Russia. He came back to New York with his hopes swelling. He cried: "I am now going to Russia! I left the land of the Rising Sun for the United States of America in February, 1919, with a determination which was epoch-making in my life and now I am to make another trip based on another decision, equally epoch-making but more serious and profound. I expect to visit the Scandinavian countries, and then Soviet Russia! My soul is leaping with thrills and expectation over what I shall observe there. The whole world has been affected by the World War. The new Union of the Soviet Socialist Republics is the only fruitful creation of the World War to remain for posterity, whose hope depends entirely on the success or failure of that new attempt at liberation. I expect to meet Lenin and Trotsky who are carrying out the socialism which has shaken the world since Karl Marx advanced the new idea. I shall see the outcome of the two years since the revolution. How could I help my heart's leaping with anticipation? I shall put through this program of mine in any circumstances or at any sacrifice."

It was not Christian humanism that brought my husband to this extreme faith in Soviet Russia. Experiences in the United States had refashioned his thinking. On board the S.S. *Frederick VIII* his jotting down of ideas continued: *"Frederick VIII* is sailing on the rough winter sea of the Atlantic for Northern Europe. It is the time for me to review my year's sojourn in the United States. It was a year of great significance for me, because of the change in my thought. Shall I simply call it a great change in my thought or is it the discovery of an entirely new idea? I have learned that the history of humankind is founded on ego. My work as a social reformer rests on ego. I see love grounded on ego. My philosophy stands on this ground of ego. I have observed America and am to study Europe and Soviet Russia in relation to ego." Thus he concluded.

The moving age was claiming its own. But the baron's plan to see Russia, despite his great determination to carry it out and although he had appropriate letters of introduction from the socialists of America, and Sen Katayama, was firmly checked. The first obstacle was the relation of Soviet Russia with other European nations; the second was the interference with his journey by the Japanese legations in Europe; and the third was his title. He could have managed to cut through the obstacles of the first and the third; but the second source of interference hindered him openly or privately until he was compelled to give up his plan completely. I wept for him when I received his letter in which he expressed his disappointment. After he realized that no effort could succeed, he changed his course through the Continent to England, his heart utterly broken.

On the road of life one makes crossings which cannot be retraced. If one takes the north path instead of the south, one's future is completely different from what it would have been if one had taken the south instead of the north. My husband had tried desperately to enter Russia, offering to sacrifice social position—even his wife and his children. His failure at that time was to him a tragedy. Had he succeeded in his heroic attempt to see his Utopia, however, I might never have seen him again. The iron bars of jail would be waiting for him in Japan if he wished to return home. Sympathizers with communism are severely persecuted in Japan.

But a hero can seldom be a hero all his life. My hero, who tried hard to be constant in his conviction, never enthralled me again by such a brave attempt. I still regret the misfortune which checked his battle for suffering humanity.

XV

My Trip to Europe

THE summer voyage on the Atlantic Ocean was pleasant. The mirrorlike waters extended over the wide space between the two continents like a large glass floor. My heart was light as a skylark's in the May air. I cherished my little certificate given by the Business Training School of New York, thinking how pleased my husband would be to see proof of my serious effort. I planned to be an efficient secretary to him so that he would no longer consider me a helpless parasitical woman. Yes, I was independent now and I should act on my own initiative, using my own judgment. My ship dropped anchor at Southampton on June 4th. I expected a passionate embrace from my husband and the joy of reunion after another six months' separation, marked by hardships on both sides.

But his expression was cold. He received me as if it were a matter of business. My heart almost ceased beating from disappointment. I wished I had remained in the United States cherishing my illusion of his love for me and his heroic determination to serve humanity. However, I expressed my deepest sympathy with him in his defeat with respect to the Russian visit and tried to be companionable. But his disappointment ran too deep for the consolation of affection. It had changed entirely his character.

We decided to spend our time in Europe for recreation and pleasure; in sightseeing and art pilgrimages. We stayed two months, visiting England, France, Switzerland and Italy together. But our eyes did not turn only on art in fact. Everywhere the post-war social unrest and distress were apparent. In England the shortage of food was still acute. We Japanese were used to a dearth of food at home, but after a long sojourn in the United States I had acquired the habit of living with plenty. In Europe restaurants furnished poor meat and vegetables at high prices, and sugar and butter were strictly limited for each person. A dose of powdered sugar was all that we could get for a cup of tea.

Among the Japanese at home, where Western clothes and the use of English were supposed to be an indication of things up-to-date, one frequently heard the jovial remark: "In the West even beggars wear Western clothes and babies speak English!" Now looking about us in London we saw long rows of unemployed, and beggars standing on the corners of the streets, miserably and inadequately dressed. My husband, who had been depressed by Germany's suffering after the war, assured me that it was not so acute in England; yet we found a great deal of misery among the victorious Allies. It was deeply affecting to encounter veterans in ragged old clothes, being wheeled in chairs along the paths of different parks by their shabbily clad relatives, ribbon decorations tragically testifying to their heroism at the front. What did the war really bring to mankind? Was it glory? Was it riches? Nothing, it seemed, but the tremendous destruction of civilization and the irreparable loss of human life and material wealth. There was no contentment or exaltation anywhere.

Physically the city of London was beautiful in June. The stroll along the river Thames brought exotic pleasure to us foreigners. Spiritually, however, we felt starved. The peace and charm of the water could not compensate for the constant reminders of war and its horrors. On our walk one day along the Embankment, a middle-aged man in tattered garments dragged his heavy steps toward us and exclaimed in a crazy tone, "Who made me so useless?" His complexion was dull, the color of mud, and his eyes blazed wildly. On his breast was a medal, indicating his valor in battle. Again and again as he shuffled along, he uttered the same cry: "Who made me so useless?" We saw another man powerfully built with a deep chest, apparently a laborer, sitting on a bench with a little child, which was sobbing bitterly. The man nursed his baby in his best, if awkward, manner but it kept up its wailing to his great perplexity. We drew near him and doubtless our solicitude was obvious. The man glanced at us with a strange expression and said:

"It's not new to me, madame, to be acting as a nurse, but this little rascal cries ridiculously."

"Your wife . . ." I ventured to ask him.

"She works. I'm an honorable veteran unemployed."

The women of England seemed less tragic to me, even well off. Now they could vote. While we were there, Lady Asquith and other women mingled with men in political campaigns making speeches and answering questions from the platform, showing their active ability and intellectual equality with men. As a traveler from a country whose women were so behind in their social position owing to their persistent feudal background, my surprise and admiration were boundless. In all the Western countries where I observed these feminist activities, I associated them with strong physiques and came to conclusions concerning the need of physical development among the women of Japan—from the delicate gracefulness to healthy and strong constitutions—if they were to hope for true elevation in their intellectual and social status.

While we were in London we had an interview with Mr. G. D. H. Cole, the young guild socialist whose literary works had been introduced to Japan. My husband asked him many questions about conditions in England and his answers explained to a great extent what we as foreign observers had found so puzzling.

"Does the younger generation of England have sympathy with New Russia?" my husband asked Mr. Cole immediately. The reply was a simple and emphatic "Yes." The next question had to do with civil liberty in England, especially free speech. Why was it that England, by all appearances, was more liberal in this matter than the United States, France and other Western countries? Would England remain liberal? And Mr. Cole maintained that the English people were less excitable, less hysterical by nature than other peoples, the result being that radicals could agitate or speak as they liked. He added, however, that England was speedily swinging in the radical direction. Consequently the government was adopting precautions such as an increase in the number of policemen and their training in rifle practice, the enlargement of the spy system and the encouragement of voluntary police organizations.

Mr. Cole's reference to the policemen made a highly ironic impression on us, since we hadn't grown up in a Christian atmosphere and were used to the idea of war lords. The idea of brotherly love had gripped us as we became adults with the full force of novelty no less than idealism. But here in London churches and policemen were the twin features of the city. The churches gave color to London, suggesting its historical background and emphasizing its religion. But we wondered why this city of Christian churches and civilized people reared in Christian principles could keep order only with many policemen. This was not true of any pagan country.

More completely I was lost in the charms of Paris. We stayed in a fashionable hotel on the Champs-Elysées where the early summer breeze carried sweet fragrance from chestnut leaves, and devoted our time to visiting art museums and places of beauty. Putting aside our interest in social and political questions, we spent our days in an atmosphere of painting, sculpture and natural loveliness and the hours ran out swiftly. At the Miike coal mines we used to study Western art at home, secondhand, by means of photographs. Now in the presence of the original works we were delighted. We also enjoyed the opera and the theater in Paris although we had been unmoved by either in other Western cities, because our eyes and ears were trained for the classical No drama and Kabuki theater.

During our stay in Paris, we consciously tried not to touch upon social questions; however, one day we left this city of art behind us and went to Rheims. Our deeper interests were revived. Surely no militarists would ever have courage to start war again if they could see the destruction so starkly and appallingly presented here. The fine old cathedral, buildings, houses, the pavement of the streets and even the trees, riddled with bullets and shattered by bombs and shells, made one think of a broken nest of bees. We saw miles and miles of trenches in which soldiers had tried to protect themselves, while they were resisting or advancing on the enemy. The exhaustion of the warring nations became more comprehensible, with military, economic, mental and physical strength all bent on this devastating struggle.

It was clear, even then, that if mankind had to fight again, it would fight with more scientific machinery and under more complicated international relations. The next war would be still more cruel, woeful and tenacious in reaching the final catastrophic decision. It was not war alone that shocked us. The aftermath seemed equally dreadful. We were greatly moved by these terrific sights of Rheims and its vicinities.

We left these tragic districts and stayed a day in the quiet old French town of Chalon, then followed on to Strasbourg in the heart of Alsace-Lorraine. Young schoolchildren of that city told us that they were taught French when France ruled the region and German when Germany possessed the land. Why must nations teach even small children to hate their neighbors? What were the Christian churches preaching to them? Those were the questions which occupied our minds while we traveled through these districts, scarred with the ravages of many previous wars.

Mountain climbing came as a relief to our spiritual agony. At home I had never thought of climbing Mount Fuji, but now that I had been educated in America to be independent and energetic, I decided to climb the Jungfrau with my husband. I was warned again and again that it was too much strain for a woman who had never climbed high mountains, but I did not listen. We started together from the Jungfrau-Joch, binding our bodies with rope, my husband going ahead, I in the middle, and the mountain guide behind us. I managed to get along very well and we reached the summit of the mountain after three hours' hard struggling in the snow. The gorgeous view with which I was rewarded made me rejoice that I had taken the risks of the ascent. Descending, however, was a different matter. I felt suddenly tired and halfway down I was so exhausted that I could not walk any more. I fell. Another step forward and again I fell in the deep snow. A thundering headache attacked me and my heart beat rapidly. But I was told that in the mountain snow no one had excess energy for carrying another; everybody had to walk by himself; if he couldn't he had to be left to freeze. It was like the road of human life where one has to live on his own strength; one has to be independent: to be born by one's own vitality and to die alone. Stumbling at every step, I finally arrived safely at the place from which we had started in the morning. I was utterly exhausted. I fainted with the headache and heart trouble, but I recovered the following day. The loveliness of the country and the peacefulness of vast spaces helped me recuperate. I especially loved the sound of the ringing bells hung on the necks of the cows in the hillside pastures. With our faces, necks and arms snow-burned and brown, with the thin skin peeling from our red noses, my husband and I continued our tour.

Every traveler who has once gone through the Simplon Tunnel knows the remarkable contrast between Switzerland and Italy. In Switzerland we saw people living, not in luxury and gaiety particularly but in comfort and contentment, so far as we could judge. But immediately across the border we at once noticed the great congestion. Our first impression of Italy was one of a superabundance of people. The landscape presented everywhere the sight of babies' clothes hanging on the lines around overcrowded houses. The resemblance to our own overpopulated nation in the East almost made us homesick.

Overpopulation, poor natural resources, and the great gulf between the rich and the poor have made Italy a good nursery for social problems. We had heard much about the difficulties Italy was facing at that time, but when we arrived at Milan we discovered we were not really prepared for what we saw. People looked tired, underfed; they wore tattered clothes. Even the horses were gaunt and weary. Human beings had to eat first and it was natural that animals should wait until their masters were fed. Waiters were striking in Milan and all the restaurants were closed, a great inconvenience to foreigners who could not speak Italian and who had to hunt for food at grocers'. We ate anything we could find, but for some reason we missed the famous national dish—macaroni.

Strikes of every kind were going on in Italy. In Rome all the streetcars were out of service and some of the carriage drivers had joined the motormen. Workers refused to transport munitions for any reason. A general strike was being advocated. The question of Fiume was like a firebrand. Mussolini and his Fascists were preparing their march to Rome, and Italy appeared to have no government. The leaders of the Social Democratic party, unable to point the way out of misery, had lost their control over laborers who were in a desperate plight. In these circumstances the rise of the fascist movement as the final crutch for the falling capitalist's power was unavoidable. This was a great lesson to us.

We had to rush our sightseeing in Rome because we were afraid that the strikers might make traveling impossible for an indefinite period. Nevertheless, we visited the Vatican, the Colosseum and other historical places and buildings. Rome made Western history live for us; her architecture and her art deeply impressed us. But we were most powerfully struck by the great power of the Catholic Church, controlling immense numbers of people regardless of their nationality or language, extending its power and influence even into politics, thoroughly coloring the life and history of the West. Church and state are kept so rigidly distinct and apart in Japan that we were amazed at the contrast. Leaving Rome with its historic monuments, commemorating the great imperialism built on the blood of slaves, we returned for a farewell visit to Paris, and then sailed from Havre to New York, our memories of our European trip a compound of sweetness and bitterness.

After visiting these countries in Europe my husband expressed his conclusions briefly: "The currents of the world are strong; one is moving from good to better, guided by the inexperienced hands of the proletariat in the face of domestic and foreign opposition; the other is moving from bad to worse, the conventional road to destruction. Egypt and Rome all over again." My own conclusion was largely that travel is the best university in the world.

Reaching New York, we took the Canadian route to Seattle and sailed for home after a year's absence for me and a year and a half for my husband. It is always exciting for a traveler to see his native land after a long absence from it. I was especially eager to see my two little sons and my parents. But, on the other hand, both my husband and myself could not avoid feeling vaguely depressed at the thought of the "heavy fetters of tradition" awaiting us, to bind us again to the past. The invisible but powerful feudal bondage loomed quite beyond the movement of the world. "How shall we fight against this power?" was the question we asked ourselves on our way across the Pacific.

PART SEVEN

BUSINESS EXPERIENCE AND SOCIAL
WORK: EARTHQUAKE TRAGEDY

XVI

Private Secretary and Shopkeeper

*I*F THE frequency of strikes indicates the awakening of a laboring class, the year 1920—the year my husband and I returned from our trip through America and Europe—showed a remarkable record in that field. Statistics indicate the number of strikes, which ended in closing factories, to be 50 in 1914, the year I was married; during 1919 it increased to 497, the highest number of cases ever reached in the labor history of Japan. Although a business depression in the early part of 1920, following the war boom, slackened the demand for labor, causing a blow to workers' activities, the rights of workers were greatly advanced during this period. Thus capitalism in Japan, which had inherited much of the psychology of our previous social system and had been exploiting to the full the laborers' sense of loyalty to their employers, as daimyos had formerly held them loyal to their feudal masters, now had to face laborers realizing and clamoring for privileges.

However, this progressive tide of the modern world had little effect on the life of Japanese ladies, still shut up to all intents and purposes in the old castles of feudalism. "Knowledge is a spring of grief," said some pessimistic philosopher of ours, and it exactly fitted my case. So long as I remained in the realm of feudalistic morality, I could conduct myself according to the virtue of harmony without murmuring, but once I was roused from the conventional code of conduct I found great difficulties in getting on smoothly within my old surroundings. I was young and energetic and eager to start cutting through the red tape of formality.

As soon as he was settled in Tokyo, my husband could not waste a moment in trying to put his ideals into practice. As a sympathizer and member of the Federal Union of Miners of Japan (Kofu-So-Rengo), which was organized within the Federation of Labor (Rodo Sodomei), he shared in its activities. He organized a group in the Federal Union to study labor questions scientifically—a great contribution to the labor movement of that time. The movement hitherto had been limited almost entirely to organization and agitation and sadly lacked proper intellectual leadership. This organization for the scientific study of labor was transformed later into an independent institute for labor and industrial research. Valuable treatises on social problems resulted. But this institute was dissolved when a law was enacted prohibiting "dangerous thought." Independent labor and industrial research were suppressed.

My husband's connection with these actual labor developments indicated his strong determination to make better working conditions his aim in life, and I was deeply interested in his ideal. He knew that his concern with labor problems would not harmonize with his position as mining engineer in the Mitsui Company, and as soon as he had presented his reports of his trip in the Western countries he resigned his post and established an independent business, importing foreign books. Up to that time the book importing business had been almost monopolized by one big firm and the prices charged for Western books were exorbitant for the people who sought the culture and knowledge of the world. And this effort to procure foreign works at a reduced cost for interested Japanese accorded with my husband's general idealism.

My own desire to be a self-supporting woman never weakened although I had come back to face thick walls of tradition and convention. I finally got a cozy little place to try my business ability as a private secretary to Miss Anna Birdsall, hostess secretary to the National Y. W. C. A. of Japan. My genuine interest in promoting international friendship fitted exactly Miss Birdsall's task of bringing East and West together socially. I helped to introduce Western visitors to Japan and to the Japanese people. This work was not heavy and I had plenty of time to look after my two little children, pay good attention to housekeeping and observe the complicated formalities of our rural life. I received fifty yen ($25) a month for my salary. Fifty yen was very little, of course, and was not sufficient to support even myself, yet it meant so much to feel for the first time in my life that I earned something by my own work. It had a different value to me from income obtained from rents on estates or interest on invested capital.

The next step we both took to emancipate ourselves from the conventional life was to give up our large residence in Koishikawa. We moved into a small house built in Western style in the Akasaka district of Tokyo. I missed the old garden and the Japanese rooms with their green mats, the polished wooden corridors and the sliding doors with their delicate paper covering, but we had decided to live more simply in order to have more time for public activity.

The big Japanese houses are designed for a life marked by plenty of leisure for the masters and plenty of work for the servants. If one could afford to spend all one's working hours enjoying the beauty in nature, I certainly would recommend a Japanese house and a Japanese garden. Even after seeing beautiful gardens in Italian or Spanish styles in many places in the West, from the most sophisticated aesthetic point of view I still give my first allegiance to the gardens of my country. But we were too young and too enthusiastic about our interest in present-day problems to be preoccupied with beauty. We did not hesitate a second to attempt to practice in our daily life the things in which we believed. Hastily we parted with our old home and started a new one, intending to be both practical and energetic. My two sons were sent to kindergarten in the Peeresses' School where I had spent my early childhood. I enjoyed the hours at home as a busy mother, and worked as a happy business woman during other parts of the day. I kept my position as her secretary until Miss Birdsall went back to America.

After a year's interval during which I went on a trip to Korea and China with my husband, I took up a business career again. One day a friend of mine, Mr. Alexander Nagai, a Catholic with a German mother, asked me if I would like to enter the wool yarn importing business. He offered me a sales agency for Minerva Yarn, which comes from America. I was especially glad to accept his offer since the object of this business was to raise a fund for the support of the leper hospital at Gotemba, carried on by a Catholic mission. I saw good reasons for promoting this Minerva Yarn business: the leper hospital, and also the prospect of using my earnings for birth control education which I was planning to start. I knew only too well that in Japan the most difficult undertaking imaginable was to raise funds for any social work on account of the absence of a sense of social responsibility on the part of a people whose interest is limited to their family circles. This would be especially true of such an enterprise as birth control education, for the idea of spacing children was not readily understood or approved by the conservative and the rich.

Besides this purpose of raising money for the Catholic charity and my own social enterprise, I had in mind another thing. It was to offset the attitude of my own class of samurai toward "material" interests. I take the liberty here to quote from Dr. Nitobe's essay on samuraiism.

"The mercantile calling was as far removed from 'Bushido' as the north is from the south. To a samurai, trade and commerce were small concerns to which it was derogatory to his dignity to pay any attention; hence the effect of Bushido upon the early days of our commerce was not appreciable. This was naturally followed by a low morality among the industrial classes. One vulnerable point of Bushido, which it shared with all class-morality, is that it meted out honor in unequal degrees to the various vocations of society—first of all to the samurai, then to the tillers of the soil, then to mechanics, and least of all to merchants. The last-named, being considered by the rest as the least honorable, naturally adjusted their moral tone to their reputation. Still, as I have already observed, honesty is a virtue easiest learned in commercial transactions; for its reward is not laid as far off as heaven after death, but at the counter or else at the court, when the bills are due." [1]

In these circumstances, the samurai were being starved while bold money-makers of another class were plunging forward with their enterprise and winning economic and political dominance. Still the feeling of horror for mercantile transactions resulting in the making of money had its root so deep in the samurai mind that it was almost a revolutionary act for a lady of the peerage to open a shop in Tokyo. I expected severe criticism but I joyously launched my yarn shop with its little school, adjoining, in which Western knitting was taught to girls and women who were anxious to make jackets and sweaters for their children and their men and shawls and gloves for themselves. Our winters are very cold and these garments would give great comfort. At the same time I planned to furnish knitting jobs to women at home in cases where they were in urgent need of earning a part or the whole of the family livelihood. My shop was in an up-to-date building in the Kyobashi district, in the same building where my husband had his bookshop, the business center of Tokyo.

The glass cases with white painted frames were filled with colorful yarn balls, and fashionable sweaters, jumpers, scarfs and ski outfits gayly decorated the shop; soft comfortable-looking dresses for children were the particular temptation of young

[1] Inazo Nitobe, *Thought and Essays,* "Samuraiism," page 354.

mothers. The customers consisted of persons who wanted something very chic and high-grade, including many ladies among the Peeresses' School graduates and even royal princesses who would order their golf-playing outfits in my shop. A few whispered that they believed in ladies going ahead in this sort of business enterprise and treated me with respect. Others behaved in the haughtiest manner, looking upon me with contempt for my mercantile pursuit. Some Kabuki actors' wives, who always tried to be ultrafashionable, came to my shop and, on finding that Angora was the most expensive yarn, with one accord decided to make their dear husbands' underwear of that precious material!

Journalists, writing about my shop, afforded me without expense the best kind of advertising and this high-grade imported yarn brought good prices. I succeeded in giving fairly profitable jobs to middle class women who learned knitting and took their work to their own homes to meet the demand for finished goods.

I published a book on knitting which sold thirteen thousand copies. I traveled to many towns to teach knitting, even as far as Hokkaido in the snow. Almost every place I visited in the interests of my knitting business brought the request that I talk on the birth control principle. So my birth control propaganda and the knitting business were strongly interwoven. I had five girls and two men at work in the shop, and several young women who helped me teach in my knitting classes.

Among my assistants was Mrs. Shigeko Nakajima, a dear young person, whose two brothers, Mr. Hideo and Mikihiko Nagata, were popular men in the literary circle of Tokyo. She was a fine example of Japanese womanhood, struggling in her unhappy married life to be economically independent while remaining loyal to her husband. She was a thoroughly gentle wife and served her husband like a faithful slave, as tradition required of every Japanese woman at home. She worked hard and competently at the office, and fairly ran back to her kitchen to prepare a good dinner for her husband and to welcome him at the close of the day. However, her husband was utterly lacking in sympathy for this sweet little woman and finally drove her out of his house. She had to find refuge in the Catholic convent in snowbound Hokkaido. Her heroic struggle was made the theme of a story by one of her brothers. It was widely read and drew sympathy from many women whose fate in present Japanese society savors of cruelty. My yarn business went ahead with unexpected success until the moment of that terrible catastrophe which destroyed everything in Tokyo and its vicinity on September 1, 1923. The Earthquake!

My example in opening a business road for women and battling with the feudalistic prejudice against commercialism may have counted for very little. However, it is since that experiment was made that our public has taken women's activities in the mercantile field for granted. Today we have in Japan a good deal of this kind of work carried on successfully by women.

While I was active in this yarn importing and selling business, I undertook one more task which also turned out well. During 1920 and 1921, a great famine occurred in South Russia extending over a huge territory and including hundreds of thousands of people. Relief work was asked of every nation. Regardless of their approval or disapproval of Soviet Russia, kind-hearted people of the world could not be callous to this great disaster, and philanthropists, religious groups, social workers and advocates of international friendship all proceeded to take part in this relief work. In Japan sympathy for the starving Russians was genuine and women were urged to give substantial aid. A relief group was organized immediately and on the committee served Madame Akiko Yosano, a poetess, Mrs. Kikuye Yamakawa, a social thinker, Miss Yuriko Chujo, a popular young novelist, and others including myself. My office at Kyobashi became the headquarters, and the actual work of relief was put under my direction. The committee labored energetically day and night and finally succeeded in raising the sum of Y 7899 ($3,949.50) which it sent to the famine districts through the Foreign Office of our government. This amount collected by Japanese women was a surprise to them and to Tokyo in general. It helped to swell the total relief administered by Japan. It encouraged our group and encouraged other women in the "progressive" attitude.

XVII

Trip to Korea, Manchuria and China

*A*FTER I had seen the countries of the West, I wanted very much to see Korea and China. My husband had already traveled there and his accounts of his trip excited my interest. Finally, in the autumn of 1922, he took me to spend two months in North China, South Manchuria and Korea. During the journey I kept a diary.

November 13, 1921.

A warm unrestrained feeling governs me, when I realize that I am starting on a visit to my neighbor countries, to see other people of black hair and dark skin. Although I have never seen them, I have a feeling of visiting brothers and sisters with whom we Japanese have enjoyed a common civilization of a long and wonderful origin.

November 16, 1921.

The face suggesting a tempo of andante, the long ragged whiskers, the primitive looking, loose, bleached cotton costume, the long, long pipe and the ridiculously small black hat—this is the meek-looking Korean man, in sharp comparison to the small and quick moving Japanese.

This was my first impression of Korea after arriving in Seoul. The Great South Gate and many of the palaces are beautiful pieces of architecture. Won't the gigantic new Western buildings built by us in front of the Korean royal palace humiliate us in later years when we truly realize that we did not appreciate the beauty of native Korean architecture?

I saw three different types of the Korean family while I was in Seoul and through them I grasped some phases of Korean life: upper, middle, and "low class" Korean families. The house to which I was introduced first represented the old native aristocracy. This family spent the sum of two thousand yen ($1000) a month for the household expenses, including the support of more than one hundred servants. This amount of money for household expenses would mean a millionaire status in Japan, yet, to my surprise, I could not find anything splendid or luxurious or even neat in the domicile. Life seemed to be on the plane of hibernation, lazy, inactive and joyless.

In this household the women's apartments were strictly separated from the men's, but husbands were allowed to enter all the family precincts. The ladies in their seclusion were meek and delicate. I could not speak to them on account of the difference in our languages but I was told that they were in family mourning which would last for three years, so much longer than in present-day Japan. As an Oriental woman, I had been thinking a great deal of the social barrier I had known in our unreasonable conventions, but here I was driven into deeper dismay by the Korean ladies who were put under more fetters and lived a more depressing life of wasteful patience!

The second of the houses which I visited was a good example of middle class family shelter. This was a friendly Christian family considerably influenced by Western missionaries in its customs and outlook.

The third family belonged to the poor and lived in what could hardly be called a house at all—a clay pit, dark, dirty, with stuffy air and queer odors.

The upper and lower Korean families alike seemed to me to exhibit a lazy attitude toward life. Everywhere in Korea I was impressed by the lack of vitality. I saw how actively the Japanese directed this annexed people. More than ever before I realized what the words "conqueror" and "conquered" meant as I traveled in Korea. Nevertheless, Korean habits and customs betrayed Chinese and Japanese elements. The food, for instance, is not as rich as Chinese but is very much like it—the delicious hot-spiced pickles made of white vegetables are a main dish. Like the Japanese, the Koreans remove their shoes before entering a room, and the architecture closely resembles that of China.

November 18, 1921.

Messrs. Leo, Lyo, Shu and Kim came to the station to see us off. Warm friendship with the native Korean people is the only hope for adjustment in the relations between the Koreans and the Japanese.

At eleven o'clock at night, we crossed the Oryokko River, the northern border of Korea. My husband explained to me about the economic and strategic significance of this river while our train was crossing the

long bridge over it. When I looked out through the window, a late autumn moon was reflected on the water, chilling the more our thoughts,
concentrated on the history of two Japanese wars—one with China and
the other with Imperial Russia with Korea in the balance. I recalled my
childhood with my old grandfather in Kamakura. How excited he was
each time he got a newspaper extra announcing another Japanese victory
in the field! How I exclaimed "Banzai" with my innocent brothers,
waving the sun-disk flag of white and red! Now, I pondered on the
way Japan is growing bigger and stronger, at the sacrifice of hundreds
of thousands of my countrymen's lives. Japan has rested her standard
of glory on the graves of her heroic patriots. She has expanded so fast
that no other nation could imitate the pace of her progress. I, too, have
grown while my country has been growing. Korea was annexed to
Japan while I was in the primary school; now in my maturity I was
visiting the conquered race. "What will be the future of Korea?" I
asked my husband. He did not answer but seemed lost in meditation
as he gazed down on the cold scenery of the Oryokko. As we entered the
territory of South Manchuria, we both exclaimed, "Bless the heart of
our Korean brothers!"

November 19, 1921.

Arrived at Mukden in the early morning. The chilly air reminded
us of the winter in New York. Suddenly my husband said, "Let's go to
Harbin." I understood the impulse, I knew his dream of getting into
the country forbidden to the Japanese had revived.

Kawlian had been gathered in. Here a vast expanse of land spread
like an ocean until it touched the heaven with no obstacles to break the
flatness of the landscape. Our open carriage drawn by two donkeys ran
over the trackless plain. In clouds of dust dimly covering this primitive
traffic on the sand ocean, we arrived at the old Tombs of the Ching
Emperors and stood among the rubbish of past splendor. The palaces,
once built with the labor of millions of human beings, now lay over-
grown with weeds and shrubs. The interior afforded safe refuge for birds
and bats, their presence intensifying the emotions aroused by the ruins
of an Empire.

November 22, 1921.

Left Port Dairen. Our boat sailed at noon for Chingtao [Tsingtao].
The short voyage between Dairen and Chingtao took only twenty-four
hours on the calm sea. Cabin passengers were few, but Chinese coolies
crowded the decks of the boat. The coolies who had emigrated from the

province of Shantung to South Manchuria were now coming back to their homeland with their small savings. They were the most important customers of the ship company. Alas, these passengers were treated in the most inhospitable way by the company! Coolies, are they not human beings? No, they are the most convenient cargoes; they manage themselves, they do not wait until the cranes lift them into the ship, they are a self-transporting and self-feeding shipload! A few women and children were among them. The whole number spent the day and night on the open deck, the cold sea wind of winter blowing continually over them! Instinctively we were gratefully reminded of the Japanese Mikado; and of the fact that there is no class of human beings in Japan as unprotected as the Chinese coolies. Nowhere in the world had we seen laborers so diligent and at the same time so able to endure a wretched standard of living. They exist only to offer their muscles or even their lives to be exploited by foreign capital, which is often their master under the beautiful name of "helping China, and developing Chinese natural resources." Without the coolies, there would be no interest luring foreign capital to this backward land. Will they ever learn to resist human exploitation? Or will they forever merely exist and breed slaves for the satisfaction of others? The pathetic picture of colonial labor saddened me.

November 23, 1921.

Arrived at Chingtao and took a room in the Pension Lineman. Chingtao is a beautiful town built by the Germans in their effort to obtain political and naval prestige in the Far East. The town faces Kiaochow Bay with the British naval station on the opposite shore. The fact that German civilization had been transplanted to this Oriental mandate could be seen in the up-to-date fortifications, and in the character of the architecture of the homes, hotels, clubhouses and school buildings in Chingtao. Today, however, the Japanese hold this territory under military occupation, ceded by treaty following the World War.

November 25, 1921.

My husband has gone to investigate some of the coal mines around the Shantung peninsula. Madame Lineman, our German landlady, kindly took me to see some of the former German residences whose charm I could appreciate due to the fact that my father's house is built in the German style from a German architect's design. One house we visited was magnificently furnished and decorated, testaments of its former social glory. Luxuriant tropical plants were growing in an adjoining green-house and on the sunny veranda, though the master and mistress had gone leaving these to the care of their Chinese servants. Only yesterday this house was occupied by a happy family. I went upstairs into the splendid bedroom of the daughter of the house, who had left there a picture of her wedding; her husband was carried away by the cruel hand of war in the midst of their honeymoon trip. The heads of two brown horses which she had been embroidering on a green silk cushion were left unfinished on her bureau. A little present intended for her father was found in the master's room unpacked. Oh, how often have such war tragedies repeated themselves since the beginning of human history, and how long is mankind to repeat the process of construction and destruction? Will not defeat some time visit our nation, now victorious?

I was shown the official residence of the commander-in-chief of the Japanese army at Chingtao—like a castle of old Europe, but with modern accommodations. A young cadet in a khaki uniform, with a red collar, led us through the house. He showed us a magnificent, ornate hall overlooking Kiaochow Bay, and pointed out to us an endless number of works of art, reiterating many times and proudly: "This is a war trophy!" Then he called attention to a huge cannon set in front of the entrance to this mansion, seemingly unaware of the way in which the artistic effect was broken by this ugly monster.

I was also taken to see the former German clubhouse, which was now used for a temporary lawcourt. My imagination conjured up a person summoned on some criminal charge to stand before its old bar, and the judge solemnly passing judgment at the back of the counter where bubbling beer and cocktails were once merrily served! The world is changing. It is certainly moving rapidly! The heavy tapestries and curtains had been resigned to the dust and the rough handling of new occupants. Again and again I asked myself: "Where have we Japanese learned such a thing as fighting with foreign nations? Are we born fighters? Do we never appreciate a civilization of high order?" My knowledge of Japanese history forbade such a conclusion. I knew enough to answer myself: "We were once a peaceful nation. We developed a high civilization of our own, distinguished for its artistic qualities. Our fighting is only a part of our imitation of what the West has done in the past and is still doing." And I longed to have my people pass through this period of imitation and realize their own creative power for the sake of human progress!

November 26, 1921.

I went to a silk factory in Chingtao, run by a Japanese proprietor, where young Chinese girls in blue cotton native clothes were working. Thousands of them operate machinery ten hours a day for a wage of fifteen sen (7½ cents) a day. Poor girls with small bound feet, recruited to serve modern capitalistic demands! I have never seen such cheap labor anywhere else. The world's laborers still have a long way to go on the road to a decent standard of living. So long as any number of them remain in such a condition, their existence will be a menace to other laborers who have gained a humane status, because capital moves into the places where labor is cheap.

I visited Tsinan, Tientsin and Pekin. I saw the ruins of a great empire everywhere, and at the same time and place Chinese people continuing their trades, haggling and peddling, buying and selling, unmolested in the streets. What a busy people they are—even the armies of beggars who swarmed everywhere and often besieged foreign travelers riding in rikishas. Poverty stared one in the face on all sides. Devoid of a strong government to protect them, without organized effort to preserve their rights, the Chinese are a woefully helpless people. They die like flies when a long drought causes famine, as it often does. They lose their houses and farms when the God of the River brings a flood, as he frequently does. Yet at theaters and in hotels, Chinese women are richly dressed, with ropes of pearls in their hair, diamond and jade necklaces around their delicate throats, bracelets on their wrists, rings on their fingers and pendants fastened to their ears, literally carrying fortunes on their persons, and seemingly oblivious to the havoc about them.

I called upon an ex-president of the Chinese Republic, General Li, and his family at his mansion in the French Concession in Tientsin. What a pity that a man of China has to live in alien territory to protect his own life and property. Young Mr. Li had been educated in Tokyo at the Peers' School and I had known him well there. I remember one day my younger brother carelessly saying to Mr. Li that the Chinese were a very dirty people. Mr. Li retorted that he knew many dirty Japanese in Tokyo. After seeing how he lived in China, I appreciated his resentment at the charge my brother made against a whole race. There are four hundred million Chinese. One must always be cautious about criticizing races and nations in sweeping generalities. My trip to China and Korea raised questions upon which one could ponder forever.

XVIII

Birth Control Movement: "Invasion of Sangerism in Japan"

SINCE the time of Commodore Perry, no American has created a greater sensation in the land of the Mikado than Margaret Sanger! Our historians have described Commodore Perry's visit to Japan in 1852 as the invasion of modern industrialism, resulting, practically, in the end of the Japanese pacific policy of isolation which had ruled for hundreds of years. Now they must describe Margaret Sanger's visit to Japan in 1922 as the invasion of "Sangerism" bearing to an island empire, distraught by its swarming millions, the pacific means of harvesting the fruits of machine civilization.

Today it is greatly feared in many quarters that overpopulation in Japan may turn out to be a world menace. No other country is really so overcrowded. Japan proper, the size of which is about that of the state of California, has a population of 67,837,577 according to the census of 1931. The average rate of increase for the last five years was 34 per thousand, adding about 940,000 newborn Japanese every year to the teeming multitude. But such figures standing alone give us no idea of their true significance. They must be considered in relation to the land of the nation. In this connection we find an average density for the population of 400 persons per square mile, making Japan one of the most densely populated countries in the world; only a few highly industrialized nations, such as Belgium, Holland and Great Britain, surpass it. The degree of density naturally varies in different parts of the country, according to their climate and productivity. Japan is gifted with scenic beauty. Her mountains provide a constant variation in the landscape by a succession of peaks. But this mountainous land is unfit for cultivation. When, therefore, we calculate the density of population per square mile, not of territory but of cultivatable area, the Japanese density is 2490 per square mile, double the density of Belgium and over four times that of England.

Who could foresee such a problem of congestion in the day when Commodore Perry lured the reluctant islanders into international competition so coaxingly with his wonderful gifts, including telegraph apparatus, a locomotive and tender, a hundred gallons of whisky, eight baskets of Irish potatoes and similar attractions [1]—exotic presents from representatives of the young republic to a dynasty more than twenty-five hundred years old!

In 1846, six years before Commodore Perry reached the Japanese coast with an American fleet, Japan's population was 26,-207,625 according to the census of the time. This figure had risen to 59,560,252 in the year of Margaret Sanger's visit.

It is clear that the Japanese population had more than doubled within seventy years of modernization. This situation was worrying many Japanese before Mrs. Sanger arrived.

Let us examine the social conditions which underlay the welcome given "Sangerism" in Japan. In 1910 Japan was shocked by a "high treason case"—a conspiracy entered into by a group of anarchists to overthrow the imperial throne by force. The loyal subjects of the Emperor were stunned. And the government felt warranted in prohibiting any social movement whatsoever. Prominent leaders of a socialistic or anarchistic bent were all arrested and the seeds of political criticism were apparently destroyed. The very word "social" came to be a synonym for "treason." Even economists had to refrain from using that word in their scientific studies. Citizens who projected reforms

[1] Miriam Beard, *Realism in Romantic Japan*, page 5.

were considered rebels against society. Any kind of social thinking was apparently crushed in the budding stage.

However, as months and years passed the buds took on new life. Through the irresistible influence of the World War, social and labor problems surged to the foreground of thought. Their pre-eminence was emphasized in the literature of an anarchistic tendency which made its way into the market at the time, and in a syndicalist labor movement which took form during the years 1914 and 1915. The March Revolution in Russia had distinct echoes in my country. It was in these days that the word "democracy" was interpreted to Japanese students by Professor Sakuzo Yoshino, then a professor of political science in the Imperial University of Tokyo. Dr. Yoshino's advocacy of democracy gained such warm supporters among the young university men and among other intellectuals that it seemed as if the democratic ideal was going to sway the whole nation. With "democracy" was associated "internationalism." So the nationalists were alarmed. Some nervous reactionaries, frightened by this new tide of social awakening, organized a society called "Roninkai" and challenged Dr. Yoshino to meet the charge of being a national enemy.

The new force of a democratic ideal and the conserving power of tradition waged open warfare. The nationalists even adopted terrorism as a tactic for defeating their rivals. Finally the dispute was submitted to public judgment in a mass assembly. An audience numbering about two thousand listened to the debate between Dr. Yoshino and a representative of the conservative point of view. Loud cheers greeted the remarks of Dr. Yoshino as he presented the progressive viewpoint. And the atmosphere of this open debate was electric with the changing currents of Japanese opinion.

After that the conservative nationalists retired from public debate. Young people grew bolder. A society calling itself the "New Men's Society" was organized among the students at the

Imperial University of Tokyo, under the leadership of Dr. Yoshino. The New Men's Society stimulated progressive social thought. But it did more than think. Its sessions not only rallied intellectuals for discussion within the group, but it sent forth young people actually to take part in the social movement, the fruits of whose labor were later unmistakable. It was the cradle of many prominent leaders of the Social Democratic and Communist parties. The syndicalist tendency in the Japanese labor movement was strengthened by the October Revolution in Russia. But in the face of other events, the labor movement as a whole veered toward political Marxism.

However, the idea of democracy still occupied the central position in our social thought. It was evident even in the social practices of those days. Errand boys, factory girls and domestic maids, who had been considered by feudalistically-minded people as belonging to a semislave class, now received the honorific "san" which corresponds to the English "Mr., Mrs. and Miss." Thus Miss Maid, Misses Factory Girls and Messrs. Boys strode to the front of the stage. This would appear a trifling act to Westerners, but in fact it was a great advance for a people so recently feudal.

The idea of democracy, accompanied by the pacifist ideal of internationalism, finally dominated a people disillusioned with respect to nationalist and conservative leadership everywhere by the results of the World War. The first Washington Conference in 1919 spurred on the new political philosophy. In Japan women of the bourgeois class organized a society for promoting international peace. Some of the advanced teachers in the primary schools started a movement to abolish warlike passages from the textbooks used by little boys and girls—an expression of the antijingoistic temper now in force—and secured deletions. Young ladies agreed that militarists were the most unpopular suitors in their marriage considerations.

Finally this tide of democratic conviction overwhelmed the

masses and the battle for universal suffrage began amid great popular excitement. The authorities tried to suppress the universal suffrage movement by force, but their persecution only inflamed the masses, and like a wildfire on a dried stubble field, the demand for enfranchisement spread. The people of Japan were acquiring self-confidence. This was in part due to the prosperity of the industrial system of the country which had advanced rapidly during the World War, giving unusually wide employment to men and women who before had thought of life and themselves merely in connection with the feudal family system and were now being individualized. But the panic which came upon expanded industry, suddenly shrinking the labor market and thrusting men and women out on the street—an army of the unemployed, sharpened the will to self-assertion. Individuals who had broken out of family confinement were unable to go back to it to be fed again in a feudalistic economy. Feudalism was weakened by the panic. Naturally this condition created social unrest and intensified labor and political struggles.

Forced to bend under the weight of public opinion, the Diet in 1924 established manhood suffrage, at least. But at the same time a law was passed for the strict punishment of "dangerous thoughts." This prohibitive measure had been planned by the authorities several years before, but it had not been enacted as a law on account of the influence of the democratic ideal. Now in the form of compromise a severer statute was inscribed on the books than that famous pact of "Ausnahmagesetz gegen die Sozialdemokratie" sponsored by Bismarck in Germany late in the nineteenth century.

Anyway this progress in the social consciousness of the people furnished a ready background for the birth control movement which I term "Sangerism." Religion was, moreover, an asset with us and not a liability as in the West. In Japan it has been separated from direct politics for centuries. Buddhism, Shintoism and the newly introduced Christianity occupy a different social position from that held by religious organizations in the western world. Religion in Japanese society never rules public opinion through clerical interference or acts as a social force through the will-to-power of the clergy. It has no reason for interfering with the birth control movement as such. However, it cannot be denied that Buddhism exercises an influence of a subtle kind on the Japanese mind. The negative morality of Buddhism, utilized by rulers, has inculcated among the Japanese habits of obedience, nonresistance and resignation. Spiritual beauty is stressed and material objects are looked upon as mere illusions. How far Buddhist teaching is from the gospel of Karl Marx!

The cardinal virtue of the former is humility and subservience, seen in all its proverbs. "You cannot defeat a crying child and the landlord." "A stake which lifts its head higher than the others will be driven down." "A tall tree is easily blown down by the wind." The main tenet is that humility means happiness. The effect is paralytic with respect to insurgent thought. The Japanese have been taught, for instance, to regard children as treasures of country and of family, which must be produced, at all costs, to the limit of potentialities. Parents of offspring whom they cannot support, however hard they work, in their poverty and hunger may often seek solace in Buddhist philosophy. And yet, despite the pull of long-taught doctrine, the cry for the cure of poverty and hunger grew sharp and bitter in Japan. There are limits beyond which philosophy breaks down. When birth control was offered as a social remedy, the poor Japanese grasped its value quicker than the ruling class. Having returned from America full of enthusiasm for this social remedy, I was hailed in the press as the leader in the birth control movement of Japan.

Then when Margaret Sanger arrived en route to China and India her dynamic personality as well as her fame lifted the movement with which I was struggling to one of major concern in the nation. The attitude of official Japan toward the visitor was reported in the New York *Tribune* as prime news justifying the space of an entire page of narration and criticism accompanied by clever cartoons. The paper gave a faithful account of her official reception. "With more than the usual amount of wit displayed by them, the Japanese policemen are calling Mrs. Sanger 'Sangai-san.' Sangai is a Japanese word which may be interpreted to mean 'destructive to production.' This is just one evidence of the extent to which Mrs. Sanger is being discussed in Japan today," said the *Tribune*.

Perhaps the futility of attempts to repress ideas by government edict was never more conclusively proved than in the case of Mrs. Sanger's visit to Japan. When she was officially restrained from making public speeches concerning birth control, the people at large heard about her and her work in a dramatic way which "took." She became the big story of Japan and the most talked-of person in the land. The day she and Admiral Baron Kato, returned conference delegate from Washington, reached Yokohama on the same steamer, the baron's picture was diverted to out-of-the way corners of the Japanese papers while large photographs of Mrs. Sanger and her son Grant, who was with her, were featured as first-class news. No group could come together, whether foreign or Japanese, in which she and her theories were not the subject of lively conversation.

The attempt to repress Mrs. Sanger truly acted as a boomerang. She was a stronger magnet than she ever could have been had she been allowed to go about undisturbed making speeches on birth control. Young Japan was in the mood just then to approve of anything the government condemned. The government thought Mrs. Sanger would introduce "dangerous thoughts." "Dangerous thoughts" were the breath of life to Young Japan. Consequently when it was announced, first, that the Japanese consul at San Francisco had refused a visa for Mrs. Sanger's passport, then that she would not be permitted to enter

Japan on her arrival in the harbor, and subsequently that if allowed to enter she would not be granted permission to speak, Young Japan decided that Mrs. Sanger must be interesting, and discussed her and her theories exhaustively.

Mrs. Sanger had been invited by the *Kaizo* (*Reconstruction*) magazine to stop off in Japan on her way to China, and while she was in my country I had the honor of being her hostess. One of the first things my husband and I had to say to Mrs. Sanger, after she finally landed at Yokohama, was that so far as the birth control movement in Japan was concerned, far more had been accomplished by the agitation growing out of the police prohibitions than could ever have come through simple lectures on the subject. The news and editorial columns of both Japanese and foreign newspapers had been full of Mrs. Sanger ever since it was announced several weeks before that she would arrive. By no means, however, had all the comments been favorable. There had been a great deal of bitter criticism and much applause for the bold stand of the police authorities. But the main thing was to get birth control universally discussed and the advertising helped enormously to do so.

"Japan watches America very closely now, just as she does all nations, since she has attained national maturity. Perhaps, like almost any other youngster lately grown past the gawky stage and attending her first grown-up party, she isn't just sure which fork to use or what to do with the finger bowl. So she watches the other guests. It is easy to see what she would learn concerning birth control by observation of American manners. The head of the police bureau of the Home Office is said to have been in New York at the time Mrs. Sanger's meeting was raided in the Town Hall. In order to prevent any such disturbance in Japan he simply announced that she could not make any speeches." This was the *Tribune's* explanation of Mrs. Sanger's situation in Japan and I think there is a great deal of truth in it.

When I was allowed to board the *Taiyo Maru* and found her in her cabin, waiting and waiting for permission to land, I felt very ashamed and sorry that our government should be treating this distinguished foreign guest and valuable gospel-bringer so rudely. But finally the matter was so arranged that she could land and could speak at public or private meetings on condition that she would not talk on the subject of birth control. It was just like drawing a dragon without its fearful eyes, if Mrs. Sanger was to be allowed to speak without delivering her message. Nevertheless, she respected the condition laid down for her entry in her address at the public meeting called by the *Kaizo*. At every private meeting which she attended she was pressed to say something in regard to her great cause. How could she refuse?

My task it was to stand at the entrance door and watch for police spies while Mrs. Sanger was talking on birth control, banned as dangerous thought by the authorities. Also I watched to see whether her speeches were correctly interpreted as it is easy for a Japanese translator, however good the intentions, to make mistakes with a speech. As I attended every meeting while Mrs. Sanger was in Tokyo, I heard everything she had to say on the subject. Among many meetings she addressed, the most significant was the one presided over by Dr. Baron Shibazaburo Kitazato, prominent as a medical doctor as well as for being the greatest authority on bacteriology in Japan. No woman, foreign or native, had ever been so well received by Japanese men as was Mrs. Sanger. The modest, ladylike tone of her voice was something of a surprise to the Japanese, who had expected to see a huge aggressive-mannered person fussing blatantly with them about their habits.

The ten days which Mrs. Sanger had scheduled to spend in Tokyo passed quickly. We wasted the first three days with the officials, seeking permission for her to speak. After it was obtained, I took her to various luncheons and dinners, which were in reality intended to be private opportunities for speeches. This made Mrs. Sanger's schedule overcrowded at first. However, we worked out a program to utilize every minute of her precious time with important interviews, meetings and receptions. She wished to be taken to the licensed prostitute quarter, the Yoshiwara district, and to Asakusa, the unlicensed quarter. She wanted to see the Kanega-fuchi cotton spinning mill and the life of the factory girls in this biggest plant in Japan. We managed all these expeditions.

Mrs. Sanger not only had a great success in Tokyo, but she was also warmly received by the people of Kyoto and Osaka. The amount she accomplished in raising interest in the birth control subject in Japan was immense, both with respect to the Neo-Malthusian doctrine and with its implications for the labor movement. She appeared like a comet but she left such a vivid and long-enduring impression on the Japanese mind that there is no possible reckoning of the true value of her visit. The birth control idea had first been introduced to Japanese intellectuals in 1902 by Dr. Wamin Ukita, a professor in Waseda University, but in the excitement attending preparations for the war with Imperial Russia, Dr. Ukita had to suppress his enthusiasm in the matter. The public hatred toward him was so great that he was called a traitor. Later there appeared several advocates of birth control from the eugenic standpoint, but their voices were weak and they made few converts.

Then this Japanese magazine invited Mrs. Sanger to Japan. In 1920, Mr. Takayuki Namaye, a social worker who had visited the United States and had had an interview with her, published an article on her work for the first time in a Japanese magazine. There appeared a complete number of a magazine devoted to birth control. But the information and opinions even of prominent people betrayed very primitive notions of the matter. Some stated that birth control was just like running away, after eating, without paying for one's bill of fare; some stated that they believed in birth control as an ideal or theory but all we had to do in fact was to observe how a woman whose name was Margaret Sanger was languishing behind prison bars because she advocated the practice of it. Clearly a thing fine in theory was harmful when agitated.

Shortly after Mrs. Sanger's visit to Japan, however, a group of interested persons undertook to gather birth control facts and study the question more deeply. Professor Isso Abe of Waseda University headed this group. It included Mr. Bunji Suzuki, the outstanding labor leader; Dr. Tokijiro Kaji, a well-known medical doctor; a prominent socialist and Buddhist, Mr. Kikue Yamakawa; my husband and myself. Its research prospectus opened in effect as follows: "The noble spirit of humanism has served to check wasteful conflict between the nations and the progress of science has decreased the ravages of diseases by revealing their causes. Hence the tendency to an immense increase in the human birth rate is to be observed. Should this increasing birth rate continue, the shortage of the necessary materials for human existence would in time be appalling, even if the advancing knowledge of science promoted public welfare. Today, our population is growing by about 700,000 new Japanese every year (a recent average is 940,000). This will cause not only severe competition within the nation, but it will become the source of international entanglement. Its distressing aspect is apparent in individual lives. Uncontrolled pregnancy robs the mother of health and raises infant mortality (we had 170 infant deaths per thousand in 1917), overburdens the family economy and prevents a decent education of children. The consequences also are late marriage, increase in the number of illegitimate children, infanticide, abortion and other social immoralities and tragedies. It is absolutely necessary to avoid any pregnancy when either parent has a disease which should not be transmitted to the offspring. But the right practice of birth control principles should not be an act of immorality; it should be in harmony with social morality. This research society is thus established for the purpose of advocating the above stated principle" (July, 1922).

The birth control work of this society was first started in the educational field. At the same time it established a clinic for experimentation placed in the People's Hospital directed by Dr. Kaji, who took charge of the clinic and medical work. I was in charge of the social and business side of this undertaking. As for the educational work of the society, we translated and published Mrs. Sanger's pamphlet, "Family Limitation," and other pamphlets: "Observing the Birth Control Question from Different Angles," which I wrote; "The Problem of Japanese Population and Birth Control," by my husband; and "Birth Control and Biological Aspects" by Professor S. Matsumura of Hokkaido Imperial University. Then we published a periodical named *Small Family* and continued our activities, lecturing and contributing articles to other periodicals. On account of the lack of scientific experience, the clinic had but small significance, but the educational attempt of our society aroused a tempest everywhere, evident in the thousands of letters we received of encouragement or of threat.

In the Osaka and Kyoto districts, there was another birth control organization, led by Mr. Senji Yamamoto who was later elected a member of the lower house of the Diet as a representative of the proletarian party—only to be killed by the sword of the reactionary party. His organization was actively supported by many labor leaders in that district, its aim being to strengthen the labor struggles by checking excess labor at its source. Mr. Yamamoto was greatly interested in meeting Mrs. Sanger, as he stated, but his understanding of the birth control principles was not wholly that of Mrs. Sanger. As a Marxist he frankly opposed the Neo-Malthusian doctrine, and his attitude carried weight in New Japan at that time, since

Marx was a great master there. However, he himself did not explain fully the inconsistency between Malthusianism and Marxism.

My activity at the front line in our birth control propaganda was a cause of alarm to the people of my own class. It was taken as the fancy of a romantic person or of one not quite sound in her head. They called me "Madame Control" and drew caricatures of me in papers and magazines. It was not seldom that people hissed, pulled one another's sleeves secretly or smiled ironically at me when they met me on the street or at any other place. Some reactionary countrymen considered me a hateful woman who brought shame on her ancestral house. Instead of urging my sex to bear as many soldiers—noble patriots—as they possibly could, I was even belittling the military glory of the nation, so they said.

However, I had friends even within my own class, such as Countess Teruko Tsugaru, young widow of Count Tsugaru, former daimyo of the Tsugaru clan, Marchioness Sho, wife of the former king of Loochoo Island, Viscountess Tozawa, Mrs. Nitobe Jr., and Mrs. Aki Hatano of the editorial staff of the *Women's Review*. They not only understood and encouraged my work but even organized a group among their friends to study contemporary thought and problems as well as to enjoy art and literature. They might be viewed as ladies of leisure toying with plants in a hothouse, but they were really serious and eager to comprehend the problems of the day no less than to heighten their cultural charm. The meeting was held at the members' homes by turn and authorities were invited to lecture to them on such topics as "The History of the Japanese Labor Movement" and "The Problems of Japanese Factory Girls," which were discussed by Mr. K. Kato, a leader in the Japanese miners' union; "Survey of the Development of Social Thought," presented by Mr. T. Nosaka, who was active in social research work and later became a member of the Communist party; and an "Interpretation of Modern Literature," made by Mr. T. Arishima, a prominent author of socialistic inclinations. Mr. Arishima named our group "Raisho-kai" (Coming Light Society) after a phrase extracted from his favorite Chinese poem.

My days were full of duties—managing the yarn shop, teaching knitting classes, giving jobs to the women who finished our knitting courses, promoting birth control and keeping my membership in the Raisho-kai. One of the treasured experiences of those days followed an invitation from the miners' union at the Ashio copper mines to talk on the general subject of birth control. The Ashio copper mines are located twenty miles to the north beyond the Nikko mountain where stands the world-famous Nikko temple and the red lacquer bridge. The mines then belonged to Baron Furukawa, one of the greatest capitalists in Japan, and this place had become celebrated for its tragic struggles between the laborers and the owner. The miners were organized into a union, which indicated their comparatively high intellectual standard. I was thrilled with the thought of standing face to face with the miners and speaking to laborers from the platform. Besides it was to be my first speech with a public audience. I hesitated, however, to practice on a critical radical group until the labor leaders assured me that my presence was indispensable. They said that the miners were willing to buy tickets for this meeting at 20 sen (10 cents) each, to raise a fund for their union. So I could not resist any more. Mrs. Horace Coleman, the wife of an American missionary, voluntarily offered to accompany me, as she was herself genuinely sympathetic with the birth control movement. Mrs. Coleman and I took an early train to Nikko, where we transferred to a local train which climbed Ashio mountain at the rate of thirteen miles an hour, Mrs. Coleman cheering me during the journey with a cup of American cocoa and a lump of cheese, partly because I had a lump of lead somewhere in my throat at the thought of the obligation I had assumed.

It was twilight when we arrived at Ashio. To my surprise and embarrassment, this little country station was filled with men and women, each with a lantern in the hand. I heard them say: "Let's see the Lady of the Peerage." When I walked out on the platform, the crowd followed, drawing near, holding their lanterns close, and scrutinizing my face as if they wanted to ascertain whether a person with a title belonged to the same or to a different genus in the animal kingdom. The meeting had already been going on a long time before I arrived. The only building large enough to house an audience of two thousand miners and their wives, carrying babies on their backs and in both arms, was the local theater. To make the miners feel that they were getting the full value of the precious twenty sen which they had paid for their tickets, the length of the meeting was one consideration. Four hours at least it lasted, with an army of speakers appearing on the platform one after another. The chairman of the meeting asked me to talk for two hours so that the audience would be thoroughly grateful. I did my best to meet the requirement but my poor throat had not been trained for roaring to a crowd in the proletarian fashion. However, I managed to keep on speaking for at least one hour and a quarter. I, too, wished to be courteous.

I began my speech with a statement of the birth control movement and went on to discuss the ideal of a planned population for the betterment of the human race, voluntary motherhood in its relation to the elevation of women, the necessity for birth control as a means of abolishing injurious abortion, infanticide and everlasting poverty, the connection between birth control and labor problems; and I closed with the moral aspects of the question. My speech was interrupted several times by the magnesium flashlights of the country press, accompanied by the sound of explosions and frightful odors. But I survived everything.

The police inspectors in grand uniforms—there were three of them—who gravely sat on the platform behind me twice corrected me for using the word "infanticide," saying it sounded too harsh for this occasion. I knew their interference was one of the formalities in a proletarian meeting, and that it was natural for the inspectors to want their presence acknowledged. Occasionally cheers came from the miners and their wives, who approved what I said. The wives were as attentive as they could be amid the duties of feeding their babies and changing their diapers. For the first time in their lives they were hearing a speech about the slavery of excessive childbearing and its relation to industry. A mixture of deep curiosity and blank amazement shone in their eyes as I gazed down upon them.

The meeting ended with little of the uproar which usually accompanied a proletarian meeting, the greater part of the audience as a rule coming to enjoy a fight between speakers and policemen. The popular proletarian speakers were those who could outwit the policemen skillfully enough to hold the platform without breaking the regulations with respect to free speech and at the same time deliver "hot shots." It was a fine art. But policemen, trained in this game to valor on their side, seemed unprepared for a new competitor like me. I got off without a scuffle.

The following day the same sort of meeting was held in another mining district about five miles away, to which place the miners who had heard me the night before paraded with their union flags in their hands, singing the "song of revolution" as they marched. Mrs. Coleman and I were utterly astonished—she the wife of a Christian missionary; I the wife of a peer! Yet we joined in the parade, though it required a great deal of courage and idealism. This second meeting was likewise held in a village theater and was packed with miners and their women, curious but enthusiastic.

In my physical exhaustion on returning home, it was rejuvenating to hear immediately that the miners' union raised enough money at these meetings to carry on its work for a year ahead. Later, I received hundreds of letters from the mining people asking for more information about birth control. They were taking the matter very seriously.

XIX

Antagonism of My Own Class

"*T*HERE'S many a slip 'twixt the cup and the lip." My social service which fixed its center in the birth control movement with a sort of league for women's economic independence tied in, though supported enthusiastically for a while, came at last upon a stumbling block. The obstacle was encountered suddenly and in quite an unexpected direction.

In July, 1923, all the press in Japan reported a sad piece of news in an ultrasensational fashion with grotesque headlines. Its substance was the story of a double suicide committed by Mr. Takeo Arishima, a prominent author and idealist, and Mrs. Aki Hatano, wife of a businessman and a member of the editorial staff of the *Women's Review,* the most progressive and popular women's magazine in Japan; they both belonged to our birth control research group, the "Raisho-kai." Mr. Arishima had been regarded as a leading spirit in the Young Japan movement. Mrs. Hatano was one of the outstanding feminists and intellectuals. Liberalism thus received what the West would call "a black eye."

The affair affected me intimately. Mrs. Hatano had been one of my close friends as well as a member of the Raisho-kai. When we discussed the social position of Japanese women and problems of life in general, she was rather inclined to a fatalistic attitude while I was full of challenging verve. Nevertheless, Mrs. Hatano was a hard worker and maintained a high standard in her writing and editing. Her strict sense of responsibility to her magazine brought results in the fascination it had for a large circle of readers.

Mrs. Hatano personally was a rare beauty. That fact

heightened the sensation over the suicide reported in the papers. She had been one of the most sophisticated and lovely young women of present-day Japan. She was a modern "Osen" of the Harunobu prints, with her delicate figure, fine oval face and long glossy hair. Her modern interests had not destroyed her attractiveness in the slightest degree. They had only enhanced it. She and her husband had lived in a neat home on the outskirts of Tokyo facing Mount Fuji, in a purely Japanese way representing the old "Yedo" style, the most urbane of the Tokugawa era. Mrs. Hatano had studied Western as well as Japanese literature; she had an intellectual grasp on modern liberal thought, but emotionally she was still a woman of the Tokugawa age. Her husband was good to her, but he lacked sympathy with her liberalism. His love for his wife was the love for a little bird in a cage. He wanted to pet her within the safe shelter of his home. Mrs. Hatano was thus an Ibsen "Nora" in Japan. When she awakened intellectually, she could no longer stay in her pretty cage. She sought intellectual and personal freedom. Like many men in the history of social evolution, Mr. Hatano tried to clip his wife's wings and keep her by his side alone. Mrs. Hatano told some of us about her domestic struggle and her story stirred our hearts.

The Nora of Japan struggled the more after she had had a bite of the sweet apple—the great author's great passion for her! The outcome was her decision that she and her lover had best die in a moment of ecstasy, for thus they could attain the immortality of spirit. So they faced death happily. By prearrangement, they went to Karuizawa where they brought life to a close by hanging themselves in Arishima's villa. Their corpses were discovered a month later. Among many letters they left at the place, one by Mrs. Hatano addressed to me explained the motive of her suicide. I was able to meet in some measure the fierce criticism of that portion of the public who tried to lay the blame for this tragedy upon me.

Mr. Takeo Arishima was a Tolstoy in Japan. He had been in the United States and was a great admirer of Whitman, whom he had translated into Japanese. His many novels and essays on social themes were popular and influential with the progressive younger generation. He inherited a large fortune in the form of estates in Hokkaido, but the Tolstoyan influence had induced him to hand over his farms to the peasants who actually tilled the soil. He gave them complete possession. There were no reservations even as to management. His sincere humanism made him denounce the system of private ownership and the inheritance of large fortunes as parasitic with respect to the owners and exploitive with respect to laborers. Though he escaped from his inconsistent position of a great landlord, he could not throw himself into the radical communist movement. Nonresistance was his creed. After his wife's death, he led a kind of hermit life for some time with his three sons. Therefore his romantic suicide was a tremendous shock to the nation.

Since this love affair between the great author and the great feminist extended beyond the limit of the social code, they anticipated that social criticism would be too severe to bear. Conservative people said: "Behold, as our great Confucius preached, there is no way to teach women and fools. Men must be careful about women, for there is always a woman at the back of a sin." Several disciples of Arishima joined in this attack, declaring Mrs. Hatano to be a hateful vamp who had lured their beloved master to destruction. It was all because of this sinful creature that their revered humanist was dead and his three sons orphaned! There was much natural expression of grief among his followers for their lost leader, but the strange thing to me was that both conservatives and progressives utterly blamed the woman and acquitted the man. The Arishima funeral was well-attended and impressive. Mrs. Hatano was buried without a single attendant other than her faithful maid who carried her ashes in a plain wooden box to the grave. "It was the punishment for her sin!" the public said.

The attitude of the public perplexed me. I could see no reason why the woman was charged with guilt and the man absolved from guilt. They had committed suicide under the same sense of responsibility and mutual agreement. If Mrs. Hatano was to be criticized, why not Mr. Arishima too? Why was man exempt from blame, and woman alone made to bear the cross? What were the liberal ideas worth in practice that these so-called progressive men bandied about? Was liberalism to be applied to men only?

With the condemnation of Mrs. Hatano went bitter censure for the entire female sex heaped upon it through attacks on her female friends. In a land still under the spell of the feudal family system, Confucianism and Buddhism, all of which conspire to belittle women, there was little chance for the criticized women to defend themselves.

The point of the argument used against me in the press was that I should have checked this extreme conduct of the lovers while there was yet time to prevent the climax. The fact that I did not do so proved that I was an accomplice in the guilt of drawing the great author to destruction; that I was a loathsome rebel against the social order. Frivolous journalism selected me for its special target since the dead woman, being speechless, was no longer interesting. I never had heard such unreasonable arguments with respect to any theme. It was true that Mrs. Hatano had often come to see me. She had told me about her struggles, but I always advised her to cut clean through her difficult situation. I never did encourage her to die. I thought she was merely romancing when she declared that she admired enormously the great actress, Sumako Matsui, who had hanged herself with a scarlet silk sash—symbol of passionate love—to join her deceased lover in spirit.

Days and months passed after her own suicide. Innumerable articles appeared in the papers and magazines criticizing women cynically or sensationally. Personally I could not whip the dead people; nor did I try to offer an explanation of their act or to refute the unkind words which hit wide of the mark. I held aloof from the discussion, leaving it for time to answer untrue charges. However, I did not escape personal injury through the suicide of my friend.

On my return from travels in the Western countries, I had broken the shackles of mean conventions little by little, had taken steps along the road to emancipation for myself and pointed the way for others. I began to conduct myself as a person and not as exploited family property. I disregarded the social prejudices against independent action for a woman. I regarded the birth control movement as the polestar guiding women from slavery and unceasing poverty to personality and culture. The more I experimented with liberty, however, the more I stimulated the jealousy of the women of my class, who, though their eager fingers were moving toward the trident, lacked courage to reach for it, to break the fetters which tied them down to the bondage of the rigid family system. Always on this hard march of mankind and womankind toward the future, the path of one who attempts to open the road wider for others must apparently be beset with prejudices and opposition from the very people in whose behalf obstructive brambles and weeds are being cut away.

So the incident of the illustrious love suicide gave the society ladies of all Japan a good chance to shoot arrows at me. The more superficial of them began at once to turn their backs toward me, and their hostility hindered my social activities. It finally forced me to retreat to the family circle myself. I was suddenly compelled to realize again the power of the feudal element in Japan still holding down the bourgeois class. I also recognized how utterly unfair even bourgeois journalism was toward women and how fickle and cowardly was the world in general which always went over to the side of the strong. I awakened to the fact that it is harder to get a person to defend the weak than to find a star on a black night. I stood alone in the midst of social protests and fury. To my great annoyance, amounting at times to despair of making headway, even the birth control movement, in which I had been so active, was called a plaything of a bourgeois woman, as if I were advocating the spacing of children for my own fitful pleasure. I felt completely deserted socially. It was hard to put faith in anybody anywhere.

I had to stop a minute and look over the world around me again from a colder and wiser perspective. Having fancied myself a strong character, after being tossed about by the rough dealings of my fellows I discovered myself to be just a poor sailor who could only row a boat in a bay of calm water. I tried to quiet myself by thinking philosophically, and watching for blue sky above the angry waves. But the stormy sea seemed to put my happy starting at naught. I had been frank, trustful and openhearted. Now I became skeptical and suspicious of everything.

However, the storms could not beat me down forever. My little bark was launched upon its humanistic course again. The fire in my heart blazed up with still more courage and a stronger will-power. I resolved that if the lack of understanding of the birth control principle caused the unreasonable attacks upon me, I would show up their weaknesses and battle more courageously for the movement. Fully aware that the poisonous arrows were shot from the fortress where feudalism had its lair and that the tactic was designed to isolate the crusader of feminism from her followers, in time I was spurred again to action in their behalf.

But I re-entered the fray outwardly calm and before long the journalistic attacks, which had been floating around like rootless seaweed, disappeared from the surface of the press. Forces invisible to the public tried to draw me back behind the high walls of feudal family traditions in a continuous pulling. Still I stood with my back against these walls as courageously as I could, carrying on my birth control movement, my business adventure, and my knitting class culminating in jobs for other women, amid the sneers and jeers of my countrymen. It had been my firm belief that I could satisfactorily take care of my position within the family as wife and mother, and at the same time take an energetic part in public work. However, I got no cooperation from the family system. It was as if I had come to a crossroad where I must decide whether I should take the path leading to individualism and be faithful primarily to myself or retrace my steps in womanly submission like the multitudes of my sex, for the sake of peace. But how could I in reality look upon my undertakings in the line of public work as lightly as I might put the match to a firecracker? I struggled to be faithful to my personal conviction and redoubled my social activities as I tried to establish a warmer relationship with my family.

It seemed that life must run more smoothly. But it did not so run. The pressure from my own dear people toward conformity on my part weighed more and more heavily upon me. My immediate family and my relatives looked upon me as a "black sheep." I could not hope for sympathy from friends whose eternal moral code was feminine sacrifice. Men regarded me as a dreadful shrew. My very husband, who had formed my personality by his insistence on my becoming an independent woman and who had encouraged me to shake off feudalistic bondage, took a neutral attitude toward my actual struggles. I could not quite comprehend what made him reverse his attitude. My love for him had never changed, but I could get no word of consolation from him. The only comfort which came to my wounded heart and body was my children's affection and health. I seemed to hear them always whispering in my ears: "Mother should be strong! Mother should not lead a slave existence."

XX

The Earthquake

HUMANKIND is gifted with a happy nature which enables it to minimize past evils even of the most tragic kind. The records of Japanese history warn us that Tokyo is to be visited by a great earthquake every hundred years. And in my home, there was a large tablet dedicated to the spirit of my husband's grandfather on which was written in beautiful calligraphy the fact that he died in the earthquake of Yedo in the second year of Ansei (1855). His son, the late Baron Shinroku Ishimoto, was saved at the time by being squeezed out from between the pillars of the house which collapsed at the first shock.

Nevertheless, neither memories of family events nor warnings of the impending destruction disturbed the complacency of the Japanese in the summer of 1923. People were just as happy and gay as ever. The city of Tokyo was a scene of hurrying and bustling as usual. With bright plans for tomorrow, the citizens looked into the future cheerfully. Our modern science had not yet advanced far enough to forecast the course of subterranean phenomena and broadcast it by radio, so the great earthquake of my time came unexpectedly at two minutes before twelve in the forenoon of September 1, 1923. When the first tremor was felt, we repeated the popular myth, jestingly, about the huge catfish, which lives underground, wiggling mightily. We were not afraid.

At that time we were living at Kamakura where we had built for the children's health a house in the compound noted for its big bronze statue of Daibutsu (Buddha). The day of

244

the earthquake I had come to my office in Tokyo in the morning as usual. I was sitting at my desk on the third floor of the Mutual Insurance Building in Kyobashi looking at my business letters when the tremor started. The building was eight stories high—a modern concrete structure. With horrible rumbling noises, the earthquake shook this building up and down and to and fro. The bookshelves and the glass cabinets in which the sample yarns were shown all turned over. I got up from my seat, but could not walk even a step. I felt a strange giddiness. Was the earth revolving? No, it was tumbling, tossing and whirling. When the first shock stopped, all who were in the room took deep breaths and looked at one another smilingly. Nobody screamed. No one could so much as utter a sound. Suddenly again and again the earth upheaved. The sun was covered with yellowish smoky clouds.

I managed to tumble across the corridor into my husband's office. "Help me to send a wire to the children!" were the words that I instinctively spoke to him. We did not realize that there would follow several hundred more shakes succeeded by terrible conflagrations which were to sweep over two-thirds of Tokyo, taking ninety thousand lives and causing seventy thousand persons to be injured or lost. I touched the telephone but found it was useless; the post and telegraph office had already been crushed. The trembling and shaking of the ground under our feet continued and I saw from the office window that many warehouses with their plaster walls were now only a heap of debris. Gray clay tiles, which had covered practically all the Japanese houses at that time, had fallen to the ground and the clouds of dust created by crumbling walls and breaking tiles mingled with the disturbed dry earth presented a ghastly sight wherever one looked. In the meantime fires had started here and there and I had no courage to remain in the office building any longer. I dismissed all the employees, closed the door and went out into the street, then full of people grown frantic. They could not scurry home for all the streetcars stood deserted on the track. The electric system had broken down.

Fortunately we had our own car, into which my husband and I jumped and drove as best we could to my parents' home. My father's castlelike house constructed on a concrete foundation stood apparently intact, but when I opened the front door I saw the porcelain and pottery vases, bronze statues of elephants, lacquer boxes and pictures—truly every bit of ornament hung on the walls or placed on the mantelpiece—on the floor, smashed into bits. The big chandeliers swung wide and almost touched the ceiling every time a tremor came. There was not a sign of a human being in the house and a strange fear seized me of some terrible calamity befalling the family.

In fact, however, my family were all miraculously saved. The big concrete chimney of their house, at the first shake, had plunged in heavy chunks through the roof to the basement, crashing through the dining room floor on its way. My parents and younger sister had just been summoned to lunch and were about to go down the stairs. Immediately the main earthquake came, and as father and sister instinctively stepped out to the balcony in their alarm, the crashing chimney carried them away in its deadly embrace. Mother was spared only because she remembered the youngest son on the third floor in time to retreat from her rush to the balcony. Luckily father and sister were more frightened than hurt when they were shot to the basement with the monstrous masses of the chimney, augmented by a large section of the dining room floor. They were not caught under the weight. They were just a part of the debris, bruised as to shoulders, arms and hips, and horribly messy. When I reached home they lay on mats in the back garden in their bloodstained white summer kimonos. Nobody dared to enter what remained of the house because of the continued quakes. If, in memory, a certain comedy is suggested by this picture, jesting is sobered by the memory of many Japanese who were killed in their Western-style houses in just that way.

To discover that my parents were safe, if bruised and shocked, was a great relief to me. But there were my children farther away. What of them at Kamakura? My husband, knowing the hazards of a drive in the car over the quivering streets amid the falling buildings, advised me to stay with my parents and help them while he made a dash for Kamakura. And as soon as he left I thought it best to follow his advice and see about food. Accompanied by my brothers and servants, armed with large furoshiki I bought rice, flour, canned goods of every kind, bean paste, sugar, salt, fruits, bread and such other commodities as we could obtain by entreaty when payment ceased to be sufficient for a sale. Seeing a good-sized ham suspended from the ceiling of the butcher's shop, I asked for that, holding out the proper price. But the butcher refused to sell the ham to me. I begged him again and again for it, reminding him that my father's house had been his customer for more than twenty years. At least, I urged, he could cut me off a portion. After some minutes of insistence on my part, the butcher, looking at my face and at the large ham alternately, said: "Madame, for a special reason I cannot sell that piece!" He smiled at me. Then I guessed his secret and had to go away laughing. It was only a handsome painted object stuffed with cotton and hung in the shop for show—a deceit not to be noticed in ordinary times.

While I was scouting around for food for my parents and their household, my husband was trying to reach our children.

He could drive his car as far as the outskirts of the city. From there, as the roads were covered with crushed houses, he had to clamber over the ruins on foot. The earth was cracked everywhere and there was practically no trace of a road. What is more, to avoid the conflagration in the low-lying Yokohama district, he had to climb up and down hills. The distance between Tokyo and Kamakura was about forty miles on the old open road, but he reached our own home only after going in the most indirect fashion and after twelve hours of walking and walking through the night. In the morning he found Kamakura in ruins—a heap of ashes and rubbish. The earthquake in Kamakura district had been followed by a tidal wave which completely cleared the shore of boats and houses, together with thousands of precious human lives. Our dwelling was one of the very few which did not completely collapse and it escaped fire too. So the children were also safe. They did not even utter a cry in the terrible disaster, we were told, for they were too small to imagine the general horror of this calamity. My maids all stayed faithfully at their post. They did not run to their own home, but guarded our children, spending the night, so fearful for them, in the garden beside the big image of Buddha until the master arrived.

My husband tried to relieve my anxiety by letting me know that the children were all right but there was no way to transmit the cheering news.

Our private family fared better than the royal family. One prince and two princesses of the blood passed away, their promising young lives cut off in the first crash of the disaster. The sad news was announced a few days later on a page of newspaper printed by a hand machine—the first printed item of public information to circulate after the destruction of all communication and traffic.

Three days were spent in an atmosphere like Dante's "Inferno." To experience an actual hell on earth before one is sentenced by the King of Hell, according to Buddhist myth, is a treat reserved for the Japanese who live on top of a volcano! Westerners have spoken of our smiling faces in hours of tragedy but we are not strangers to fear. Continually terrified by rumors of what was happening and developing in the downtown district, my father's household, including myself, huddled together the first night in the dark garden.

My two sons, Arata and Tamio, in their kindergarten days

A tennis match at my father's farm

The ruins of my father's home after the earthquake in 1923

We were told that the whole district downtown was aflame and that men, women, children, houses, bicycles, horses and automobiles were all caught in the blaze, there being no means of escape from the holocaust. We climbed a nearby hill and saw with our own eyes a fire start from a chemical school about a mile distant from our house, but there was no wind to bend it in our direction. There was terrible heat. Immediately the water service was cut off entirely, and the electric and gas services were ruined too. So we realized that we might be caught in a fire ourselves, at any moment coming from any direction. In that case we should have for our protection neither water nor police. Firemen were helpless throughout the city. Fire was King, as the Americans would say. Red flames began to burst everywhere we looked from beneath the debris of crushed wooden pillars and beams. Rapidly they increased in number and vigor. Between earth tremors we found courage to rescue essentials for living and family treasures which we hid as well as we could in a hole we dug in the ground. It was fortunate that we had a well in our garden, and fresh water in our thirst.

On the second day, the huge fires, which had been extending westward, turned toward the east and toward us. One of them reached the school building at the other side of our hill. As I watched the building burn, the heat scorched my cheeks. The fire drew nearer and we decided to carry more of the family treasures to safer spots as our godown had been shattered.

Unable to do anything for my children, I wondered whether I could do anything about the fine old paintings which belonged to my husband—handed down to him by his father. These had been placed in storage in a bank in Kyobashi, when we had given up our big house in Koishikawa. It may be that the thought of material losses at a time when hundreds of thousands of human lives are being injured or destroyed is unworthy of man or woman. Certainly I was grateful for the safety of my relatives. Yet I worried over the possible loss of works of art which could never be replaced. And on the second day of the earthquake I learned that the bank was completely gone. My grief rested on something more than personal deprivation. Such art! The effect of this grief was to make me resolve to save at least the collection of old paintings, picture scrolls and screens which my husband had collected himself and stored in my father's godown. The picture scrolls were rolled up in their narrow long wooden boxes, and some of the boxes were quite heavy, but I carefully and tenderly carried hundreds of them, one by one to a place which I thought would be secure from fire.

The horrible second evening passed and the third morning came. The fire had almost lapped our garden wall when it veered in the opposite direction, to our unexpected relief. Only then, worn out with the hard labor of moving furniture and other objects round about, did we all take some rest. But first we had to appease our hunger a little bit at least.

The end of our woe was not yet on the calendar. On the evening of the third day the fire consumed all the small houses which surrounded ours. Foreseeing our doom, we carried chairs and other prime comforts to the street running near the outer moat of the Imperial Palace—to the fire barrier. Sadly we bade farewell to the dwelling enjoyed for so many years. As we sat down on our chairs by the moat, my mother and I looked back—to see, as we thought, our house turn into flames! Mother uttered no word. She gave forth no cry. She was the daughter of a samurai. But I was less repressed. "Ah! everything is gone, our house, our treasures, all our material possessions!" I exclaimed. In that instant I knew the futility of large material possessions. A whole city, amazingly beautiful, built by hundreds of years of toil, representing incalculable wealth, was destroyed by a single act of nature!

Having nothing to do, our group sat on the street packed with people who, like us, had come away from fallen houses or from the fire which had consumed them. A few pieces of the small Japanese furniture and apparel wrapped in handkerchiefs and carried on their backs were now their total property. But our eyes were busy, if our hands were idle, as we watched the swarm of men, women, big children and crying babies passing to and fro or squatting beside us exhausted, some even sobbing on account of weariness and defeat, one occasionally screaming out in pain. There were those who had left behind, in the crushed house, their dear relatives, having been unable to rescue them from the weight of the fallen roof or the fast-pursuing fire. Some had already walked and walked for three days without a cup of water to drink or a grain of rice to eat. They had still to walk on and on—to what destination they did not know. I gave away the biscuits and the water I had brought with me.

Quickly I learned a new lesson—the antisocial effects of the rivalry for material possessions and the brotherly love inherent in economic equality. Here we were—we Japanese—from every class and every income stratum, looking backward. Once competitors and enemies, now on a common level of no possessions, we were friends and co-operators in a trice. My entire family spent that night on the sidewalk of the dusty street sinking to the ground for a little sleep among the piled-up furniture. Amid the noise of destruction and the cries of the refugees who streamed by me endlessly, exhausted in mind and body, I took my meed of sleep.

My father must have been born under a very lucky star. Swept by a crashing chimney into its heap of ruins, he got up only somewhat bruised. His house, which the flames had apparently chosen for their prey on the third day of the conflagration, loomed up sound and imposing as ever on the fourth day. It is true that the small teahouse in the corner of the garden, had perished like all the green trees, but fire could not penetrate the dwelling's walls coated with cement, or its windows of thick glass which we had closed tightly before we left. The records of the earthquake mark my father's home as the spot where the fire stopped of its own accord. We could not see that clearly as we sat beside the moat. Eventually we came back home carrying our furniture and treasures, dragging our exhausted bodies, our souls sick from witnessing so much suffering.

As the terror of immediate fire lightened, my anxiety about my children led me to dispatch messengers to Kamakura. One tried to make the trip by bicycle. But each time the man could go only halfway and had to turn back on account of the cracks in the earth and the debris—once cities and villages—on his way. On the seventh day I heard that transportation by boat to the Yokosuka naval harbor had been opened and so the next day I got a man to take me to this boat. I hoped to reach Kamakura in this manner. Since police protection had vanished and in the abnormal physical and mental conditions murders were becoming common, it was by no means safe for every woman to move about at will. Hence I dressed myself as a peasant, hoping to be ignored. I covered my head and face with a white and blue cotton cloth, tenugui, put on a plain cotton kimono, tied up my sleeves and turned up my kimono skirt, making a dirty petticoat and bare feet the high points of the disguise. Thus appareled, I walked across the ruins of the city to Shibaura harbor where the boat was anchored.

There were no trains, no stations, not even a recognizable harbor. Government buildings had been wiped out, schoolhouses crushed and burned, penal and charitable institutions laid in ruins. As I looked over the confusion of twisted telegraph poles, wires, skeletons of high buildings, burnt corpses and swollen ones floating on the water, frenzied parents seeking their lost children, and deserted children crying for their parents, I thought about the last days of Pompeii of which I had often heard from Uncle Yusuke in my childhood while fancying then that the like could happen only in stories.

At the Shibaura harbor, I pressed into the crowd of refugees and sailed for Yokosuka. The blue summer sky high above us seemed as serene as if nothing of horror had happened on the earth. While I sat with the crowd on the deck of the cargo boat without shade from the burning sun, I listened to what the others were saying. One tragic tale after another ran around the crowd.

I landed at the equally wrecked Yokosuka naval harbor, and from there walked back ten miles to Kamakura. As I passed through the ruins of this town, I saw everywhere, on the fallen and deserted houses, pieces of wood and bunches of burning incense sticks marking the spots where corpses were lying beneath the debris. As I hurried across the garden by the Daibutsu Temple, I caught a glimpse of my two children playing, unconscious of tragedy, on the lawn. Chairs, tables and dishes were in evidence, for the house, though not in ruins, was turned halfway around and these had been carried outside. My sons ran up to me and I embraced them without a word. But tears of gratitude to God, who had protected them from the deadly calamity, flowed uncontrolled. Arata told me that he had been fed with macaroni every day since the quake, and that he wanted to eat something else. Tamio, the little one, utterly unaware of the menace to himself in the earthquake, told me how amused he was when he saw the opposite house and the tall pagoda in the temple garden tumble down. The food distribution had been unorganized in this district and the first thing I had to do was to get some potatoes and fruit from the vicinity for the children who had eaten nothing but canned stuff for a week. Extra bedcovers and blankets which I had in my house I gave to neighbors who had lost their all in the fire.

As soon as the railroad was put in order, we closed this half-burned house and came back to Tokyo by a freight train in the manner of horses and cows. It was better than walking. Since everything was so chaotic as to plans, I decided to take my children temporarily at least to my parents' house in Tokyo. We had to think about our own reconstruction while the government pondered on city reconstruction. How to start again from the bottom and in the ashes? I had lost not only family treasures, but the commodities at my shop. However, when one has to make a clean start one ceases to think in terms of better and worse. As soon as the temporary repair of the damaged office building was finished, I opened my yarn shop again.

It cannot be denied that there were thousands of irreparable tragedies caused by the earthquake of 1923. Among the three and a half million victims, countless human beings failed to recover from the wreck of matter and the crushing of their world. Yet in the upheaval the Japanese woman made one astonishing discovery. She found herself! Without waiting now for men to take the lead in social organization, women proceeded in remarkable numbers to take care of those in need. They began with the distribution of milk. When this form of municipal relief was taken up by the city fathers, women turned to distributing food and clothing. And while they were permitted full play for their talents in relief work, a really comprehensive woman's movement came into being for the first time. The women of Tokyo learned to co-operate instinctively on a large scale, it appeared. Within a few days after the calamity, they had formed a federation of women's societies to meet the larger demands that would be made upon them after the immediate emergency had been met. The earthquake occurred on the first of September. This organization grew so rapidly that by the end of November at least forty-two groups of women had affiliated with it. Social, educational, industrial, political and labor sections, formed within the federation, were setting about the most varied kinds of work.

PART EIGHT

SEEING THE WEST AGAIN

XXI

America at the Zenith of Her Capitalistic Glory

DESPITE the backwardness of his country, my husband's baptism in the liberal thought of the West, coupled with his foreign experiences, held him loyally for a while to humanistic ideals. His free position after he left the Mitsui Company, his wealth, and his generosity to others, however, tended to divert him gradually from humanistic action. Petty men with selfish designs used his friendship to promote their personal schemes. Little by little the brightness of his nature and his intellectual sensitiveness were smothered under a poisonous crust steadily thickening and hardening with the flattery bestowed upon him until his interest in general social advancement weakened and he became more aware of the obstacles to reform.

With the darkening of his social idealism, the traditions in which he had been reared renewed their rivalry. It was easy to fall back into ways of ease. The career of hardship which he had elected came to seem foolish to him, as the pressure for his return to ancient loyalties intensified. Because the lotus flower blooms in muddy water, he fancied that he could mingle in a moral quagmire and retain the purity of his character. Retracing his steps at this mid-point of his life, his sympathy with his wife's ideals faded and he began to demand her return to the old shell of feudalistic subjection from which he had pulled her with his own hands.

It was he who had encouraged me to launch on an independent career, and be brave and daring. He rang the bell and woke me from my peaceful dream of parasitism. I would not have thought of attending the business school in New York to get a professional training if my wedded guide had not constantly preached to me the virtues of self-support. I would have had no urge to be a businesswoman without his prodding. Nor without his help would I have had courage to participate in the birth control movement. Now, the steersman of my boat was trying to reverse its charted course while the oarsman wanted to pull straight ahead. Naturally a melancholy mood took possession of me. Being a Japanese wife in a period of economic and political transition, I faced two roads leading far apart: one to women's economic and personal independence; the other to renewed feudal subjection. The more I tried to unite them, the wider they seemed to branch.

The damage which the earthquake had done was found to be even more decisive than we had calculated at first. Our shop commodities, family treasures and other forms of wealth were destroyed, while our debts remained untouched. However, I did not, and could not, break down at this calamity. I started my business again and expected that my husband would be pleased with my undefeated soul and strength. But this met with a totally unexpected attitude from him. Instead of giving me warm encouragement, he even began to meddle in the trifles of my business enterprise to its disadvantage.

I had to realize that no individual life is to be segregated from community life; that no woman can expect special treatment as a favored person while her sisters move in an atmosphere of submission and dependence. Perhaps it was natural that my husband should change in his mood and begin to treat me as other men treated their wives. As I observed his mind alter, I had to consider the future seriously. Mental struggles, social work and the strain of the earthquake badly affected my health. I could not solve my problems by myself, though I tried to put them in the form of clear questions. "Have I selected independence merely to war against my beloved husband? Why does my personal growth separate me from my husband, instead of fulfilling my primary purpose to co-operate with him for the advancement of his own work?" I still felt great responsibility toward my husband who obviously had likewise lost his peace of mind, although its immediate cause was the too complex nature of human society which, with its hard and ugly facts and complicated troubles, had shattered much of his youthful optimism.

So I closed my Minerva Yarn Shop, which had been a notable success, willing to make the sacrifice if I could win home life in the process by restoring our mutual happiness. I also felt the need of rest. In the circumstances we agreed to make another trip to America, for which country we both felt especial affection.

The charm of the United States had been enhanced in our minds by her kindness to Japan at the time of the earthquake. Men and materials had come to us from America as first aid in the relief work. The citizens of Tokyo and Yokohama cheered with gratitude when they saw the big khaki-colored motor trucks distinguished by the mark U.S.A. distribute flour for bread, cans of food, blankets, shoes and clothes—even though some of the garments were twice or even three times too big for the small Japanese—and medical provisions. The American ambassador, Mr. Cyrus E. Woods, was the center of admiration for the sufferers of the ruined cities. The hearty sympathy of the American citizens across the ocean, beautifully named the Pacific, made a deep impression on the Japanese and moved my husband and me to revisit America instead of choosing some new objective for our trip of recreation. Taking my younger sister, Kiyo Hirota, we left Tokyo when the signs of reconstruction could be detected by the smell of fresh timbers lying where the old had met destruction. Yokohama was still in a wrecked condition and the piers were half sunk in the water as we sailed away on the U.S.S. *President Grant,* May 13, 1924.

The United States in 1924 was at the zenith of her capitalistic glory. Her industry seemed to be expanding to limitless proportions. The great Empire of America was reaching to the highest stage in the history of mankind from the standpoint of material power. The financial axis of the world had shifted from London to New York.

But it was not this phase of America which lured us there. New York had for me the charm of a second home. One may feel intense affection for a place where one has met conflict and yet won victories. Light footmarks on a smooth path may have a feebler appeal. So on reaching New York I went over the old ground of my New World challenges and, in doing so, took fresh stock of myself. This time, however, we lodged at the Plaza instead of in a rooming house.

This was a different perspective on New York but I had not forgotten my sympathetic landlady, Mrs. Nelson. She had died since my first visit, to my deep regret. The school where I had taken a business course had not changed during the five years and I was happy to renew friendships there. It was a joy to see again Mrs. Sanger who had been my inspiration and guide as a promoter of the birth control movement in the Far East. Dr. and Mrs. Charles A. Beard, who had been in Tokyo before the earthquake and who returned on the first steamer to reach Yokohama after the disaster, were likewise my friends. Dr. Beard had been municipal adviser to the mayor of Tokyo, Baron Shimpei Goto (later Count Goto), and when the mayor became Home Minister charged with the reconstruction of Tokyo, he again sought advice from Dr. Beard.

My whole time did not have to be given to schoolwork during this second New York visit. I had leisure for seeing old friends. I made many new ones. It was a great treat to be taken to the home of Mr. and Mrs. Howard Mansfield, whose collection of Japanese kakemono is of high value. Mr. Mansfield's understanding of Japanese art was, I thought, a more powerful factor in the promotion of goodwill between our two nations than all the diplomatic speeches of empty formality lumped together. When a people who have reached a high peak of aesthetic taste and a people who have attained heights of industrial efficiency can associate sympathetically, a basis seems laid for amity, with potentials for a fine superstructure of international culture. We Japanese are very proud of our art. It pleases us to our marrow to meet Westerners who are sensitive to the sources of our pride. No doubt, too, the West likes reciprocity in this respect.

I was also entertained by Mr. and Mrs. Frank A. Vanderlip, in their home at Scarborough-on-Hudson which includes among its numerous rooms one suggestive of things Japanese. Guests to whom I was introduced there had a fellow feeling for our art. Mrs. Vanderlip was then undertaking the heavy task of raising the reconstruction fund for Tsuda College, a girls' school in Tokyo for the study of English especially, founded under Christian auspices. Its buildings had been destroyed in the earthquake and the students were trying to go on with their work in barracklike quarters set aside for the emergency. The present Tsuda College, some miles outside the city of Tokyo in a beautiful spot among the pines, is a tribute to the energy of Mrs. Vanderlip and her American finance committee. All the Japanese regard this institution, in such handsome surroundings, as a splendid demonstration of international goodwill. Mrs. Vanderlip also presented the federation of women's societies with a fine working library of feminist literature.

I now had an opportunity to talk with many American feminists, notably Mrs. Carrie Chapman Catt, who kindly gave a luncheon for me, and Mrs. Harriot Stanton Blatch. In association with them I came to understand better the amount of persistence and sacrifice that the women's movements demand. I had not realized before how hard the English women had battled for enfranchisement. Or the American women's long battle either. I never tired of listening to the stories of how they contended for the vote; how they made speeches from soap boxes; how they paraded all in white! I wanted to know all this history for I felt it would have to be repeated in Japan. Mrs. Catt sent me a copy of her book, *Woman Suffrage and Politics,* with these encouraging words written on the flyleaf: "To Baroness Ishimoto who, I predict, will lead the women of Japan to their emancipation from outworn traditions." The sympathy of these American leaders strengthened my resolves. I thrilled at the idea of mutual respect and understanding overriding the barriers of distance and race.

On this trip we explored more of the American continent than on our previous sojourn in the United States. I traveled with my husband and sister to many American cities. I stayed with friends in New England and went south to New Orleans, along the beautiful Mississippi. Everywhere the active, happy and healthy American women fascinated me. They never seemed afraid of anything. What they wanted to do, they apparently tried to do and succeeded in doing. They worked seriously but they enjoyed themselves heartily. What a contrast they presented to Japanese women, indifferent to personality or rights or the power of will, bound by the chains of tradition and conventions—two extremes divided by the Pacific! One typified joy and freedom; the other, wasteful martyrdom.

Another great difference between West and East which gripped my mind was the divergence in the living conditions of the two worlds. American civilization was revelatory of material and mechanical progress in home surroundings; Japan sank down, by this comparison, into the shades of domestic poverty. I got the impression that, come what might in the way of political repression, American women would never be reduced to servitude.

Even my short stay in the United States restored my health and cleared away the gloom that had settled upon my spirit. The youthful democratic country worked like magic on the subject of an ancient state. I felt fresh energy springing up within me. I was ready once more for the battle at home.

XXII

Europe in Transition

*J*APANESE who go to Europe before seeing America, almost without exception become pro-European; those who visit America first become pro-American in their sentiments. Men who think of "My Great Britain" like to don derby hats and wear white spats over their Oxford shoes. Those who put the "Yankees first" emphasize neckties and indulge in American slang. In some such fashion Westerners divide into "pro-Chinese" and "pro-Japanese." My husband and I tried to imagine ourselves seeing America and Europe at the same time in order to be objective and impartial. At least we went on again to England and Europe from America. I was anxious to see my niece who had been born in London—a darling little creature, so dark of skin, with thick black hair and big dark eyes, that she looked like a little bear on the lap of her fair-skinned and blond-haired English nurse.

England was now on the eve of labor ascendancy. Bourgeois liberalism seemed to have regained its sway on the Continent. Social unrest in Italy was being subdued under Fascist power. Anti-Soviet propaganda in France was sweeping the Communists aside; while all dissension was by no means allayed, outward signs indicated a social truce, if involuntary.

We were invited to lunch by Professor Keynes of King's College and asked him many questions pertaining to the economic situation of the world. We also visited Mr. Harold Cox, the former editor of the *Edinburgh Review,* who explained to us the leading national traits of the British people and em-

At the Minerva Yarn Shop in Kyobashi, Tokyo

Working with yarn at my home

Myself in New York in 1924

phasized their superiority in the matter of self-government, pointing out many historical facts and customs by way of illustration.

I talked with Dr. Drysdale, president of the Malthusian League, and Mrs. Drysdale, about whom I had heard so much through Margaret Sanger. I was particularly anxious to know what Dr. Drysdale thought about the Neo-Malthusian theory in relation to women's economic and political emancipation. He was very hospitable and kind. He was patient when I questioned him but he appeared to be concerned only with the protection of motherhood. In view of English conservatism, he had displayed a heroic attitude in this cause at the birth control clinic in Woolworth Centre, and public opinion now seemed more favorable than in America, where a puritan repression was hampering the movement. I also visited Dr. Stopes' clinic, but she was out of town and I missed the pleasure of meeting her. However, I was shown all that my eyes could take in. London taught me invaluable lessons.

Berlin was a hitherto-unknown capital for me. Its people looked so exhausted that I was shocked. Political order had been restored by the republicans and industries were recovering. But unemployment was rife and the streets were crowded with persons obviously in dire need. A feeling of despair was settling like a pall over Germany, induced in part by the Dawes Plan which goaded the Germans to labor and yet refused to buy their goods. There was no glow in the German eyes and no buoyancy in the German manner. Anxiety about personal and national existence was uppermost in their minds and hearts. The lean men in patched suits and the women in torn shoes talked endlessly about the heavy burden assigned them by the Versailles Treaty. The war was started without popular consultation, but the result affected every individual. Whether the load could be carried another year everyone doubted.

German protest against the treaty was countered by the Allies' threats, as everyone knows. So German complaints found no remedy. The atmosphere of Berlin was charged with melancholia.

During my short stay there, I visited some of the girls' schools and public institutions. It was hard to find any girl or teacher wearing decent shoes. There was no style in their dress and any garment was better than none, of course. I looked into the pots which contained their luncheon, and learned that hot potato soup was the main nourishment for youthful hungry stomachs. The rationalization of industry, encouraging dumping and national starvation, coupled with the policy of inflation, which caused increasingly high prices within the country, were Germany's attempts to survive while conforming to the Versailles Treaty. But resentment against the treaty poured from the lips of every German with whom I came in contact.

At Cologne, naturally, the French army occupying the Ruhr District was the focus of attention. To the aliens who admire French art and German science, the French and the Germans are alike so admirable, each in their way, that the idea of their being such fierce enemies is almost incomprehensible. I pictured to myself the people of the working classes shaking hands across the borders of these countries as a common protest against their mutual enemies whose territorial and imperialistic ambitions do so much to prolong this belligerency. I left Germany with the feeling that I had seen a truly defeated nation, its population as a whole fatally punished without personal sin. This suffering seemed to me a warning to my own country whose people have never been defeated in a foreign war through two thousand years of insularity, but instead have been flattered by success in extending territory and markets for industrial output as a result of modernization.

From Germany we went to Switzerland. In Geneva we had the delight of being with Dr. Inazo Nitobe, then vice-chairman at the Administration Office of the League of Nations. It was like being with my own father to chat with Dr. Nitobe. And at this center of international politics and diplomacy, he reassured me with regard to my private ideals. He took us on a drive around the beautiful lake and to historic spots in the country. He described the League's work, and introduced us to many prominent people of different nationalities. I was proud to have Dr. Nitobe in Geneva, not only as an officer of the League, but as a representative of the internationally-minded and cultured Japanese.

Marseilles was our next station and there we boarded a French boat for Naples. As all the tourists in Naples do, we strolled through the excavated city of Pompeii. But in Italy as a whole with its long history, its excitable race, its artistic tradition and its physical conditions—mountainous land and poor natural resources—we experienced the sensation of being Japanese at home. Italy is so like Japan! Even the religious climate suggests analogies—the herdlike obedience of the masses to blind instinct; the official policy of noninterference with the course of nature, which the church deems best for a suffering population; and the inevitable outcome. Walking through the slums of Naples—it had been my intention to escape these— on the way to famous spots I saw the actual results of large-family adoration. Crowds of ill-fed, ill-clad children, some of whom were crippled, others blind, and all pale and malformed, crying on the dirty streets and in their dark warrens, made me sick at heart. These slums seemed even worse than the slums of Japanese cities, since Italians obviously did not object to sharing their shelter with donkeys and cows—a thing never found among the Japanese with their devotion to personal cleanliness. It was clearer to me than ever that birth control must be understood by religious people; that human children should not be born to live the life of pigs and swarms of flies. A beggar's existence is not worth having. Noble thinking does not correspond with the quest for a copper to buy an immediate morsel of bread, with only despair for tomorrow.

Leaving behind the city of Naples with its blue sky, colorful roofs and walls, and its green foliage, our boat went on to Palermo, the Sicilian town of ancient charm offering fascination comparable to that of turning back the leaves of a historical picture book.

So our foreign trip ended. I had spent six months abroad this time, now as a provincial woman on a sightseeing tour, now as a student of birth control and women's problems, again as an observer of political and economic development in different nations. Within a given space of time I had seen many races and nations. I had come to the conclusion that the American women hold the most enviable position of all women. I saw how others lived and operated. I compared other peoples, other conditions of life and labor, and other ideals and programs with the Japanese people, their social setting and their intelligence and I reached a firmer ground for my personal determinations.

XXIII

Women of the World

THE best angle on one's own country is often gained by traveling in others. Thus it was through my second trip abroad that I was led to inquire what the industrial achievements of Japan had brought as benefits to Japanese women? It is said that the Japanese army and navy have caught up with the best Western standards. Have the women of Japan also advanced their front line as far as the military men and the merchants of their country have advanced theirs? How do our conditions compare with those of American and other women of the West? A re-examination of the Japanese women's status went on in my mind.

It is true that Japanese women are no more the mere objects of romance under cherry blossoms in long-sleeved kimonos; nor are they now the puppetlike creatures once versed only in tea ceremony and flower arrangement. They are entering professions in increasing numbers. About 85 per cent of the women of Japan, that is, those between 15 and 59 years of age, are engaged in some kind of work.

Among the occupations in which our women are engaged, agriculture—including sericulture—comes first, numbering 1,300,000 workers.[1] Industrial workers number 800,000,[2] of whom 70,000 are employed in the mining industry—chiefly in coal mines—and 730,000 in the mills—spinning and weaving cotton and wool. The third rating as to the number of em-

---

[1] From the first official census, 1920.
[2] Official statistics, 1924.

ployees occurs in various lines of large-scale commercial enterprise, which total 630,000 [2] among whom the entertainers—geisha, restaurant waitresses, hotel maids, café-girls and dancers—take first rank; the office and shop girls and the telephone operators are not as numerous as the girls who serve the amusement industry. The fourth group of working women numbers 400,000 [1]—manual laborers who work courageously in teams chanting peculiar songs to mark time while they perform such hard tasks as driving piles into the ground for sewer construction, or tamping the ground before a house is built by means of a great pounding stone pulled up and down with a block and tackle. The fifth group comprises laborers in small-scale manufacturing, numbering 320,000,[1] that is, those engaged in the medieval kind of factories which employ less than five laborers each, to make toys, boxes, baskets, knitted goods and other articles depending more on manual skill than on machinery. The sixth group is composed of girls in the transportation business, numbering 50,000 [1] most of whom work on urban buses.

Business and professional women come last, listed as 260,000,[2] and within this group 37 per cent are engaged in the medical profession as doctors, midwives, nurses and pharmacists; 31 per cent in educational work mostly as primary-school teachers (75 per cent), but with some high school and college teachers (25 per cent) as well. We have girl typists and secretaries. We have girls in beauty parlors, in press and magazine work, in the musical profession, and to some extent in nearly every modern field.

Though the enumeration of women in business and the professions is impressive, except for a few especially favored professional women they are not paid enough to support themselves. Take the city of Tokyo, for instance. The Social De-

---

[1] From the first official census, 1920.
[2] Official statistics, 1923.

partment of the Tokyo Municipal Office reported, in 1934, that business and industrial women numbering 137,000 represented about 14 per cent of the whole woman population of the city. Of these working women, 27 per cent handle businesses of their own. Office workers and technical experts amount to 19 per cent; and 54 per cent of the employees take orders merely.

Examining their incomes, we find that only 10 per cent of these women, including medical workers, popular musicians, actresses and college professors, get above 100 yen ($50) per month; 10 per cent are receiving a monthly income of between 100 yen ($50) and 60 yen ($30); another 10 per cent are earning less than 60 yen ($30) and above 35 yen ($17.50) per month. The employers force them to labor long hours for small pay, taking advantage of their meekness—of their sacrificial spirit.

Japanese women are humble in the presence of men, and their relation toward society in general is one of submissiveness. The old feudalistic habits are responsible for this. Women have been driven out from sheltered family life to become industrial workers, but their ideas of the social proprieties remain unchanged. They view their occupation only as the means of subsistence in a situation in which the men of the family have no actual power to support them in spite of being the heads of families and cultivating dignified manners as the masters of the houses. Girls, who have been brought up to regard the family, and not the individual, as the social unit, ignore the fact that they are cruelly underpaid for their efficiency and the amount of labor they are giving to society. They consider their service a temporary expediency to be ended by marriage, or to go on afterwards as a sacrifice for the sake of the family system. Only the labor unions have as slogans: "Equal standards for the sexes! Equal pay for equal work!" These cries as a rule sound foreign to the ears of both employers and employees. The deep-rooted sense of humility in service, entertained by the workers themselves, and the traditional feminine modesty have caused the cheap labor of women to be a tragic anachronism in this industrial age.

In spite of the millions of tributes to the gracefulness and high moral standard of Japanese women, paid by men—and women—of the upper strata of society, in reality the average Japanese woman is a dreadfully exploited creature. Among the thousands of primary-school teachers in Japan, only one woman has held the chair of a principal. It is an unwritten law that no woman can become the head of a government school. It is not a question of ability, but our fatal custom that holds woman in subjection to man—a ridiculous tradition which does not remain so intact even in China, the birthplace of Confucius!

Japanese women have not yet gained the right to vote, either in national or municipal elections. A Japanese woman cannot be a higher official than a teacher in a government school. None of us can be a judge, a lawyer or a public notary. The elimination of every personal right, such as the ownership of property and independent action, from married women is a terrible disgrace to our country. Our law forces us to serve men as half-slaves. On every side our way to equal opportunity and independence is barred. As I face these realities, cold and cruel for my countrywomen, who are human and long for the freedom to be happy themselves while they try to make others happy, I am attacked by melancholy. What a tall wall to break through! What a long tedious path lying ahead of us! But without striving toward a goal we have no hope of making any progress whatsoever. Our Japanese men have not yet realized that to encourage women to develop their personalities will bring more happiness even to men, for the sexes are deeply dependent upon each other in this as in all other respects.

Then away with the so-called feminine attitude of dilly-dallying! Away with shyness, timidity and slavish servility! Cut the chains which bind the whole feminine population of

Japan to the old feudal system! Through such courage alone will the women of Japan be able to fashion life and labor in harmony with women's needs, and advance into the future hand in hand with men. Only after the women of Japan shall have removed the fetters which cramp their thought and action will their real womanly graciousness shine forth beyond dispute! Today they are automatons afraid of their own shadows!

PART NINE

MARITAL ISSUES INTENSIFY

XXIV

Domestic Women and Geisha Problems

IN *The Travel Diary of a Philosopher,* Count Hermann Keyserling refers to the Japanese woman: " . . . She cannot be taken seriously as a personality, and to this extent those people are right who place her beneath the European woman. On the other hand, it should be remembered that any perfection is better than none at all. No matter how perfect many European women are whose type belongs to past ages—I do not know a single one among the modern women who signifies more than a hasty sketch of her specific ideal. Therefore, for this age I must give the palm to the lady of Japan." [1]

Ten years have passed since this book was published and it may not be strictly fair to quote from Keyserling in such a changing period. But he continues: "The Japanese lady whom I have in my mind will also belong to the past ere long, just as the European grande dame does already. No æsthetically sensitive man will envisage this fate without melancholy. With her, one of the sweetest charms on earth will pass away, and nothing of equal value will replace her soon, no matter how much effort is extended in this direction." [2]

The melancholy of the German philosopher would be the grief of all the Westerners who love to dream of Japan as a "Land of Romance." Occidental men like to think that there is still some country whose women do not argue but always gently obey—women who can be managed without any fuss at all. Indeed, it may be a pleasant relief for some of them to come

[1] Page 202.
[2] *Ibid.*

277

to a country where mankind is still considered absolutely superior to womankind. But have they never realized that sweet obedience is a heartbreaking code for Japanese women in this transition period? The *Travel Diary* goes on: " . . . Thus, the perfection of the Japanese woman is the direct product of her position in life, which she has occupied for centuries; whatever may be said against this position—we owe to it the Japanese woman as she is. How miserable is the argument that she deserves a better fate, since she is so charming!" [1]

The feminine type to which this Western traveler completely lost his heart has likewise been the object of praise among the Japanese. Our men explain: "See how Westerners praise you! Don't lose this national pride. Don't be silly enough to imitate others and thus allow your virtue to degenerate!"

What, then, are the elements of this so-called perfect feminine quality which the German philosopher, and other æsthetes, Occidental and Oriental, admire so much? The elements seem to be: exquisite beauty and grace unconscious of themselves; the absence of pretense; naïveté; unselfishness. With this compound a woman becomes a doll. A living thing, she has a heart—a delicate heart—but positively no soul! As heavy iron chains fasten prisoners in their cells, so the masterful pens of Westerners lauding Japanese women's doll-like feminine charms serve as bonds strengthening native weapons of control. Nevertheless, modern Japanese women are chafing at their jailers and saying that the praise of women devoid of personality is an intellectual and social disgrace.

At the same time we are taking the influence of education into account. The *Great Learning for Women,* written by Kaibara Ekken (1631-1714), a great teacher of the Tokugawa feudal times, was through long years the prime guide in female education. Our ancestral mothers all tried their best to carry out

[1] Page 203.

his ideals. And it was this body of "wisdom" which, as I have said, my devoted and beloved grandfather willed to me at his death. Its fanatically rigid discipline is disclosed in such quotations as follow.

The honorable teacher says:

"Woman has no other place but her husband's house to live in, and so in Great China woman's marriage is called 'returning home.' Even if her husband's house is poor, she should have no regret. Poverty is the misfortune Heaven bestows on her, and she should, on no account whatever, leave her husband's house. This is woman's way, taught by the divine masters of old. . . .

"If a woman dishonors her way and is divorced, she carries a lifelong shame with her. There are seven reasons for which a woman may rightly be divorced. These are called the 'Seven Rules for Putting Away a Woman.'

"Rule One: put away a woman who does not obey her parents-in-law.

Rule Two: put away a woman who does not bear a child; for woman is needed to beget the heir. But if she has the right spirit, good manners, and is not jealous, she may stay and adopt a son within her family. If a concubine of her husband has a child, the childless wife need not be dismissed.

Rule Three: put away a woman if she is lax in morals.

Rule Four: put away a woman if she is jealous.

Rule Five: put away a woman if she is leprous or has other undesirable diseases.

Rule Six: put away a woman if she is talkative and impertinent, for a talkative woman causes discord among the relatives and breaks the harmony of the family.

Rule Seven: put away a woman if she steals things."

Elaborating these domestic principles, the honorable teacher continues:

"When a woman is divorced after once marrying, she is disgraced all her life, even if she is married again to a rich husband, for it is against the way of woman. . . . A woman has no master but her husband whom she should serve with respect and humility, never with a light attitude and disrespect. In a word, the way of woman is obedience. To her husband she should be submissive and harmonious, serving him with gentle and humble expression of the face and speech. Never should she be impatient and willful, proud and impertinent. This is her first duty. She should absolutely follow the husband's teaching and wait for his direction in everything of which she is not sure. If the husband puts a question to her, she should answer in the correct manner. An incomplete answer is a piece of incivility not to be excused. If the husband gets angry and acts accordingly, she should fear and be ruled by him; never contradict him. The husband is Heaven to the wife. Disobeying Heaven only incurs righteous punishment. . . .

"The common evil natures of woman are: (a) to be willful, (b) to be offended easily and be reproached, (c) to be inclined to abuse others, (d) to be jealous, (e) to be shallow-witted. Seven or eight out of every ten women have all these five sins. This is what makes woman inferior to man. She should know herself and conquer her weaknesses. Above all, shallowness of mind is her worst fault and is the cause of all the other evils. Woman is the negative principle, like night and darkness. Therefore woman is ignorant and does not foresee anything; does not know what is despicable to the eye of others; what is a hindrance to her husband and her children. Her ignorance is even such that she reproves and bears ill-will toward those who have no cause for being reproached and cannot tell her who are her true enemies. In bringing up her children, she merely follows instinct and not reason; so she cannot educate them properly. Utterly devoid of wisdom, she should humbly follow her husband in everything. . . .

"In the ancient teachings, it is said that when a girl baby is born she should be laid for three days under the house floor. This is because man symbolizes Heaven and woman, Earth. Therefore woman should follow man always with humility. Even when she has done something plausible, she should never be proud of it. If she has her faults pointed out by others, she should acknowledge them at once and make amends with humbleness of heart, in order never again to be put in the same disgrace. Even if she is scorned, she should not be offended but be patient and prudent. If she follows these teachings, there will be harmony between man and wife, peace in the family, and a long conjugal honor to the woman. . . .

"Woman should always be careful to keep herself blameless. She should get up early and retire late, never lie down during the day, keep busy, not neglecting spinning, weaving and sewing. She should not drink much of such things as tea and sake wine; should never see and hear such lewd drama as that at the Kabuki theater, popular songs, and Joruri music. Also she should refrain from going to shrines, temples and other crowded places, before she is forty years old."

Reviewing these teachings, we now understand how negative our feudal education was. The author of the book was not particularly hard on women considering the tendency of the age, and yet he never thought of elevating or even improving a sex held in ignorance, from which all these feminine evils could not but spring, and for which the only cure was, in his opinion, "earthly" humility. In truth the teacher may be called fairly reasonable, when we remember that the perfection of the family system was the aim of every woman's education. For the tyranny of the family system, women had to be mentally killed— deprived of the strength with which to ward off the disgraces heaped upon them. The last of the "Seven Rules for Putting Away a Woman" says: "Put away a woman who steals things." This emphasis on stealing indicates that the married woman, who is necessarily propertyless except for her clothes, given to her by her parents at her wedding, is sometimes tempted to use for herself or pass on to others the family properties without her husband's permission. It is a sin which she cannot avoid sometimes and yet it is so fatal to her honor! What Western woman of the twentieth century can imagine the position into which some of her Eastern sisters are still driven?

My father has been progressive enough not to force this moral standard unconditionally on his daughter, but I have watched my mother conduct herself all through her life in a literal following of what is written in this great book of morals. A new social system and a new social consciousness in harmony with it seem to me never to arrive together. People's ideas always lag behind economic events, even though they live to all appearances in a changed age.

Although those Japanese women who are working in their own retail shops with their husbands, those girls who have entered the army of factory workers, those women who work in the fields side by side with their men are still bound by feudal notions of good and evil inherited from their mothers, in reality their lives are not confined as rigidly to feudalism as those of upper-class women. Workers of any kind are more than obedient dolls. And yet while Japanese women are participants in modern productive methods for reasons of family income, they usually try to model their behavior according to this ancient book of ethics.

While carrying the heavy yoke of labor, Japanese women have thus cultivated the power of endurance to a remarkable degree. Their negative strength has been developed amazingly. For instance, the women of my class never betray their agony at the moment of childbirth; nor do they use any sort of medicine to reduce the pain. At the moment of a great sorrow or a mental shock, they know how to control themselves and face the circumstances stoically. This is their great price of personal pride. This is our national pride in them.

However, these negative virtues of the Japanese women have surely led men to extreme self-indulgence. It is this everlasting patience of women in the presence of men's dissolute practices and unfair domestic conduct that perpetuates the geisha system in Japan. The geisha with their teahouses and the licensed prostitutes of the Yoshiwara section of Tokyo and many other cities of Japan are often an exotic lure for Western tourists. Some foreigners spend just a few days in our country but, however crowded the schedule, they seem never to forget to exploit the "gay quarters" and set down in print their impressions. Usually they are extravagant in their praise of the geisha while condemnatory of the Yoshiwara girls. But occasionally a Westerner is able to look at the system of entertainment by courtesans, which exists in almost every Oriental country in some form, with a keener insight and even extend co-operative sympathy to the native social reformers who seek to abolish what is to them a blot on Eastern society.

Count Keyserling describes the geisha institution from a very masculine point of view. He says: "The geisha have the privilege and the duty of fostering the old traditional forms; thus, they are the guardians of the Holy of Holies. . . ." [1] His pen goes on: "In Japan, baseness seems unknown, even to the lowest wench. Here all femininity is bent on charm, and charm is inculcated in them as an end in itself. Since the women do not see anything dishonoring in selling themselves to a strange man for money, and the man sees nothing shameful in visiting these pleasure houses, an atmosphere of harmless cheerfulness prevails in these establishments, just as, in Europe, among children round the Christmas tree." [2]

Is he commending our society? Or is he making fun of it? Perhaps the German philosopher really speaks for men at large. I do not wish to be too severe on this distinguished writer. Tasty wine has its medicinal virtue and gentle entertainment by young girls of exquisite charm is not bad in itself for any man. Japanese teahouses are undeniably lovely and the geisha have learned through long training how to make themselves attractive to men in such surroundings.

To spend the evening playing, laughing and being amused by beautiful women, with nothing but men's happiness on their minds, is apparently a masculine idea of Paradise. But teahouses have been valued not only as congenial places for relaxation; they are also important council rooms for statesmen and clubs for businessmen. Austere gentlemen who enter them stiff and formal, after drinking cups of sake and chatting lightly about nothing with girls taught to make them unbend, often open their hearts and reveal their purposes as they would

[1] Keyserling. *Travel Diary of a Philosopher*, page 190.
[2] *Ibid.*, page 194.

never do elsewhere, least of all with their wives. They discuss with these young women the theater, movies, boxing and wrestling matches, politics and markets. Every possible line of contemporary interest is chatted about, the girls always appearing sympathetic, even when they tease. Because of the need of it, many geisha are learning English, putting their little notes on vocabulary into their paper-handkerchief bags, hidden between the folds of their brocade sashes. The girls now in teahouses dance the foxtrot with their guests to the rhythm of jazz bands. They are trying to be up-to-date when modernity is in demand, while preserving their traditional skill in Japanese dancing, singing and playing of instruments.

Almost every important function in Japan must still have feasting on the program and geisha for entertainment. The stiff and artless wives are entirely expelled from conviviality. They are allowed to attend wedding ceremonies, memorial services for the dead and celebrations of old age, with their relatives. But they stay away from affairs in the teahouses. When a gay party is to be given there, or at a public restaurant, the host calls upon the proprietor to have ready the required number of geisha. No cooking is done in the tearoom but food may be sent in from outside. When a man invites his friends to a restaurant, he must have permission from the police to bring in the geisha. Generally the entertainers for a large party include girls called hangyoku, from about thirteen to sixteen years of age, dressed in colorful kimonos with sweeping sleeves; maturer girls from about sixteen to twenty-four years of age; and a few older women, corresponding all in all to the number of invited guests.

After entering the room with polite bows, the entertainers take their seats, one in front of each guest, to whom they serve sake only, the food being carried around by plain maids. At the guests' command and during the eating and drinking, the geisha play the samisen, sing and dance. The teahouse proprietor charges the host for the girls by the hour. The music and dancing are an additional charge. So this kind of Japanese entertainment on an accredited scale costs at least thirty yen ($15) per person just for a short evening's pleasure, which is twice as much as the cost of a grand hotel dinner in Japan. Away from the geisha, our upper-class Japanese men are usually so frigid of manner that a Western type dinner becomes hopelessly punctilious if they try to show honor to tourists in that way.

In the geisha business, the popular girls often cover many parties in one evening. Even a brief appearance is expensive for the host. But the young entertainers do not get the money for themselves, though their fine apparel is expensive. Hence a popular geisha, almost without exception, has a patron who pays the bills for her purchases of seasonal kimonos and accessories. Men are often generous about the sums they bestow upon their favorites, for these gifts help to build for them the reputation of being wealthy. But almost none of them would spend so much upon his wife. On the contrary, a man takes it for granted that a wife has no need to show off her attractions outside the family, since she is thoroughly protected in the home. Besides, it is her duty to be thrifty and to devote herself to household economy, letting her husband have a wide range for his devotions. The patron of a geisha is also responsible for the bills incurred in connection with her frequent music and dancing rehearsals; again, for a public performance where her prestige calls for fine costuming, stage setting, accompanying musicians and the distribution of rich gifts, he must open his purse without stint. If the man pays all her debts to her proprietor for her education, and interest on the proprietor's investment, usually calculated to be a sum ignoring the rule of arithmetic, then he can either marry her or have her as his mistress and let her own a house for him alone to visit. Often he buys for her the privilege of running a geisha establishment herself.

It is not so simple to become a famous geisha as to become a movie star. The training for the geisha is longer and far more precise. As a geisha is supposed to be an artist, or it would be better to say since she is an art performer, her discipline is rigorous. A handsome appearance is, of course, an essential requirement and poor parents with good-looking daughters often maintain themselves by selling their offspring at a tender age to geisha houses. In such cases the girls are commonly adopted legally as daughters of the house to avoid the actual form of human trade. The young apprentice in turn calls her mistress "mother" and her elder mates "sisters." Filial duties and absolute obedience to the commands of her elders are enforced upon her. Often the whip of discipline lashes the little girls severely, but as elders may own juniors there is no legal redress. Outsiders are helpless to stop this kind of cruel treatment, but it cannot be denied that the strict training is what gives distinction to a Japanese courtesan.

The education law requires that the very young apprentices shall be sent to a primary school in the daytime, but after school hours they pass to the teachers of dancing, singing and musical instruments. In some cities there are geisha schools where girls can combine all their lessons under one roof, which is a very convenient arrangement for them. Scarcely have the little creatures finished the elementary grades when foster mother and elder sisters begin their polishing. This work starts on the girls' sunburnt faces from which is removed every sign of vigor in order that they may appear like excellent white dolls.

The well-polished butterflies captivate men's hearts or curiosity by whispering a thousand words of love as their profession requires them to do, but none of them is supposed to make real love to any man, unless she is so ordered by her mistress. But it is far from the truth if a Westerner thinks that these human beings see nothing dishonorable in selling themselves to any strange man for money. The whole business is regularized. A code of honor prevails even in this system. Girls who evade its pattern are called, by a term of disgrace, "coming (lying)-without-seeing-the-man" geisha, which adjective is often used for other misdemeanors such as a politician's unfaithfulness to his party. There is no dishonor, according to this code, attached to a geisha's prostitution at the bequest of her mistress. Nevertheless, a popular theme for that department of our literature which specializes in the "underworld" is a geisha struggling against the foster mother's command to sell herself to a hated patron, for usually a rich but coarse and elderly male is abominable to a young girl who would rather have a handsome youth for her sweetheart, even if he is too poor to please the geisha's owner.

There is no escaping some kind of patron. Someone must pay for the debut of a grown-up apprentice. After the debut, usually at the age of sixteen or seventeen, the debutante, to indicate her maturity, changes her costume entirely, cutting her sleeves to the ordinary length and dressing her hair in the adult fashion.

But visitors to the teahouses must also conform to certain rules. It is not supposed to be shameful for men to be entertained by a company of these pleasant women, in a group. A personal intimacy with one of them is not considered proper. At the first-class teahouses, only customers of long acquaintance or new customers with reliable introductions bearing names indicating high social position are acceptable to the mistress in charge. She is generally a woman grown stout by alcohol, and always a person of political and business ability. She manages men of power and wealth as easily and skillfully as a Chinese juggler trifles with his balls and plates. The mistresses are really very influential women, governing this "flower and willow" society, made up of teahouses, geisha establishments, Kabuki theaters and actors, teachers of the various arts of amusement, and the men who visit these places, not forgetting the diseases which they bring.

While the women of our intellectual class are hardly earning their own bread, while not a single chair of a highly responsible kind in the universities is spared to any of them, the women of the underworld are running this peculiar business on a large scale and many of them are getting enormous incomes in the process. Their power over the prominent gentlemen of Japan is gained not by challenging in the open but by artfully and tactfully whispering.

The secret politics of the country, business negotiations and conspiracies of every kind are talked over in the privacy of the teahouse. A group of men with attending geisha may be thoroughly secluded in a quiet compartment in the teahouse without fear of facing others unpleasantly. Absolute privacy is guaranteed. The quietness which reigns in such places giving, in the midst of the city, the feeling of having come miles and miles away to a country villa, is hinted at by the wooden gate and stepping stones well-sprinkled with water which lead toward the entrance hall. The clogkeeper kneels to receive one's shoes—clogs or sandals—and put them carefully away with the canes. Then a sedately-dressed maid makes obeisance and guides one along the zigzag corridors of polished wood or mat-covering which enclose a small inner garden picturesquely landscaped with a pondlet, stone urns, and a little grassy hill upon which a plain wood or red-laquered shrine for the Fox God is placed to invite prosperity to the house. Finally one reaches the reserved room, not large necessarily but very neatly furnished. The paper sliding doors, the screens, the soft-colored walls and the carefully selected wood of the tokonoma pillar are all calculated to create an atmosphere of refined taste. The setting for teaism forbids a gaudy effect.

Many Japanese writers practically live in these houses, for they say that they can work efficiently only in this congenial atmosphere. However, because of the unwholesome economic and ethical, if artistic, surroundings, public opinion in Japan is becoming critical of this way of life, for doubtless it is the source of dark shadows on Japanese society and, as a matter of fact, whenever there is a social scandal, a teahouse or teahouses are always involved.

When a customer arrives at one of these retreats, not for a party but for quiet pleasure, the customary procedure is to have one of the maids telephone to his wife that he will not be home for supper. A gentleman who is waited on at all times will not steal away to spend an evening with other women so boldly as to neglect to notify his wife of his absence. He is too formal for that. The gentle wife, who has been preparing her husband's favorite dishes in expectance of his homecoming and a happy supper table, now has to eat alone or with her children only, knowing full well that her beloved husband reposes in the amorous air of the teahouse listening to the flatteries of the geisha. But the wife waits and waits as the clock turns to the limit of the day, stirring the dying charcoal in the brazier in the wintertime to keep warm, and burning mosquito sticks endlessly in summer. The august mate returns late in the night or early in the morning with hot face and staggering feet, to be bowed gracefully into the house. If he is reproached, it is not then and there. Contrary to the customs of our neighboring country, the Japanese girls often send their tipsy guests home in the dead of night!

Prominent statesmen, high officials, leading businessmen and others have the privilege of leading a life of this sort, unhealthy and expensive, without much influential criticism. The wives of such men, of course, feel chagrin in the circumstances. Courageous middle-class women are inclined to rebuke their husbands frankly, but the ladies of the upper class cling so religiously to the behavior established for "well-conducted wives" that they make noble attempts to stifle the call of their hearts. Combativeness avails little, so long as these ladies are economically helpless. Thus men enlarge their opportunities for pleasure while wives cling to the interminable household tasks like goldfish in the pond, having slight chance to see the world at work or at play.

There are about ten thousand women in the geisha profession in Tokyo alone and about eighty thousand in the whole of Japan. Those geisha who hold the first rank have incomes four or five times larger than those of women in intellectual professions. But the geisha "mothers" usually control these incomes, and the girls are obliged to spend so much for the sake of prestige that there has never been a geisha in the millionaire brackets. It is hard to keep pace in this profession after physical attraction is gone. On account of the constant smoking, drinking, irregular eating and thick powdering, the lack of fresh air and outdoor exercise, the geisha lose their youthful charm much earlier than ordinary women. Some of them marry men whom they like or by whom they are purchased with money. Some spend their lives as private mistresses. Some run geisha houses of their own, either inherited from their geisha mothers or bought for privilege. Some become teachers of music and dancing for the younger girls. A few remain professional geisha as long as they live, a seventy-year-old geisha not being a monstrosity! Those who were once most popular and clever in entertaining people make the most popular proprietors of teahouses or restaurants catering to the trade.

Yoshiwara in Tokyo, Shimabara in Kyoto and other licensed prostitute quarters present a separate problem from the geisha quarters and teahouses, although there are common problems which they raise. The license for a geisha carries permission to sell one's art only; that for a prostitute is what is literally indicated in the word. There are in Japan about fifty-two thousand women who come under the pitiful brand of licensed prostitutes (1931). Some low-class geisha have the two licenses together. However, before we decide upon any practical and effective measure to do away with this shameful institution, we have to take account of the fact that it has been a deep-rooted historical phase of our social growth.

Prostitution seems a universal social phenomenon, though it may arise from different causes in different societies. In Japan it existed from ancient times in the form of religious rites practiced by sibyls and priestesses. All through our ancient history and with the formation of the samurai class about the twelfth century, the prostitution of women was given a semireligious warrant. There was a large class of slaves in those days, but prostitutes were not so ranked.

With the usurpation of power by the samurai, the sexual morality of the warrior class was gradually refined, especially on the women's side. A high sense of chastity was maintained by the wife, and beside her restraint prostitution seemed more immoral. However, it never declined. On the contrary, it grew with the increase in the precariousness of the warriors' lives rendered unavoidable in a feudal society, and with the brutality of feudal wars marked by the selling of women captives. It developed rapidly throughout the country, spreading wherever a town rose under the power of a local daimyo; until at last in 1528, the bankrupt Ashikaga shogunate achieved the idea of taxing immorality, thereby giving it special recognition and destroying its secret machinations. Licensed prostitution flourished in the open from this time on, accompanied by a prosperous traffic in women. Daughters of unfortunate samurai, of indebted tradesmen and of hungry peasants were bought and sold in a thousand ingenious ways.

It was the first of the Tokugawa shoguns who segregated prostitutes, enclosing the brothels in licensed quarters. This was the origin of our Yoshiwara and other so-called Pleasure

Enclosures (Yukaku). Miserable women were gathered here by cold-blooded brokers and brothel proprietors, and shut up, in most cases, for life; in the case of the physically exploited, the run of life was short. With the return of peace and the rise of the bourgeoisie in the last stages of the Tokugawa feudal regime, the Pleasure Enclosures became the center of social life for men, offering refuge from the rigidity of the family system. Some produced grand courtesans, refined and proud, who raised the standard of men's cultural tastes, and so introduced the professional entertainer—the geisha of today.

Shocking but tempting must have been this peculiar institution of Japan to the Western visitors of early Meiji times, for many a Madame Butterfly and Okichi, with many of the more practical Madame Chrysanthemums, became familiar figures to gallant foreign gentlemen. However, the Meiji government was thoroughly ashamed of this barbaric institution and within five years of its establishment it prohibited the traffic in girls and declared the abolition of licensed prostitution. This sudden reform only distributed the evil through the entire society and, in less than a year, the government reinstated the licensing system with the proviso that the women were to be regarded as employees, and not as human chattels to be bought and sold. A physical examination was strictly enforced on the licensed prostitutes.

It would be far from just to condemn as immoral the Orient as a whole on account of its licensed prostitution. More than ninety per cent of these girl victims sink into this shameful servitude not because they want to, but because they must help their poverty-stricken families by this means. It is natural that Keyserling should observe that the atmosphere of the Japanese brothels is not unclean. The relative refinement of these places springs from the girls' sense of filial duty. Natural depravity and vanity have not thrust them into this inferno.

However, no matter what have been the reasons and background for the existence and growth of these professions, both the low-class prostitutes and the geisha are the enemies of domesticity and, as such, enemies of civilization in Japan.

Owing to the recession of feudalistic sentiments among men and women amid the change from complicated formality to free and open conduct, the demand for geisha and licensed prostitution is decreasing, though its rate may be slow. Unhappily, café waitresses, professional entertainers whose service is within the restaurants, girls in the public halls who dance by the ticket system are new professionals replacing the old.

Our licensed prostitution is a grave problem for us, and it has become even an international issue. There have been many attempts to remove this blot from our society, but so far none has succeeded. One thing that impressed the public with the cruelty of this institution was the Yoshiwara tragedy at the time of the great earthquake. The women of this quarter, unaccustomed to liberty of movement, lost time in running from the pursuing conflagration after the earthquake and many of them were burnt to death. This horrible fact roused righteous indignation among the Japanese, and especially among the women of Tokyo who, having learned to organize while taking part in the relief work after the earthquake, now resolved that there should be no permanent handicap of this kind for their sex, and determined to end the licensed prostitution for all time. The national Antiprostitution League, which had been organized some time previously, now met with wide support from various women's organizations, notably the Christian Women's Social Reform Organization (Fujin-Kyofukai) and the Alliance of Suffragettes. At present, Japanese law sanctions the right of licensed prostitutes and geisha to free themselves from forced restraint, if their debts can be paid in some other way; so the Salvation Army and several women's civic organizations are doing their best to protect these "reformed women."

Reform movements and organizations are, no doubt, doing much good in purifying our society ethically. But more is involved than ethics. Even if they succeed in freeing prostitutes and geisha from their cruel bonds, so long as there remains the need to exchange one's personal charm for rice their profession, whether licensed or not, will remain. It may even expand if the depression throws more economic wreckage into the streets. Nor have the greatest among Western countries yet succeeded in destroying this evil at the root.

I have had a number of opportunities to meet geisha girls in the past either at men's parties at which I have had the rare privilege of being present or in personal association which I enjoyed especially during the time I was taking dancing lessons with some of the geisha. As party entertainers, they all look pretty, merry, and bold, but when I talk with them personally, I find them modest and peculiarly melancholy. As personal friends they may show some individuality, but as professional women they are all alike, being clipped and trained after a certain standard of beauty, which is no more than the prettiness of uniformly shaped, sized and colored carnations and roses raised in a commercial hothouse. They may dazzle our eye a moment with their well-studied painting and dressing-up, but not for long.

The geisha are regarded by men as commercial articles and they are manufactured accordingly, each with a price mark, tagged on the neck, somewhat differentiated with reference to age, art and talent. At any rate they are ready-made beauties, and are, like other ready-made things, uniformly patterned. We often see them in trains accompanying men on pleasure trips. At such times, they try their best to look like wives, with their quiet clothes and restrained hairdressing. But at a glance anybody can detect the difference. Even when properly married, they cannot look and act like ordinary wives. So markedly standardized is the making of the geisha.

The beauty of the geisha can be put under one category

of "iki" which is a unique word in the Japanese language, since the geisha are a class peculiar to our society. No foreign tongue can give even an approximate equivalent for this singularly Japanese expression. A friend of mine, Professor Shuzo Kuki, in the literature department of Kyoto Imperial University, who is an authority on the cultural history of the West as well as of Japan, interprets this word "iki" in his book, *The Analysis of Iki,* as something a little less simple and common than the English word "smart," as a refined coquetry a little more specific and narrowed than the quality expressed by the French word "chic." It is analyzed as the Buddhist spirit of resignation and apathy combined with the inherited pride of the Yedo people which could spurn power and wealth if honor was at stake, this pride appearing in the geisha as their strong revolt against men's tyranny. It refines the geisha's forced professional coquetry and creates a peculiar beauty. Within the definition of this word I can recognize and admire the geisha's beauty and charm in a detached way. I am not one of those Confucian Puritans who despise these girls merely as evil women. I know too well what they suffer.

It is undeniable that the existence of the geisha is a grave menace to good housewives and a force destructive of the peace of family life. However, I am not so blind as to overlook the social forces that call it forth. Geisha are simply driven into their profession; they know they are grieving the innocent wives and are heartily sorry for it. The puppet play by Chikamatsu based on the life of a public prostitute, Koharu, later made into a Kabuki drama, shows best the fated relation of the geisha and the wife. The story is a triangular plot, of course. The geisha, Koharu, and the Osaka merchant, Kamiji, who is married, fall in love with each other in spite of themselves and decide to commit a double suicide—the conventional solution in the Japanese society of Yedo days. Even in their last embrace, Koharu, tenderly thinking of her lover's wife, proposes to die separately in order not to put her to too much shame. She apologizes herself at the final moment for taking the man away from his angelic lady. But she never triumphs over her love. The wife, on the other hand, does not blame her husband for idling in the gay quarter, for she knows well how the pressure of the family system kills every bud of human pleasure and causes the reactionary outbursts in the geisha quarters. She is sorry for him and in order to shield him from the strict father, she often pawns a precious kimono to take care of his debts. It is not servility, but the purely unselfish love of a good wife. There is something in this play everlastingly appealing to the Japanese mind long nurtured in a feudal society, and this one of the Kabuki plays I myself never weary of seeing.

I think that the geisha have never, since of old, been happy in their profession; that they have not lured men, of their own free will, into dissipation. On the contrary, they are pitiably ashamed of their position and almost unduly conscious of their sinfulness in stealing the money and attention of husbands due their wives. I am sorry for those who are forced by our singular social circumstances to take up such a calling, to be gaily dressed but terribly exploited workers. I grieve over their misunderstanding of the meaning of our traditional "filial piety," which persuades them to be geisha in order to relieve temporarily with their own persons some family distress. It is a too-nearsighted view to regard them as the direct enemy of the oppressed wives. It is our society that not only tolerates but in fact sponsors the existence of such a profession. Men should be ashamed of taking advantage of it. Awakened women cannot but feel it their duty to work toward the removal of this horrible disgrace, imposed on their sex.

Only where security is assured to those who work can love and marriage properly exist. Conversely, only where love and marriage are both enlightened and possible to all can prostitution disappear. The welfare of the state is intimately bound up with this issue.

XXV

A Japanese Husband

*A*S I LOOK back even over my short life I see there repeated
challenges of the new against the old, the perfect feminine
in the old sense trying to put down the struggles of the new
feminine aspiring to express itself in a progressive world. It
was my own mother who regarded it as her great work to
cast her daughter into the mold deemed so admirable by Occidental and Oriental "philosophers." When mother bought a
kimono or an obi for me, she was always particular to select
one elegantly quiet in color and design. I was not to look
younger that I was actually; nor was I to be the focus of all
eyes by reason of some splashing decoration in my apparel. If
my garments were costly, the fact was not to be strident. My
manner she hoped to make accord with the refined modesty
of my dress. A naïve grace was the desired effect. Even my
speech was to be free of such assertions as "I think," "I like,"
"I want," "I, I, I . . ." the *I* never coming first, unlike the style
of free Western girls. My mother warned me that I must listen
to others always, smile at whatever they said, and express as
little as possible of myself.

While my mother was eager to make a dainty bride of me,
the man I married was writing in his diary: "O God! bless my
heart! If Thy will is to make me Thy faithful servant and let
me work to bring Thy Kingdom on earth, then select for me
a wife with whom I shall work to bring glory to Thy Name!"
Again he wrote: "I am not hoping that my wife, Shidzué, will
be a baroness of the sort depicted in fiction or drama, leading

an elaborate life amid luxurious surroundings; what I really hope for her future is that she will concern herself with the great problems of her countrywomen!"

After our marriage and while he found inspiration in working for labor, he watched with interest my growth in social consciousness. As soon as we had settled in a cottage in the coal mine district in western Japan, away from the traditions and complication of the old family system in Tokyo and its guardian mother-in-law, my husband began his constructive task of educating his girl bride into a "real" person. He insisted on my changing my attitude even toward him from a meek feudal wife to an alive, liberal and understanding companion. He did not permit me to sit on the mat without a cushion as I had done in our Tokyo house—a true Japanese is supposed not to use a cushion in sitting before his elders—but assured me that I could behave as an equal. I must admit that I enjoyed the cushion. When he took a bath, I asked him whether he needed assistance, as is the way of a proper feudal wife, but he replied scornfully that he did not need a slave. His persistent call to me to rise from a stage "too delightful to behold" toward that of the "self-conscious woman" changed even my appearance.

After his long and hard effort to put spirit into a doll-like creature, and just as his labor began to bear fruit—that is to say, just as I learned to express myself, my husband said to me one day that he thought my appearance was losing charm for him.

Now he frankly declared that the beauty of a Japanese woman lay only in her naïveté. He pointed to the delicate feminine figures in the old prints, pronouncing them his ideal. What a contradiction! After having so long admired the sturdy women of Millet and the powerful masterpieces of Rodin! He who once had undertaken to educate his wife with a view to making her as active and independent as any English or American woman was now gloating over Japanese dolls in the old prints as types to emulate! But as my husband had always been ahead of his time, so his reaction against liberalism was a sign of the newest national tendency.

It now seemed foolish in my eyes for a man to take off his hat in the elevator when a woman entered, to rise from his seat in a train if a woman were standing or to help a woman carry parcels. He reverted to the "good old" ways of his people marked by masculine hauteur. The "inferior sex" could stick to its grace and modesty. He would not lift another finger to change habits and customs.

What brought my husband to this sudden reversion of attitude? What made him move from one extreme to the other —from progressivism to conservatism? He had been such a zealous crusader for human rights! He had been ready to risk everything in an effort to get into Russia regardless of what this implied for his wife and children, and when he was prevented from seeing that great social experiment at first hand his disappointment seemed deep and genuine. He had thrown in his lot with the laborers of Japan, sympathizing intellectually with their class war and aiding them directly in many ways. What had robbed him of conviction and loyalty to the common people? What had transformed him into an antifeminist?

His diagnosis of the movement of history seems to have been the basis of his mental and spiritual change. Having believed in a swift reconstruction of Japanese life from top to bottom, he was unprepared for the slow and tedious march of events toward that goal. As the reactionary forces at home grew bolder, he grew correspondingly discouraged and soon felt that idealism had been irrevocably betrayed. Immediate realities curbed his imaginative flights and eventually he was completely overcome by the influences of his bourgeois environment. There he was at last—a mere man of aristocratic urban culture, captivated by the conventions of his own class!

His second trip to America and Europe had driven him backward instead of forward and nothing I could say or do or pray had any effect. He lost faith in the downfall of capitalism, within his lifetime at any rate, after he saw the status of the Western countries in 1924. It was disillusioning to the young Marxist, indoctrinated with the idea that capitalism was a frail thing, to discover how stanchly it was, to all appearances, entrenched despite the World War. On returning from his second trip to the West, my husband whitewashed his socialistic internationalistic colors, and repainted them with vigorous nationalism. In this respect, too, he was a pioneer adjusting himself to new conditions. He put aside all his work of a socialistic nature, and let the petty profit-seekers gather intimately around him.

Having awakened from his romantic dream of quick social reconstruction, he was hungry for capitalistic enterprise which lured him by its covering names of "national policy" and "the reconstructive project of great Japan." Now he laid a plan for rice-field irrigation in Korea, for the establishment of a financial organ and a railroad business in North Korea and East Manchuria, among other things. His money and his labor went into such schemes as these.

But no enterprise under the sun of capitalism can flourish without profits. And this man, ingenious as he was in the realm of ideas, was less gifted in executive talent. Actual experience was also lacking as a basis of success. Naturally record after record of failure struck fatal blows at the family fortunes. But he refused to admit defeat. He learned to picture himself as a great empire builder—a forerunner of Asiatic statesmen who were to play a new role in the mainland, especially in Manchuria. The more fixedly he bent his head in this direction, the more purely he symbolized Oriental heroics.

In family life in Japan, as it must be everywhere, the husband's mental outlook directly affects the life of his wife. This ancient truth, known to my ancestors of course, I now took to my heart. Hardly had I become conscious of myself when I had to face this reactionary wave at home.

If the ensuing domestic problem and struggle had been but an isolated private affair, my melancholy plight would have been of little moment as a story. But my story is a common one among the present-day Japanese women who are trying to emerge from the condition of nonresistance to events however meaningful and take their place in the shaping of events in their own interests, in the interests of the race and of the nation. So in talking about myself, I am really talking about countless members of my sex in Japan.

Several courses lay before me in the circumstances I have just described. I could try to forge straight ahead working for the realization of my dreams as a social innovator. I could spurn my husband's protests and remind him bluntly of his own responsibility for my new interests and convictions. I could subside completely and revert, if I tried, to the type of feudal woman beloved of my class. I could battle to restore my husband to the idealism of his youth—make him again the humanistic crusader; the man among men, his handsome aristocratic figure distinguished among copper-colored miners and other laborers as that of a person who owned himself; the strong individual able to work twelve hours a day in the dark pit and find satisfaction as a toiler; the guide and friend of woman in her effort to rise out of slavery. Images of his former power and charm floated before my eyes incessantly.

So I chose the latter course. I attempted to win my husband again to the path he had believed enlightened. I thought that a seat in the House of Peers would enable him to give voice to his appreciation of the facts and problems staring him so starkly in the face and that he could utilize his abundant knowledge of politics and economics in the interests of national progress. At the same time I fancied that if he took his seat among the peers he might give up harmful friends and assume new obligations. So I urged my husband to start a campaign for membership in the House of Peers. Now this plan does not imply that such a campaign for membership in the upper house of the Japanese Diet is like an English contest for membership in the House of Lords, with English ladies openly and actively taking a hand. For the seats in the upper house of the Japanese Parliament are inherited by princes, marquises and counts, while viscounts and barons receive this honor only through the unanimous vote of the peers of the same rank, over which the council of powerful elders within each rank has entire control. Naturally a candidate must thus fulfill requirements pleasing to the conservative eyeglasses of the elders. In this situation I had to face a severe inner struggle of my own, to advance my husband's status.

When he discussed the proposed entry into the Diet, his friends with one accord insisted that the wife of a candidate for the House of Peers must absolutely conform to the feudal code. She must not talk about women's rights and women's personality; there could be no suffrage campaigning on her part. They scarcely needed to assure him that his wife could not work for birth control. There was clearly no chance for his winning a seat among the peers so long as my "dangerous thoughts" continued to find expression.

To give up all my social interests and maintain a dead silence even within the narrow walls of home was like being sentenced to prison. But my devotion to my husband, my effort to bring him back to his better self, made me pay any price for his sake. However, after paying the heavy costs of this campaign, opportunity for which comes only once in every seven years, he failed to win the seat. It was claimed that his own too-radical years were his handicap. It would be years now before he could live down his past sufficiently to stand again for the House of Peers. To expect membership in any case meant that his wife must hold aloof from social activities in the future. My coworkers in the social movement attempted to draw me out from this status of spiritual imprison-

ment, but I was determined first to regain domestic happiness.
I never thought of sacrificing my husband's career for mine.
Gladly I resolved to sacrifice mine, for his.

As I spent unhappy days in praying for a bright passage
to open for my husband, he proceeded to discover a dark one
leading in another direction. His injurious friends led him
to shadowy corners. Their first project was to remove him
from my watching eyes. They made every effort to keep him
away from his family. Geisha and the teahouses were the
fortresses for these men in this gloomy battle—fortresses which
the wife could not assault.

My husband has been and still is a very honest man. He
has been unable to doubt other people, whom he always takes
to be just as honest as himself. This good nature of his is
found in many men who have been brought up in the wealthy
or well-to-do families of Japan. And this simplicity led Baron
Ishimoto more and more into the entanglements of a dis-
honest and complex society. With the world-wide depression
financial difficulties arose and grew until they overwhelmed
him. He thought that he must not let his wife know the real
state of his finances, and instead of telling everything frankly
and counting on a natural approach to the solution of difficulties, he resorted to proud defiance or sullen silence as a way
out. In his effort not to lose the honorable husband's dignity,
he conducted himself almost like one deprived of reason.

So after all I had a regular feudal lord at home. The only
thing that was absent from the picture was the perfect feudal
wife. The days and months wore on as if we were traveling
over a desert. But my devotion to my husband never changed;
I continued to pray that I might be able to rejuvenate idealism
along progressive lines. I aspired to conduct myself as far as
could be done according to what is taught in the book of great
learning for women to which I have referred. It was not because I approved of this blind feudal code as such but only

because it seemed to offer the only means of restoring a friendship held so precious and vital.

To my infinite regret, the gentler I tried to be the harsher
was my failure in reaching my goal of rehumanizing my
husband. Often the image of a grindstone came to my mind
during those trying years as if I were set to polish it with patient
and unerring labor. But I had other tasks as well as grind-
stones to think about those days. So many duties dropped
upon my shoulders.

My husband's interest in the railroad works in the northern
border of Korea and in Manchuria deepened, and most of the
time he left me alone except for financial problems while he
traveled about bent on elaborate business schemes, dreaming
about Cecil Rhodes of Great Britain, writing Chinese poems
dedicated to Prince Ito, the man who succeeded in annexing
Korea to Japan. It was during his many trips to Korea and
Manchuria that he published pamphlets taking for their theme
Japan's national policies in relation to Manchuria and Mongolia. With his historical knowledge of the East and the
West combined with ideas of Japan's future economy, he looked
forward to a national drive toward the huge natural wealth
in Manchuria and Mongolia, declaring in his fiery manner like
a pioneer and prophet that to exploit this unutilized land and
wealth was the true mission for the Japanese nation.

Meanwhile he wrote me no real letter to console my lonely
and difficult days at home. Nor did he let me know what he
was actually doing. The happiness of wife and children was
a trifling matter for a man who was solving great national
problems and framing national policy. Tenderness would be
a disgrace in an Oriental hero at work on a state issue! There
could be no wasting of affection on one who was only a wife!
And a woman! I heard from him very seldom, and when I
did his letter was written on a long piece of rice paper with
India ink and brush, filled with the most exaggerated form of

the classical Chinese expressions representing the stiff formality of the old school. He seemed to have forgotten that I was his wife. The thorough orientalization of my husband made me recall the story of a wise emperor in ancient China, who, during the time when he was a loyal subject entrusted with the diking of a great river, was so heroically absorbed in the public work that he passed the front of his own house three times without once entering it during the three years of his responsibility. It has often been considered a great virtue or even been taken as a matter of course for a man to neglect or sacrifice his family for a noble cause.

When I replied with news of what I had been doing for my husband and for the family during his absence, mentioning some of the difficulties and anxieties, the answer was wont to be only a few lines stating casually that "The Japanese nation will be grateful to you, as I consider you meritorious in managing the difficult family affairs, as a good wife should do to help her husband who is fighting in the front line in behalf of a national policy." Great Heaven! I never thought of being recognized by the nation. My dreams soared no higher than acknowledgment by my dear husband. This did not come and my heart was finally broken.

One day when I felt as if I were plodding through mental darkness, I received a postal telegram from my husband in which he very abruptly said: "A bear is arriving at Tokyo station by express this evening. Go and get it." Was he planning to establish a zoo in our small garden beside this crowded street of Tokyo? I asked myself. Or was it just a stuffed bear to be a toy for the children? I was not sure of my husband's recent state of mind, as I could not guess at it through his inexpressive Chinese letters of grand formality. However, I had no time to speculate. I had to prepare at once to welcome this strange guest from Korea. Taking one of my younger brothers and my two little sons with me to help fetch this fearful present, I went to the station. We had entrance tickets and on the platform we waited half-dazed for the express train to arrive. As usual in an old community like Tokyo, one's circle of acquaintances is large. Thus I met several people whom I knew well and we exchanged greetings. "Is somebody arriving?" they asked me. "Yes, I came to meet . . ." I could hardly say that I had come to meet Mr. Bear of Korea!

Busily and happily, all the passengers left the train after their long journey from the western edge of Japan proper. We were still standing on the deserted platform as if we had missed somebody. "There it is, mother! The bear! The bear!" came a sudden cry. The children had discovered a big wooden cage being carried out from a freight car in the rear. On one side of the cage, a large white square sheet of paper was pasted containing the inscription, "Baron Ishimoto's possession" and beneath this were a few words in smaller letters, saying, "Give him water as soon as he arrives." I was quite embarrassed when the baggage master came up and told me that he had been asked to deliver this unusual cargo by the Shimonoseki station-master who in turn had received instructions from a provincial governor of Korea. This governor, a friend of my husband, had given him the bear. It was not one he himself had hunted in the mountain.

The bear, a large brown one, peering through the iron bars, nodded his head to everyone who was watching him, with the most cheerful manner, as if he felt no fatigue after his long journey. But when I got nearer to it, I was almost stunned by its terrible smiling. My sons were excited and fed him with the pieces of biscuits they had brought from home as a welcome for their new friend, Master Korean Bear. The procession home began. It consisted of a truck and a motorcar. Through the crowded and gay evening streets of Tokyo, it made its way and disbanded at our gate. Our young maids were frightened when they encountered this happy animal and its tremendously dirty smell. That which annoyed me most was the fragile look of the cage which suggested the danger of this wild beast's escaping. So that night I had the bear placed in the dark small barn in the corner of our back yard where we kept our charcoal and firewood, and I wanted to close the door of the barn so that I could sleep safely at least until the next morning. The children were not satisfied with their mother's treatment of the animal, however. Both Arata and Tamio insisted that if we closed the door of the barn so tightly the bear would be uncomfortable in the stuffy air. We must leave the door open, they said. Arata, the elder one, eagerly started to draw a plan for a concrete cage wide enough for the bear to move about freely; he even designed a spare room for the animal to go into while the other part was being cleaned. The children were friendly and trustful toward beasts—universal traits of the young!

Soon the bear had a new cage a little larger and stronger than the former one, but it was not the ideal imagined by the children. I had to tell them that I had no intention of keeping the wild beast around the house so intimately in this crowded city life. When it turned warmer the smell of the animal became almost intolerable and when I tried to clean the cage with a long-handled brush and a hose, the bear took in everything he could catch with his paws, and pulled it into the corner of his cage where he kept his trophies in a heap. He gnawed the hose and pulled it about. His strength was so great and his growling was so fearful that I could not make headway against him. At times he was very amicable and ate well. We fed him cooked rice, potatoes, beans and sweets. He was fond of bananas, oranges and every kind of nuts. The children fed him with their own fresh fruits from the table, while their mother was thrifty and fed him only with leftovers.

When summer came, the bear was less active unless we urged him to move by turning the hose on him twice or three times a day. This took much time and care. I wrote letters to the masters of several zoos and of some circus shows, asking whether they would be interested in adopting this untamed member of our family, but no one was. Once some men came and looked at the animal. "A brown bear? Uninteresting," was their verdict. All others said the same thing: they were not interested unless the animal was of an unusual type. During this time we had to move once, carrying this unwieldy object with us. Finally, after seven months, I succeeded in giving it to one of the small zoos in a country town. I suppose Mr. Korean Bear is still nodding and eating there in the country zoo, delighting other children with his cheerful manner.

My husband's interest in wild animals was as strong as his enthusiasm for a great national policy. It was his delight to hunt wild beasts wherever he happened to be traveling and send home his catch. It was my presumptive delight to take care of them until I could dispose of them courteously. One day I saw the picture of a beautiful pair of wild deer in the Asahi *Graph* beneath which it was stated that these deer were to be an honorable present to a royal prince from Baron Ishimoto. I was frightened, anticipating the care of another set of wild animals when our dear bear had not yet been disposed of, in spite of every effort.

My husband came back home shortly before these deer arrived. The female deer was pretty sick at the end of her long trip by water from the northern border of Korea, on account of the want of exercise and proper food. But the two were elegant creatures as compared with the plebian bear, even if they did require good care. It would be a shame if we failed to present these animals to the prince since the gift had been announced to the public in the *Graph*. My husband left this heavy responsibility entirely to me, and I did not feel equal to the burden.

The male deer was about five feet high and had a pair of horn bags on the top of his head. The female was shorter than her mate, and gentle-looking, with a white and brown dotted skin. Her round black eyes shone beautifully like obsidian jewels. I liked this aristocratic-looking animal with its clean habits much better than our dirty bear. As it was impossible for them to get enough exercise in our narrow garden, we had to close both the front and the back gate once in the morning and once in the afternoon and let the pair race free for a while in the whole enclosure, around the kitchen, in front of our drawing room or behind the closed gate. It might have been splendid to fasten chains on their elegant necks and take them for a walk in the park to start a new fashion, but these animals were too wild to let us get that close to them.

When the children were at home they loved to take care of the deer, but their school hours were so long that they could not attend to the job except on Sundays, so the maids and I had to drive the deer, after the animals had taken daily exercise, into their cage which stood beside the bear's. The female deer was very meek and got into her place easily, but the male rascal ran here and there all around the yard every time his turn came to get back into his cage. He never behaved well. While they were loose, they ate all the leaves from the trees in the garden, both the dead brown leaves on the ground and the green ones on the branches. Finally they bit even the young branches in the wild manner which they had enjoyed in the wilderness of the North Korean mountains. For the sake of their health we had to indulge them, every day adding to the number of bare trees.

While my husband was working to get the royal prince's consent to accept Baron Ishimoto's gift, an approval which had to pass through much red tape and formality, the spring came with every bud and sprout bursting from their long winter sleep. The horn bags of the male deer, which looked like wens, daily grew larger until they were broken and a pair of real antlers appeared, becoming taller and taller and spreading out like beautiful tree branches on his head. As his horns grew the animal became wilder, kicking, jumping, charging right and left, and running after the female deer in a mad way which brought an unspeakable worry and fear to me.

One late afternoon in those windy spring days familiar in Tokyo, as I was about to change my kimono for an outing—above the creaking of glass windows and paper screens which trembled every time the strong wind shook them, I heard the scream of a kitchenmaid, while another one dashed breathlessly into my dressing room. The strong wind blowing against the poor back door of the yard, she said, had weakened the latch of the gate; finally it gave way completely, permitting the male deer to race into the street. While he was giving a fine demonstration of fast running to the city people, the kitchenmaid was dashing after the animal, crying: "Help! Help!"

"Helpless!" I thought. "What shall I do?" The promised gift to the royal prince was running away! The next moment I, too, ran out on the street with my sash half fastened. Men, women, errand boys and children, all stopped to watch this strange sight! The animal fled swiftly until he came to the wide thoroughfare where he saw the tram cars and automobiles rushing by. These must have terrified the country fellow, for he turned back through the narrow street. My faithful young O-shin bravely shouted still: "Help! Everybody on the street!" And she added: "He won't bite you, so help me please!" The people who heard that the animal would not hurt them gathered together and made a human fence as a barrier against the racing deer with its fearful-looking horns. Finally the rascal was caged once more.

When the pair of wild deer were accepted by the prince—a great honor for my husband, of course—I was at least relieved of a great burden. The royal prince took the animals to one of his huge estates. Recently this estate was presented to the City of Tokyo.

XXVI

Escape in the Philosophy of Caricature

*T*HE uptown residential quarter in Tokyo can be very
dead on a winter night. On one such night I was sitting
as usual on a cushion on the mat floor of my room, leaning over
the charcoal fire in the brazier with an open book on my lap.
The children were asleep and the maids had retired to their
rooms. I was looking into the pages of the book, but concentrating all my attention on my ears, that I might not miss the
rumbling sound of my husband's motorcar outside the gate.

"Indeed, I thought it over and over again last night," a
woman was saying in my book, written by Ippei Okamoto,
a popular cartoonist. "Taki-san is a good man, but he makes
me mad by his looseness. If I want to talk to him heart to heart,
he makes fun of the effort and turns it into a mess. If I weep,
he says 'Gosh!' and goes out. Is that the nature of men?"
The woman continued: "Oh, I wish I could meet a man even
once in my life, who would turn his whole heart to me, no
matter how slow or stupid he might be. Am I wishing too
much, wanting to find such a man in this world?" This was
the wife of a sandwich man complaining about her merry
husband.

I turned the pages. An old priest appeared, to chat quietly
with the village lads and women gathered around a fire. To
them he remarked: "The way of Ukiyo—this fleeting world—
is crooked, curved and twisted. If you try to go forward
straight ahead into it, I am sure you will dash your head against
the wall and you will disgust and be disgusted, losing every
bit of charm in life."

The simple and plain speech of the aged country priest led me to investigate further the cartoonist-author's philosophy of life. In its light I began to take stock of myself. I saw myself as a young woman stepping out from the warm guardianship of my mother, under the gentle protection of my father, to sail my boat onward and onward always with a favorable breeze aiding me, until my good luck ended. There I was lost in melancholy and grief. Indeed, I despaired of everything in life: the world seemed twisted round just as the old village priest was saying to his neighbors.

When my broken spirit was floundering in the dark valley of despair, the book of the cartoonist with its delicious drawings and humorous view of life suggested to me a way of escape. It taught me to laugh at life, tease it, smile at it and scold at it too. I had been shown many angles of vision. But here was a perspective revivifying in its freshness and geniality. Now I felt able to cut a path through the marsh of skepticism. I was strengthened again to look at the world with a fresh attitude.

"A striking idea sprang up in my mind," a man says in another story written by the cartoonist-philosopher. "Let's dance! Let's dance! Let us all dance and laugh at our ignorant selves! Yes, let's dance and laugh, putting everything together, business, fortune, happiness, and even gods and Buddhas, putting all together, to dance and laugh! Let's laugh at the whole of life!" A character in this tale who was honestly, simply and seriously suffering in this world of cruel inconsistency, finally turned to folk dancing for relief.

"O. K. Start at once!" a teacher of jolly folk dancing commands his melancholic patient. "Kids and lads who come to me to learn dancing are all like you, being persons with delicate nerves, but possessing a larger worm in the stomach than others which makes them provoked and disgusted (this being a Japanese belief). Let's dance, let's dance happily and merrily."

My uncle, Mr. Yusuke Tsurumi, and myself on Long Island

Mrs. Hiroshi Saito, wife of the Japanese Ambassador, and myself

Addressing the miners at a country theater at Ashio. The posters in the background carry slogans: "Prepare for May Day!" "Birth Control for the Working Women!", etc.

The command fascinated me. I began to dance too. But the woman patient suffering from melancholia did not make her choice of a teacher versed in the rollicking folk dances. She selected one of the prominent masters of the Hanayagi School of Dancing—an old-fashioned art. Hanayagi and Fujima are the two main inherited forms of symbolical rhythm underlying all the dancing and gesturing on the Kabuki stage.

When one begins to study the centuries-old complicated but extremely aesthetic rules behind the Kabuki drama which include formulas for coloring, costuming, singing, the playing of instruments, dancing and making gestures, one is surprised at the infinitely varied phases of this art. A closer and longer study inevitably creates intense enthusiasm for it. I needed to study as well as to dance.

A friend of mine introduced me to Tokutaro Hanayagi, one of the leading teachers of the dance. It was my first peep into this circle of Japanese society. I had been taught the feudal social manners but here was tradition of another kind preserved unchanged for centuries. It bore a close relation to what the Japanese call the "flower and willow society" which I mentioned in connection with the teahouses.

This theater circle stands quite apart from the intellectual circle of present-day Japan, the latter being so much influenced by Western ideas and manners, the former so purely Eastern that I was received almost like a stranger when I called upon the dancing master whose house, nevertheless, was near the main thoroughfare—the Ginza. This being a new adventure on my part I took with me the cultured wife of a well-known businessman of Tokyo. Each of us wrapped a certain sum of money in thick white rice paper, tied it with a red and white cord and under the cord as decoration we slipped a lucky symbol, in the center of which we wrote "a humble cake." This was going to be our offer to the teacher of an entrance fee.

The relation between the dancing master and his pupils

is more feudalistic than I had expected. As a master of the inherited art, the teacher is almighty in the school and pupils are placed in the position of disciples rendering absolute obedience. When I began to study the Kabuki drama, the teacher and his wife, both excellent dancers, had several young men and women living with them. These were their real disciples endeavoring to equal the master. The lessons went on from eight o'clock in the morning till five in the afternoon, every day. There were stepping, gliding and turning all the time on the platform floor, no matter how slowly the depression was lifting in the outside world. Love, nature, animals, birds, ghosts, gods and Buddhas, in a word, everything in the universe was beautifully symbolized on the Kabuki stage.

The disciples who lived with the teacher were bound to him by a contract of practical servitude for a certain length of time, perhaps for three or five years; he, on his part, undertook to make them instructors of this art within that time. Many were sent to him by their parents. They not only learned the art but they did the dusting and cleaning of the house and waited on the master and his guests. Other pupils were mostly geisha girls, both young and mature. A few children of the Kabuki actors were enrolled on the books.

The master, almighty in the dancing house, instructed the pupils in the technique of stage love-making, humming as he did so amorous sonnets of a human warmth not permitted in the rigid family fold. The instruction hall was always packed with gaily dressed, pretty girls interspersed with boys. When one opened the entrance door of the house, one would see on the stone floor of the porch rows and rows of colored wooden clogs, red, brown, and black lacquered, or mat covered, with silk or velvet toe-pieces. The flaunting hues of these might create suspicion about the manners within the school. But everybody behaved quietly and solemnly as if he or she were in some religious temple. The girls never chatted with one another or sat in a relaxed pose while they were waiting for their turn at the lesson; they watched eagerly what others were learning. In the presence of the master, all the students were reverential and, to my surprise, the girls waiting on him were happy to bring him a cup of tea or to fan him, anticipating his smallest desire. The teacher seldom spoke, but always the girls read his mind through his facial expression.

A strict code of etiquette prevailed. If anyone should violate it, he would be immediately expelled from the circle. With the advance of democracy we may lose the advantage of discipline before we have really assimilated the advantage of liberty. And democratic brashness can be observed in many phases of contemporary Japanese life. The menace of social conditions worse than those which marked feudalism is not a thing to be lightly dismissed.

Our teacher wisely guessed that the two new pupils would not have the courage to take their first lesson in the presence of the watchful geisha. So we were asked to wait until the other lessons were over. Then the teacher asked us to stand upon the stage platform. We bowed to him politely again and did as we were bid. We were asked which song we preferred to try as a start. I was confused, for I knew almost no song of this school; my previous life had never allowed me to become acquainted with love sonnets. But how could I say to him that I was there as a miserable patient who was seeking some medicine or treatment to make her life happier?

My dancing-mate was a naturally cheerful little lady, but she was seriously disturbed about the geisha who were stealing so much of her precious husband's time and money. As neither of us could give any proper answer to the teacher, he chose a song for us to start with—"A Dance of Kamuro."

Kamuro were the little girls of six or seven who waited on the grand courtesans in the gay quarters of the Tokugawa days. Their duties consisted of bringing and filling tobacco pipes and fetching other small things to the mistress, who was attended by ten or fifteen of these little girls, as we see on the Kabuki stage depicting that older time. The dancing of a little girl of that age with a battledore and shuttlecock in her hands is utterly innocent and cunning. It sounds simple but in reality it is difficult and interesting enough for a great actor such as Kikugoro VI to perform in the popular theater of our day. Kikugoro, now the greatest Kabuki dancer, who is middle-aged and weighs two hundred pounds, still takes this little girl's part so charmingly that one forgets he is not a real kamuro.

But a lady, five feet and four inches tall, three times bigger than a kamuro should be, struggling with her long limbs to symbolize a little girl of the gay quarters, looked ridiculous beyond measure at the dancing school! She and I could not help laughing and laughing at each other's funny style.

"When I saw my partner on the stage, dressed up in a dandy manner with his front teeth so ill-placed [the reader must realize what ill-placed Japanese teeth look like], I could not help bursting into laughter." I recalled a passage in my cartoon story. And the jolly teacher in the story remarked, scoldingly: "Listen, don't show sensitiveness!" It took me some time to cast off all self-consciousness and try to become a faithful depicter of human life, through the dance.

My friend and I, wiping our faces, necks, arms, perspiring as if we had been in a race, bowed again when our first lesson was over. Before we left the teacher we asked about the fee. He replied, gently: "In our circle we do not sell our art for money. I cannot calculate my art in terms of silver." He still remains aloof from the commercialization of his art. We were so grateful for his instruction, however, that we made up a purse containing more than the average sum bestowed upon him by his pupils.

While I was absorbed in studying this art, gracefully as I

could but energetically, I regained strength and my melancholia lessened. Besides succeeding in my primary purpose, I had mastered a number of stage performances and added to my knowledge of the native culture—a profit and a joy for me.

Although my melancholia was somewhat alleviated by the dispersal of the gloomy cloud in the performance of my dancing, I did not regain true mental happiness while my relation with my husband was dangling in the air. It may have been burdensome to him to have a wife whose disposition was not meek enough to be controlled under an absolute despotism. But apparently in his mind, busily occupied with varied enterprises, with his ancient Oriental attitude of heroism, with his wild interest in animals, his kind of wife had no place. She could not slip into his heart again.

During the later years of this unstable situation, I began to take part in such social activities as the woman suffrage movement, but my mind was more concerned with family problems than with public duties. One day I was invited to go to Kobe to speak about women's enfranchisement, the question being agitated in a lively fashion. I was glad to go on this occasion, because my husband was then just coming back from Korea after spending a severe winter in the heavy snow, struggling with a railroad construction problem. Not only the weather, which had been severe, but the whole condition of his business was unfavorable and he had to return uncomfortable and humiliated. With the deepest sympathy I wanted to welcome him at the station; so after I had finished my talk in Kobe, I waited for his train from the west and met him. An intimate friend of ours, who was then living at Kobe, suggested our going to Arima Hot Springs over the ridge of the Rokko Mountains to rest. I thought it would be a rare occasion for me to talk quietly and honestly with my husband. Our friend kindly led the way to Arima, about two hours' drive from Kobe, up hills and into the mountains. We stopped at a neat-looking Japanese inn. All of us enjoyed the mountain springs and we spent the afternoon together in a cosy little mat room with a tastefully decorated tokonoma in the corner. There was a garden in front of the room and a big magnolia tree with its tightly closed buds casting shadows on the white shoji-screens. A nightingale was singing, hopping from branch to branch on the tree without knowing that we were looking at its shadow from behind the closed shoji. A peaceful atmosphere governed the room.

There on the mat was set a kotatsu (a fire box resting on and covered with thickly-padded silk quilts) to keep our feet warm. A quiet conversation was begun. Our friend surprised me by saying to my husband suddenly:

"Don't you think that Japanese wives are, as a rule, too much neglected by their husbands? I think a man should consider it a duty to open his mind to his wife and consult with her as to what he is going to do in the future or what he is doing at present." My husband was silent. I was killing my breath wondering what this spokesman of my interest was going to say next—the spokesman who voluntarily entered the lists for me without premeditation. "Times have changed," she went on. "No one of us present-day Japanese women will be happy if she is ignored intellectually and expelled from being her husband's mental companion."

"I have a different opinion from yours, my dear madam," my husband replied. "A man likes to keep his ideas and ambitions sacred and solemn in the inner court of his heart. There lies man's heroic conceit. Solitude is the pride of strong men. In the history of our great forefathers, or the ancient Chinese heroes, I have never heard of a single man so despicable as to confide his ambition to his woman! It spoils masculine heroism. It will ruin great enterprises!"

"Oh! no, that's not fair!" The lady was excited. "You treat women without sympathy. You don't understand their problems. You are ignoring woman's intelligence, sensitiveness and even disturbing her heart! If she were ignorant, if she were uneducated, if she had no sense of right judgment, your philosophy might be justified, but I do not think this is the case, baron!" She pressed her argument. I did not utter a word. "It's man's selfishness! Too much egotism. He expects his wife to stand every phase of hardship, as his partner. Men today count on their wives' being intelligent enough to bring up their children, while they neglect to treat their wives as persons. It is customary for wives to co-operate with their husbands to an extent where, with any mishap occurring, the wife is to be blamed equally with the master of the family. And if that is the position woman has to take in our society, naturally she should be trusted to look into every corner of her husband's mental life."

"Please go ahead, my dear woman suffragist! I don't care what other men think or do. I won't follow suit. No, madam, never shall I be weak enough to have to consult a woman!" My husband laughed.

"Oh, dear baron, you are being very narrow-minded," he was told.

"I am sorry that you don't understand the psychology of Oriental men. But, madam, I shall never agree with you or follow your advice on my attitude toward my wife!"

The spring sun vanished quickly behind the shadow of the hills and the room was getting dark. The nightingale had flown away while we were arguing around the fire. Gloom settled over us, and my heart was heavy under the pressure of despair. My friend called a maid to bring in a samisen and she tried to create cheer with her music. But my heart only sank into a depth of sorrow with the realization of a broken love. From the early days of my marriage, I had followed my husband's pace. From humanism to liberalism and realism to radicalism, I continued. And now I had to realize that

I was unable to follow him any farther on his way to Oriental heroism.

I had to determine to give up trying to follow and let my husband go alone on his way with my prayers to a kind providence. This was indeed a tragic conclusion to my married life as it had started with such happiness and enthusiasm. However, it had to be accepted.

With the sorrow of a broken love but with gratitude to the man who had been my guide toward mental maturity, I set out on a path of thought and action—alone.

PART TEN

WHAT BUDDHISM OFFERED

XXVII

Sects and Religious Attitudes

*I*T IS natural for the suffering soul to seek solace in religion. Try as I might to cure my melancholy by dancing and laughing at the humors of life, light diversion proved inadequate. I longed for unbetraying truth and spiritual contentment. If Buddha would but open his benign arms, I felt that I could throw myself upon his infinitely wide and deep bosom and find peace. My heart was being starved by lack of nourishment. In the hope that it might develop harmoniously with my reason, giving new strength for life, I drew nearer to Buddhism.

Up to this time I had been indifferent to religion, like most of the people around me. In the early part of the Tokugawa feudal regime, Christianity was rigorously driven from the Island Empire, because our rulers thought it had brought too much trouble in our politics. And in order to abolish this newly introduced religion they persecuted its devotees, and many Christian martyrs died in Japan. This policy of the Tokugawa shogunate forced every Japanese family to be registered in one or other of the sects of Buddhism, the established national faith. Thus Buddhism entrenched itself in the family system. It remains the pivot of our social system. The Buddhist religion has thus been taken for granted and has evoked very little critical thinking about the soul. Religious rites have been performed punctiliously—not intellectually.

According to our official history, Buddhism came to Japan in the sixth century A. D. And the Japanese people have done with this exotic religion what they have done with everything that has been brought to them from abroad. Buddhism was accepted simply, humbly, in a sincere and almost childlike fashion by the Japanese, but they laid the stamp of their own transforming genius upon it.

It immediately made converts among the mikados and in the royal circle. After many centuries of development under their powerful patronage and with the appearance of great scholars and saints among its priests, Buddhism became Japanized and made definite contributions to the world's religious thought and to its by-product: the arts.

Since the Meiji era, however, with its constitutional guarantee of religious freedom, Japan has been friendly to Christianity and a considerable amount of capital and intense spiritual effort have been expended in missionary work in this "heathen" land. Christian missionaries have succeeded in establishing schools and hospitals. They have several hundred thousand Christians in Japan to their credit. On the other hand, Buddhism, although it is not now an official state religion, has been rooted in Japan for centuries. Approximately 75,000 temples and 150,000 clergy are registered in its books and nearly sixty million adherents profess loyalty to its tenets. Truly so far as religious organization is concerned, Japan is one of the largest Buddhist countries in the world today.

Under the influence of Buddhism, for centuries most of our daily habits and even our racial traits have been molded. Generally speaking, tenacity is not a striking characteristic of the Japanese people and its absence I attribute to Buddhism, which has taught us fatalism. The fatalist view maintains that our present life is the karma of a previous existence, and that the same law of causality will operate for continuous reincarnation, the nature of which will depend on what we do or desire for ourselves now. The concept behind our endeavor to build fine habits and conduct ourselves well is happiness in the next world—not the betterment of the present world. A certain kind of behavior may lead us to reincarnate as cats; another, as monkeys; the dogs barking at our feet may have been princes or even kings, who did not act in ways conducive to a human existence. Fatalism holds that the parent and child relation is limited to this world only, while the husband and wife relation continues to the next world, which will be a shock to some people!

Our present life, as Buddhism visualizes it, is too frail and pitiable to be inspiring. "The Moon is easily overshadowed by clouds, and cherry blossoms are often disturbed by cross winds while in full bloom; thus uncertainty is the rule of our life. . . ." In this fashion we are wont to begin letters of condolence to friends and relatives bowed with grief. I was taught to make this salutation a fixed ritual. This conception of the uncertainty of life coincides with our sensitiveness to all sorts of natural phenomena, certainly a striking characteristic of the Japanese!

Japanese Buddhism has had tremendous influence on the whole nation. There were periods in its history when that influence was invigorating. But after being protected by the Tokugawa government as part of its state policy, Buddhism became decadent. Flattering the powerful, through Confucian accretions Japanese Buddhism grew formalistic, preaching only conventional virtues, forgetting its original role as a critical philosophy of behavior and a profound philosophy of the universe.

So its priests have for some time been emphasizing in Japan the negative virtues, such as endurance, self-repression, restraint—a code of resignation and subjection which offers nothing but sadness for the soul. My mother declares that she does not like the smell of incense or joss sticks; that it makes her gloomy. Many people have the same feeling, indicating the true effect of Buddhism on the human spirit, however expressionless the Japanese face may appear.

Buddhist teachers have had very little to say about the problems of the practical world. They do not touch individual life

and thought in that relation. They betray no positive understanding of love between man and woman. On the contrary,
they belittle woman by insisting that it is as hard for the woman
to become a Buddha as it is for a rich man to enter the Christian
heaven. Buddhism upholds the following doctrine: (1) that
life is pain; (2) that the law of predestination rules three worlds:
one's pre-existence which, if unfortunate or evil, causes the
present existence to be full of trouble, and the future existence
will be determined by the present one; (3) that constant effort
should be made to accumulate good traits for the sake of a
better life in the next incarnation; (4) the cause of sorrow is
desire; so long as one has endless worldly aspirations there is
an everlasting struggle leading nowhere.

Though they may be superficial in so interpreting Buddhism, the Japanese take the doctrine at its face value. They
revere the images of Buddha; they send contributions to the
temples and priests; they try to be benevolent even if only
on a small scale. A calculating person may donate money to
temples when he gets old, asking that favorable prayers be
offered for his salvation in the Pure Land to which he cannot
carry his purse. The poor offer their manual labor to temples and
the public works connected with them, believing that Buddha
will recognize their humble devotion expressed in this way.

This low general level of Buddhist instruction has irritated
the intellectual Japanese and the preaching of the Buddhist
priests has lost its dignity for them. The modern generation has
largely outgrown the influence of this gospel in its old form.
Recently there have arisen new Buddhist movements imitating
the propagandistic measures of Christian enterprises, sending
missionaries and social workers all over the world on the tide
of the Pan-Asiatic movement. This new Japanese Buddhism
reveals innovations in doctrine, such as the righteousness of sex
equality. It is building its temples in modern-style architecture
with Otis elevators to carry the bronze images of Buddha. Its

leaders preside over Pan-Pacific Buddhist conferences. It has the semblance of an attempt to introduce Americanism into Buddhism, by destroying the ancient charm of quietness common to all Oriental religions and introducing the nervous rush and uproar more characteristic of Occidental faiths. But its future is still in doubt. How far it can go in this direction and how much social leadership it can exercise remain problematical.

On the other hand, religious lethargy has been more and more noticeable among the Japanese during recent decades. There are those who see no inconsistency in marrying and vowing loyalty to the spirit of General Nogi at the Nogi Shrine in Tokyo—formerly the residence of the heroic general, and now a popular place for wedding ceremonies—and burying their dead according to the Buddhist sutra, chanting and burning incense. But the conquest of spiritual matters by the almighty force of modern science has created a new trend of thought among the intellectual Japanese, away from any sort of traditional religious formality. This may be illustrated in the will of my uncle who ordered that his funeral ceremony be performed in an airplane entirely apart from sutras and incense vapors.

This uncle, who passed away a few years ago, was an electrical engineer and had been president of one of the government technical schools. His will stated that there should be no religious rites at his death, no gravestone to mark his burial place; his body was to be cremated in a modern manner and his ashes scattered in the air from a plane. His widow and sons were willing to carry out the funeral according to the will; but the police objected, saying that there was no precedent and that it would bring confusion in police regulations if many people began to follow this strange fashion. So my uncle's will was not fully executed, but the box containing his ashes was carried into the sky on an airplane and was tossed overboard to land at the center of the schoolground, amid the cheers of his students. Though my uncle had desired that the clouds of mystery and divinity surrounding the dead be dispersed by his attitude, his wife sorrowfully complains to us that she has no temple or graveyard to which she can take flowers in memory of her husband. She is released, however, from the trouble of repeating the complicated anniversary memorial service for the dead! I did not approve my uncle's revolutionary funeral arrangement, for I felt sympathetic with his wife who was denied the opportunity of experiencing the spiritual significance of his death while the airplane roared his farewell.

Too swift a modernization of Japan and the Japanese may be a danger. In planning modern cities, for instance, there is the temptation to abhor avenues of fine old cherry and pine trees and destroy the arch-shaped classical bridges—simply to do something new. The beauty of many old things would be charming even in modernized towns.

Viewing religion from this angle, though there are many aspects of Buddhism with which I am not sympathetic, it has an appeal for me, just as one loves to keep an old and cherished habit even though it may be a useless one. My husband taught me to read the Bible of the Christians in the early days of our married life, but it gave me the feeling of reading a book of alien sentiments and I always missed something there.

My uncles seemed to make a great point of their funerals. Another and younger one had a Christian burial. He had been consul general in one of the cities of the United States. Called back from this post, he was ill in bed for a whole year. While he was prostrate at Kamakura, his wife succeeded in converting her dying husband to Christianity, and a minister was asked to baptize him shortly before his death. So my uncle's spirit found a place in the Christian heaven. His funeral took place in a church so simple as to resemble a barrack; a young minister presided over the ceremony, reciting prayers in the modern Japanese language, the words sounding uncouth in their direct transliteration from the English Christian vocabulary. A harsh

My sisters and myself at our father's home in 1927.
Kiyo (center) is wearing her wedding robe

*Myself in the fifteenth century dance costume
of the famous Kabuki theater*

air reigned in the crude church. Such imagery as the "Good Shepherd," "lamb" and "green pastures" were utterly incomprehensible to the Japanese mourners who had never seen sheep except in the zoo. There was no sweet and solemn emotion such as springs from ceremonies in our historical temples of Buddha or in the Christian cathedrals of the West.

This miserable service made me realize the weakness of words. I recalled the high solemnity of my grandfather's funeral, which was performed in an old Zen-sect temple in Tokyo. How impressed I was by the sight of the noble-looking priests in their robes of gorgeous silk brocade indicating high ecclesiastical dignity, followed by rows and rows of other priests in purples, greens, browns and yellows, each in a different costume glittering with silver and gold, advancing slowly and softly in snow-white tabi-socks over the tan mat floor of the temple hall! They moved with measured steps, according to the formalities of the rite, reciting numbers of Sanskrit sutras in unison to the accompaniment of various holy instruments. I looked once more at my grandfather's coffin at the north side center of the hall, decorated with numerous artificial lotus blossoms of gold, silver and white, all enveloped in thick vapors of burning incense. The tall gilt image of Shakyamuni on the dark altar gazed down benignly on the coffin and with magnificent gestures the priests handed over the dead to the merciful Buddha. The sutra chanting lasted long and no lay person understood what it meant at all, but I never tired of this grand performance which certainly elevated the mind and soul as one knelt in silent prayer for the friendly acceptance of the departed spirit into Buddha's Land.

In his book, *The Pilgrimage of Buddhism,* J. B. Pratt discusses the mysterious power of language, pointing out that one's speech may obstruct the meaning of one's own soul. For the human being is more than any of his verbal assertions. In this sense the Protestant prayers loudly uttered in church are like the puerilities of schoolchildren in the classroom. "It is this essential inadequacy of language to the inner life which explains the very real advantage which a foreign and sacred tongue so often possesses in the expression of religious emotion." I fully agree. Pratt says, again, that "reverent sounds, which are to the worshiper both less and more than words, do not compel him to sign on any dotted line or to confine his meaning to any stable proposition. They suggest but do not hide. They are like music." From my uncle's Protestant Christian funeral, we were finally rescued by an *Ave Maria* played on a violin, an instrument which my uncle cherished to the last moment of his life. A celebrated woman musician added this fine touch.

My search for a satisfying temple took some time. There are in Tokyo many temples with holy-looking priests, but none of them caught my heart at once. I love the old Zen-sect temple, in whose graveyard the ashes of my ancestors lie peacefully under the ancient trees. Its priests are impressive at funerals or Bon festivals, but they failed to convince me that they were my spiritual guides. My mother's family temple, to which I occasionally go to visit my grandparents' graves, is tended by young and old nuns clad in black robes and bonnets that impart charm and grace to their small shaved heads. But they look too delicately simple for me to put before them such a problem as the salvation of one's soul.

As a member of the Ishimoto family, I am supposed to belong to a temple of Jodo-shu (Pure Land sect) at Hakusan, Tokyo, but I have regarded that temple and its priests as a part merely of family business affairs, requiring our regular contributions at the middle and the end of each year, and on occasions such as the anniversaries of our departed relatives. Beyond that business relation, I have had nothing to do with the clergy of the temple. The head priest is a modest middle-aged gentleman. At the seventh-day ceremony of my late mother-in-law, he offered to Buddha a big round tub of living loaches wriggling and twisting their small snakelike bodies in the water. While he chanted the sutras he scattered white and pink artificial lotus petals all over the temple hall. The offering of living loaches meant that, after the ceremony was over, when the live creatures were turned loose in a river human mercy toward every living thing, such as birds, fish and even insects would be demonstrated; that Buddha would be pleased; and that the salvation of the newly departed spirit would be assured. I do not know what the scattering of lotus blossoms signified, but it added to the picturesqueness of the ceremony, which was very elegant if artificial. Undoubtedly one function of the clergy as professionals is to sell the Buddhist ceremony to the satisfaction of their customers who desire different formalities on different occasions.

This Pure Land sect to which my husband's family belongs is unlike my own family's Zen sect. While a rigorous practice of stoicism is preserved in the latter, the former is very worldly. Honen Shonin, the founder of the Pure Land cult, recognized the human nature of the priesthood, permitting them to marry and to eat meat and fish; whereas in the Zen temples no women, no meat, and in some of them no alcohol even, is allowed. I love the clean atmosphere of a Zen temple where the great priests are really men of high culture and profound scholastic attainments; in the Pure Land sect, on the contrary, the priest-hood is usually an inherited family profession and I have often seen baby clothes hanging in rows behind its temple and young and old women chattering in the priest's residential quarter behind the altar room.

There is no assertion of subtle individual faith in any of the Japanese religions. A Japanese woman, born in a family which belongs to the Zen sect and married to a family belonging to the Pure Land sect, has naturally to follow her husband's family religion, never thinking faith a personal issue. There is no such complication for her as in the case of a Catholic girl married to a Protestant man.

The Pure Land sect is one of the six largest among more than a dozen Japanese Buddhist sects now in existence. Honen Shonin, not satisfied with the mere ascetic teaching of Buddhism, founded it in 1175. His beloved disciple, Shinran, then started his own sect called Jodo-Shin-shu. These two together are called the Amida sect; it believes in salvation through the grace of Amida given freely to all who have faith in him—an analogy to "Our Heavenly Father" in Christianity. The ritual of the Amida cult is simple and emotional. One has only to repeat the name of Amida, "Namu Amida, Namu Amida, Nammamida, Nammamida, Namu Amida Butsu . . ." with all one's heart, whether walking or standing, whether sitting or lying down. But there must be no cessation of the practice for, as the founder of the sect said, these words must be recited almost breathlessly. Honen and Shinran, the founders of these two branches of the Amida sect, stressed the point that faith means complete trust in Amida—a doctrine similar to that advanced by St. Paul and Martin Luther. "By grace are ye saved through faith; and that not of yourselves; it is the gift of God."

Faith, which means complete trust in either Buddha or God and renunciation of self-help, may be fascinating to religiously-minded persons, but it is difficult for the logical-minded. The way of salvation shall be given even to the ignorant or the sinful if they merely repeat "Namu Amidabutsu." This is naturally an attractive gospel and there are, it is said, more than twenty-six million Japanese chanting "Namu Amida. . ." almost instinctively. The sect has nearly thirty thousand temples and fifty thousand professional clergymen. It is the greatest religious force in Japanese society today.

If not keenly logical myself, I aspired to find a logical faith. My quest continued.

XXVIII

Meditation in the Zen Temple

If you wish to seek Buddha,
You must search your own nature;
For this nature is Buddha himself.
It is like water and ice,
There is no ice, apart from water,
There is no Buddha, apart from yourself.

If you have not seen into your own nature,
What is the use of thinking of Buddha,
Reciting the sutras, observing a fast, or keeping the precepts?
Not knowing that Buddha is near you,
Foolish to seek him afar;
Like the cry of thirst, in the midst of water;
Like wandering in a slum, being born in abundance.

Hundred causes of your trouble come only
Through your mistake, trying to bow to external objects:
Wandering, lingering, complaining.
There is no end of sorrow in your journey in darkness,
If you let light into your mind, Pure Land is not far from you.
The mind is Buddha, Buddha is the way, and the way is Zen.

If you see the Truth is here,
Your voice is the chanting of the sutras,
This place is the Land of Lotus,
You Yourself are Buddha![1]

[1] The above is the translation of one of the masses in the Zen temple, which I try to put into English according to its meaning and not literally.

"AM I BUDDHA?" "Yes, you yourself are Buddha!" The sutras in Sanskrit chanted in unison sounded like music to my ears, but the one translated above is sung in the native tongue and so remained longer in my mind, setting themes for meditation. My mental helplessness brought me at last to one of the Zen temples, for I could not surrender to Amida who asked me to resign myself completely to the Great One's strength. The religion or philosophy which arrested my attention was one which challenged my own strength.

The Zen sect of Buddhism was introduced to Japan from China late in the twelfth century, and a division in this sect was brought about early in the thirteenth century. Zen stresses the development of the individual spiritual life, and this has appealed especially to the samurai class. In the aristocratic days before the Meiji restoration, Zen was chiefly the church of the samurai—the intelligentsia of those days—and its adherents to-day are largely the descendants of the old samurai families. We now have over twenty thousand Zen temples in Japan with thirty-five thousand Zen monks, and more than eight million lay adherents. The Zen sect is one of the most influential in Japanese Buddhism. It stands second only to the Pure Land, or Amida, sect. However, the figures for adherents cannot be taken as an accurate measurement of the influence of any religion in Japan at the present time; they are not obtained in any precise way. A count is made of the persons whose families were listed in the different Buddhist sects under the command of the Tokugawa government. As I have explained before, I was born a member of a Zen-sect family and married into the Pure Land sect. Nominally I was first a member of one sect and then of another, but until these later years, when I began to take religion seriously as my own spiritual matter, I had given no consideration to the streams of thought in Buddhism— to the teaching of self-strength or the teaching of reliance on another's strength as the means of salvation. Of what sect, then, was I actually an adherent?

Now, however, I became deeply interested. The profound teachings of Zenism are said to be very simple in form. But "simple" is not always the synonym for "easy." Zenism is the philosophy of "Thisness," signifying self-examination. Shakyamuni, according to Zen teachers, never preached a word about "Thatness" during his exhortatory career of forty-five years. Dharma (Bokhidharma), the powerful Hindu teacher of Zen who went into China, floating, so the legend says, down the Yangtze River on a reed (one of the favorite subjects in Buddhist painting), appeared before the Emperor Wu, of the Liang dynasty, in 520 A. D. The Emperor was a munificent patron of Buddhism, and the conversation between the great teacher of Zen Buddhism and the Chinese Emperor is one of the popular subjects in the Zen philosophy text books.

The Emperor asked: "You will be interested to hear that I have built many monasteries, distributed scriptures, given alms, and upheld the faith. Have I not indeed acquired merit?" "None at all," Dharma answered, betraying the Emperor's expectation. "In what, then, does true merit consist?" asked the Emperor. The Dharma answered that in the obliteration of Matter through Absolute Knowledge, not by external acts, lay true merit. Dharma is said to have sat in silent meditation for nine years with his face turned to the wall, wrapped in red cloth, in his mountain monastery, and the Japanese children sing: "Dear Dharma-san has no legs, tightly closed lips, and large shining eyes. . ." What Dharma declared on his first opening of the tightly closed lips after nine years of za-zen, was this: "Above and below the Heaven, the Truth is here in one's self."

Za-zen is a method of obtaining spiritual power by controlling physiological movement. That is, it is organic feeling —a balanced relation between mind and body. To reach the psychological goal a certain form of meditation is necessary.

Half sleeping, half awake, like one insensate and yet trying hard to think, in the Tokai-ji Temple, I began practicing za-zen in the meditation hall. The chilly air in late January seemed to kill every germ in the air, under the ground and in the water; and to purify the human soul likewise. Dead silence was maintained by everyone within the temple room. About thirty men and a few women were my companions.

I was able to sit in the same posture more than half an hour without moving or uttering a sound, though this was a short duration of time compared with the famous meditation of Dharma. I drew my breath through my nose deep enough to hold down my abdomen, and sent it forth slowly and quietly, repeating the process in a rhythmic tempo. Faithfully I tried to hold my breath while I counted from one to ten and, after ten, breathing; then began from one again, repeating the process over and over, endeavoring to concentrate my mind on this thing. My lips were tightly closed like divine Dharma's; my tongue pressed against the roof of my mouth. Like the people around me, I sat on a rough hard cushion in a squatting position. All the time, I kept my body erect so that the tip of my nose and my navel should be in one perpendicular line, and my ears and shoulders on a horizontal line. I crossed my legs in front, putting my feet on opposite thighs. My hands rested lightly in my lap.

As I kept my eyes half open during the whole period of meditation, I could see only four or five feet ahead of me. On the dark mat floor of the hall the flickering candle-light cast faint shadows. There were only four or five candle stands in this spacious meditation place, which scarcely gave enough light for the two young barefooted monks to move about stealthily on the icy-cold mats. Each of them held a bamboo club five feet long with which he tapped those who had fallen asleep when they were supposed to be practicing the art of putting their mind in a vacant condition, sinking themselves willfully into the universe; giving up every attempt at self-guidance; letting the subconscious forces control. Though this emptiness of the mind which is sought in za-zen is far from unconsciousness or sleep, many of the practitioners do lose consciousness.

To practice the evacuation of one's mind must be queer enough to the Westerner. It is queer to the Japanese of the sects as well. But Zen teachers go further; they believe that the mere sitting and practicing of meditation does not produce the spiritual capacity to create the unity of thinking that any human being possesses as a personality. So in order to attain this purpose the pupils are given "koan," or problems, designed for unified thought. It is said that there are something like seventeen hundred koan in Zenism, and every one of them is a surprise to the uninitiated. They puzzle the pupils of Zen to the highest possible degree. They induce the direct opposite of logical argument or a scientific solution.

Those pupils who are interested and enthusiastic enough are assigned Zen problems for solutions. One usually struggles with a single problem week after week—or months and even years—whether awake or asleep. If the answer which he brings to the abbot is wrong and he fails to pass the examination, he has to keep on thinking about the same problem until he finally works it out. Often the teacher beats the pupil who is too stupid to answer correctly. The external words spoken are not very important. The teacher judges his pupil's victory by his face, manner, or perhaps by his footsteps as he approaches through the long corridor from the meditation hall to the examination room. I was afraid that I could not find a proper solution to any of these queer problems and that I might be beaten every time I appeared in the presence of the abbot. I did not have courage enough to advance to that step of Zen. But I learned what the koan are and what solutions and explanations are set forth in the books of Zen philosophy. This was very interesting and helpful in my study of this cult.

It would be fruitless to attempt to explain here the contents of koan problems and their answers, because their meaning depends so much on the original Chinese words and characters, as well as on the habits and manners of Zen living, and it is impossible to transfuse them into any other language. However, many college students and other intellectual Japanese are struggling with them, simultaneously with their efforts to pass college examinations or carry on the business of daily life!

The outstanding character of the Zen sect is the stress placed on experience and on life itself; cult, theory and learning are secondary. The koan problems are based chiefly on the endless series of anecdotes recording the minutest happenings in the lives of famous Zen monks and their trivial sayings. But from the Zen point of view, behind these trifling acts and sayings lies a deep significance. The pupil in struggling with these problems is supposed to obtain the mental power which was once possessed by the ancient Zen masters. "Fire is cool, if one denies the mind's consciousness." Thus declared Ezan, the distinguished Zen divine; in the sixteenth century he was burnt in his temple by General Nobunaga who destroyed hundreds of religious edifices to eliminate the political influence of Buddhism at that time.

One is able to gain the Zen mental strength by constant drill, just as one obtains physical strength by continuous discipline of one's body. The koan is often a question full of apparent inconsistencies or it is planned to lead one's thinking into the trap of inconsistency. If one's knowledge is limited to plain common sense learning, one repeatedly faces sudden irrationalities in practical affairs without preparation from orthodox religious teachers. It is a pity, the Zen teachers say, for one to be caught in this immense illogical maze unable to cut his way through with his limited knowledge. So Zen furnishes the mental practice as a result of which one may free himself from confusion and despair.

Reading such an abstract explanation of this queer za-zen may even put my readers to sleep. But I know what it means to try to ward off the sleepy devils while I am struggling to find the Buddha myself. In spite of my hard drill in za-zen during the severe winter nights, I did not accomplish very much. On the contrary, I detected a peculiar brusquerie and cynicism in most of the Zen practitioners, which may be the result of denying the reality of the world too much and playing to excess with abstractions, for one cannot live wholly out of society. I found myself not quite contented with Zen and I left the temple in the late spring when the peony blossoms were in full flower everywhere in the temple court and around the gray gravestones. Nevertheless, I retain a warm, lingering affection for this sect, whose quiet atmosphere is very dear to me.

XXIX

Nichiren, the Sun-Lotus

THOUGH I did not go much further in Zen philosophy, I gained a certain mental strength with which to overcome my restlessness and the ill state of my nerves, caused by leading an active life like many people of the present age, a life of rush and struggle in the midst of various anxieties. A certain serenity of mind I have since acquired, and I must attribute a great deal of it to the teachings and meditations in the Zen temple.

I grew to believe, however, that Zenism is a sort of cowardly attitude to life whose solid realities it purposely overlooks. The spirit of Zenism has not, of course, always been a negative and cynical thing in relation to actual life. There have been divines who were men of action as well as spiritual force. But Zenism has often been abused and it has been bent, to a great extent, in a wrong direction. I observe most of the people who are absorbed in this religion toying with mere metaphysical arguments, cynically and lazily pretending to be indifferent to contemporary social problems. I could not find one bit of happiness for myself if the ultimate happiness of mankind were out of the picture. And this excluded me from strict Zenism.

On my religious pilgrimages I reached the goal of spiritual enlightenment, not in Mecca nor in India, under the bo-tree in Buddha's Nirvana, but on the dusty bookshelves of my husband's library. There I found many works on the sect which was founded in the thirteenth century by Nichiren, whose name is a synonym for brave action related to ideals.

"I am Jo-ko Bosatsu! I am here to preach the gospel of the Lotus Sutra! Shyaka himself prophesied my coming. I am here, and shall be the great eyes to the Land of the Rising Sun!" So the prophet Nichiren spoke (the literal translation of his name is Sun-Lotus). He was born the son of a fisherman in a village not far from Tokyo. His mother dreamed of this child as the product of a sun's ray shooting into her body, the kind of legend behind the birth of every great religious leader. Being an unusually clever boy, he was sent to a temple near his village, in those days the only place for one to obtain knowledge. While he studied in this local temple, his clever questions and profound eagerness for the further study of Buddhism led the elder priests to send this young monk to the Tendai Monastery on Mount Hi-ei near Kyoto, which contained at that time a wonderful university for Buddhist students as well as the great cathedral of the Tendai sect. After many years' study and meditation he came to his enlightened conviction through the gospel of the Lotus Sutra, and all through his life he fought for this gospel, bringing on a revolution in Japanese Buddhism. In his later years he set a firm foundation for the Nichiren sect which still remains quite an active one among the Buddhists, though it is a pretty noisy religion on account of its mass processions with the vigorous beating of drums and the chanting of "Naum Holy Lotus Sutra!" Nichiren's fiery devotion to his faith and his effort to live in accordance with his ideals were rare in the history of Japanese Buddhism. While Japanese history is replete with feudal heroes, there have been few comparable religious heroes.

If Zen is the religion of solitude, an argument for nihilism, Nichiren is the religion of social righteousness requiring action under persecution and every difficulty. It is aggressive against social injustice. It is the only sect of Japanese Buddhism which declares the unfairness of ranking women below men. Nichiren's affection for his mother made him resent the point of view so generally held by Buddhists that womankind is sinful and unworthy of salvation.

In opposition, he declared: "Man is pillar and woman is frame; man is wing and woman is body; if the wing is separated from the body, how can it fly?" However, my interest in Nichiren is not in its doctrines as a cult, but in Nichiren himself. As in the case of many other great religious leaders, there are many miraculous stories told of him; these do not affect me. Their origin often may be traced to the zealous imagination of his followers, who make their master a superhuman being and thus spoil his real value as a person. My interest in Nichiren has to do with his spiritual strength and the courage which never failed him even when faced with the threat of death.

After many years of study and pilgrimages to the great divines of his age, Nichiren finally stood forth as an independent Prophet. He appeared alone on the streets of Kamakura, the capital during the Hojo feudal regime. Nichiren openly denied Jodo, Zen, Titsu and Shingon, the sects which did not preach the Lotus Sutra. He was alone. The rulers and the whole nation were against him. When he cried out, "Heaven and the four seas will come under this holy Lotus Sutra!" the people shouted, "Hey! this crazy monk!" They threw stones at him and burned his hut to drive him away.

"For shame!" the leaders of other sects declared. "Don't leave this insane monk free to preach on the streets and insult the whole of Buddhism!" They were enraged and appealed to the shogunate to suppress the insolent fellow. He was exiled and deserted on a small rocky island in the sea. Nearby, however, was a fisherman's hamlet and soon he was taken there by its humble and warm-hearted folk. His banishment gave Nichiren a chance to preach his gospel among these simple people and he made new converts. After that, whenever he was compelled to wander, he added to the number of his followers and was the more confirmed in his own conviction by their response to his preaching.

After he was recalled to Kamakura from his exile, he wrote his famous *Discourse on Social Righteousness and National Defense,* and dedicated it to the shogunate. He denounced the shogunate's policy and prophesied the foreign invasion which occurred a few years later when Kubla Khan, the great chief of the Mongols and the Emperor of all China, sent his fleet to conquer this little island empire at the end of the thirteenth century. At that time Japan was in a state of economic and social confusion, distraught by frequent earthquakes and famines. And to the shogunate this accurate forecast by Nichiren was but an added insult, making Nichiren a supernuisance. Accepting his enemy's accusation of him, the government imprisoned this Lotus Sutra prophet and finally sentenced him to death on the charge of treason.

His reply was: "Nichiren, being born on this land, shall obey its law physically, but shall never succumb to this command spiritually." He then turned to his followers and commanded them as follows: "Do not any of you be coward enough to deny that he is a disciple of Nichiren! Do not be drawn back from your faith for the sake of your estate or family! In the infinite space of time in the past, the number of those who dedicated their lives for the sake of the feudal lord, or of the family, has been innumerable like the sands on the shore, but a single life has not yet been dedicated to the honor of Lotus Sutra! Do not hesitate to be the honorable soldier for this Holy Gospel! To dedicate our humble lives for the sake of Lotus Sutra is like exchanging a stone for a mass of gold, dung for rice! If you fear the threat of the mere master of this small island state, how can you prepare yourself to stand in the presence of Great Emma, the mighty lord of hell! Having sworn to serve Buddha, timid servants are worthless! What is the significance of life and death to you? There is only life and death in the truth of the Holy Sutra of Lotus!" What spiritual force! What conviction! Sneering at earthly power, which ordered him to die, he described his persecutor as a mere master of little islands!

Nichiren faced death as calmly as if he were facing home. With a volume of the Lotus Sutra in his hand, he was led to the place of execution on the sandy Kamakura shore. The brave preacher chanted the Sutra loudly as he sat on the seat of death. He was fifty years old at the time. The autumn moon was casting her pale light on the silently grieving disciples who had assembled for the last earthly look at their great teacher. But Nichiren's chanting voice alone echoed in the whole place against the silver tide flowing and ebbing.

The warriors whose duty it was to cut off this holy prophet's head were almost paralyzed by the sight of their undaunted victim, whose spiritual force so inspired them that it was scarcely possible for them to raise their swords against him. After having struggled in vain to do so, they finally knelt down before Nichiren and confessed how deeply they were impressed. Just then a horseman arrived to deliver a message from the authorities announcing the release of Nichiren from the penalty of death. He was again exiled, however, to a remote island in the rough Sea of Japan far north of Japan proper. It was like deportation to the icy wilderness of Siberia.

The snowy winter had already come to this northern island of Sado when Nichiren arrived. The shogunate authorities, who were afraid of killing this prophet with their own hands, planned to let him die alone in the cold of the northern snow and the bitterness of hunger. A wretched hut six feet square in the Tsukahara valley was his only permitted shelter. In this tiny hut he lifted a small image of Buddha from the bosom of his torn robe and began his holy chanting of "Nam-Myo-Ho-Ren-Gekyo, Nam Holy Lotus Sutra." The snowflakes fell on the earthen floor and heaped on Nichiren's lap, covering the image of Buddha. He passed nights protected merely by a straw hat and a grass raincoat. When the snow got deeper and heavier, Nichiren's meals, which were supposed to be brought from the neighboring village, were cut off. Many days in the snowbound valley he did not eat. Yet he never worried about his food; nor was he ever afraid to die for the sake of his faith. His voice, chanting the Sutra, was never silenced.

The man Nichiren, who with steadfast faith and conviction always pushed ahead in the promotion of his cause, moved me the most of all religious forces. My husband himself was not unlike a Nichiren disciple in sacrificing his family—not for the sake of the Lotus Sutra but in action through a faith in the national policy which he considered as holy and important as the Sutra. But alas! his wife, who had been brought up in well-to-do circumstances, naturally, like every wife suddenly cast into the wilderness of economic insecurity, was worrying terribly about financial reverses. However, since I was deeply inspired by the spiritual power of Nichiren, who feared neither hunger nor death, who never worried about shelter or clothing, I reached a wonderful calmness of mind, never to be disturbed again by uncertainty, grief, anger or momentary pleasure.

The calmness of my mind is, I should say, an attainment not to be explained to others by words, as many teachers of the Buddhist philosophy would agree. Satori is the Japanese word which indicates a special state of enlightened rest. This satori, the teachers say, may be defined as an intuitive looking into the nature of things, in contradistinction to the intellectual and logical understanding of life. Modern science maintains that man should always be protected with proper shelter and food to keep him in good health. So-called civilized people are driving themselves into more entanglements by analyzing every element contained in the daily diet and clamoring for specific calories. But my enlightenment came when I saw something, —which I cannot explain by the logical process,—when I responded to the life of Nichiren. The teachers explain this process as the unfolding of a new world hitherto unperceived in the confusion of a dualistic mind. Or we may say that with satori our entire surroundings are viewed from quite an unexpected angle of perception. In the midst of financial problems, I could now take a deep breath as if under the shining spring sun.

The teachers explain that, whatever the satori is, the world for those who have gained a satori is no more the world as it used to be; even with all its flowing streams and burning fires, it is never again the same. Satori is a revolution—a revaluation of the spiritual aspect of one's existence. This change of mind came to me, not through my hard practice of za-zen meditation, but as the balance sheet or gross sum of my years' hard thinking and labor, and the various experiences of my early life. Indeed, it is a pagoda to celebrate my triumph over my serious mental conflicts. Hereafter I shall be able to carry my message forward with *never defeatable courage* and conviction though the road be of thorns!

PART ELEVEN
THE FEMINIST FRONT IN JAPAN

XXX

My Relation to Feminism

"MAN and Woman complete a human being. Both sexes supplement each other," Kant declared. Could there be anything in fact less applicable to Japanese humanity than this statement? The Japanese women are toys to be petted by men; slaves to be driven by owners. Their awakening and self-development do not please men. The relationship between man and wife in a Japanese home is not that of two supplementary personalities, but that of master and servant. It is the relation between the absolute possessor and the property. Indeed, in the presence of others a Japanese wife refers to her husband usually with the term "master," and is called by him something like "sirrah!"

Naturally when this human property goes out from home to work, she has to assume a position of independence quite contradictory with that of slavery. Various stimuli she receives in the course of her public life necessarily train her personality and cultivate her intelligence. Thus she may develop into a new being while her husband remains as he was. So long as the husband fails to understand and trust his wife in the changed circumstances, the contradiction between home life and her public activities will never be resolved.

Trying to resolve that conflict by sacrificing public life, I adopted a stoical attitude for a while. This was a time of inner enrichment. I lived quietly. I read and I thought about life as a whole. Even later when I made an effort to laugh at life and dance away my grief, questions pertaining to the social system, woman's position and the relationship between woman and the industrial system still haunted me. In an effort to answer them, I tried to form a theory of my own. First of all I studied the history of Japanese women for more knowledge of changes in their surroundings through the ages. Then I read over and over August Bebel's book on the history of women in general. To this I owe the greater part of my birth control theory, especially the thesis that it could be the agency of woman's emancipation.

The Neo-Malthusian doctrine had hitherto attracted me to birth control. Nor do I now deny the general adequacy of this doctrine in relating population problems to birth control problems in a capitalistic era, but I cannot now agree with its unconditional assent to the fatal assumptions made by Malthus, who for one thing ignored the creative power of science and the cultural growth of mankind. I was never fully satisfied with the Malthusian doctrine even while I was upholding it. And a re-examination of *An Essay on the Principle of Population* was a revelation of errors.

Next I studied *The Philosophy of the Poor* by Karl Marx, a theoretical opponent of birth control in that he makes the class war the key to emancipation and well-being. Given a "just" distribution of wealth, he maintains, more of mankind could survive on a comfortable basis and be infinitely happier. Marx's theory is that it is the development of capitalism which drives laborers and peasants into extreme poverty and his theory seems to find convincing proof in Japan as elsewhere. My intimate contact with the poor in the mining districts of my country had opened my mind to the social evil of poverty. Its prevention was a major consideration with me, as a fundamental of human development irrespective of sex. Convinced though I was of the value of birth control as a means of emancipating women, protecting motherhood and establishing good eugenic practices, after reading Marx I decided that I had been too narrow in concentrating on its advantages for a single sex. I likewise came to the conclusion that even with a larger acceptance of this agency, the problem of poverty would probably remain. So I became less feministic in a bourgeois way and more humane in my thinking.

This does not mean that my interest in birth control as a method of liberating women from masculine subjection weakened. Or that the feminist movement in Japan lost my allegiance, for the very existence of such a movement is evidence of the need.

Two streams form the Japanese feminist movement: the middle-class struggle for equality with men and the proletarian struggle for class equality. Bourgeois feminism accepts the present capitalistic social order, and within the boundary of its operations attempts to lift the position of Japanese women to the standard set by the most advanced Western women. Proletarian feminism is on a more rebellious basis; it denies both the justice and the excellence of the present social system, and calls for socialism.

The bourgeois feminists fought, and are still fighting, though greatly hampered, for the elevation of women's position in connection with legal rights. Their demands include:

(*a*) The abolition of the restrictions imposed by civil law on the married woman's conduct. For instance, a wife can enter into a legal contract only with her husband's consent. She is thus in the position of a minor who must have the approval of the parental authority for any legal procedure. If she fails to get the necessary consent from her husband, the contract is not valid. The unmarried woman over twenty, legally possessing full contractual rights, loses them the moment she marries. Too obviously our law denies a married woman's personality.

(*b*) The establishment of married woman's property rights. The Japanese husband has the right to use and gain profits from his wife's property, but the wife can do the same with her husband's property as well as her own only when she is the head of the family—a post arrived at only by the legal adoption of the husband into her family. Furthermore, a daughter usually does not inherit property, getting only a small share even of her trousseau; only by special prenuptial arrangements does the wife bring wealth to a marriage. In the case of divorce by mutual consent, the husband is under no obligation to guarantee the livelihood of his wife. Her fate in the circumstances depends on his sense of moral obligation if he is a person of means. The children belong absolutely to the father. Whether a woman is born in a wealthy family or marries a wealthy man, she is not legally entitled to a penny of the riches, except by special arrangement. This forces the Japanese woman to submit to the existing family system—a slave in a domestic autocracy.

(*c*) The removal of the inexcusable inequality between man and wife in the case of adultery. The husband is liable to penalty only when he is sued by the husband of the woman with whom he committed the crime, and in no other case; so that no matter how questionable his conduct may be in the so-called gay quarters and even with any other unmarried woman, he is treated as a respectable gentleman by law as well as by society. Whereas, when the wife commits the same crime, regardless of the position of the man thus involved, whether married or unmarried, she can be punished by her husband immediately. This unfairness not only insults the Japanese woman, but necessarily leads to the moral degradation of society by overlooking the husband's indulgence and condemning the wife's.

To eliminate the legal unfairness toward women, our bourgeois feminists are convinced of the necessity of obtaining the suffrage, the right to vote and the right to hold office. But the truth is that the Japanese woman has no right to join a political organization of any sort. Even the right to attend a political meeting and to hear political speeches was withheld from her until 1922. Hence the immediate step toward enfranchisement scarcely goes beyond a request for the freedom to join political parties.

The proletarian woman's movement has similar objectives but it starts with an attack on capitalistic tyrannies. It identifies itself with the class war. Consequently, this group has the same and wider objectives than the bourgeois women's group.

These two branches of the Japanese woman movement conflict with each other ideologically speaking, but practically they have much in common, such as the desire to change the feudalistic rules and views of life and to elevate women's legal position. Despite the mutual objectives, these two groups have often been rather hostile.

For certain domestic reasons, I had to choose an independent path and join neither of these women's parties. I accepted the fact calmly for a while, believing that there was too much sentimentalism and excessive sex antagonism in the feminist movement anyway. For a sounder approach to the issues raised, it seemed to me that deeper study was required and that we must have a woman's institute.

I found coworkers for the institute in Miss Fusaye Ichikawa, Miss Natsu Kawasaki, Mrs. Ito Niizuma and Mrs. Shigeri Kaneko, whose acquaintance I had enjoyed since our relief work for the Russian famine. Other friends gave us support. Our purpose in establishing our "Research Institute" is to be found in the following prospectus, dated October, 1925.

Women have lived in the past in a condition quite different from that of men. Naturally there has been a world peculiar to us marked by phenomena exclusively concerning women. This divergence was true not only of the past, but is true today, and even if the time comes when our social circumstances shall be entirely identical with those of men, problems will still remain in some form, caused by the differences of sex.

However, there has never occurred in the past a single worthy study of those phenomena of the women's world. Such studies as have been published have all represented men's views. Again, there is a great deal of breath spent in the daily papers on the transition in circumstances that women today are facing; yet no concrete substantiation of the statements accompanies them.

Lately there have sprung up a number of women's organizations with professed purposes of elevating women's position and obtaining women's rights; but most of them have sentimental motives only, with very little reservation for sound thinking based on accurate facts.

In this situation, we venture to establish an institution in which one can study the history of women's social problems and make detailed investigations into the fundamental relations of man and woman. Consequently, this institution restricts its activity to research. It does not participate actively in movements. And without restricting ourselves to any one school of thought, religious sect, or class, we pledge ourselves to study impartially the problems of women on a factual basis.

Lastly, however, we add that, although primarily established for research as distinguished from propaganda, this institution shall offer every moral support in its power to the cause of elevating the position of women and advancing feminine rights.

This institution, based on the above prospectus, competently furnished to some of our women's organizations, overwhelmed by mere excitement, the scientific materials with which to operate more intelligently.

This institute had not a small part in promoting the higher education of Japanese women. In 1919, "The Society for the Advancement of Women's Education" was organized, mainly by men educators of women; it met with little success. About 1922 or 1923, the time when our feminist movement was vigorous, the cry for equal educational opportunity commanded attention. It was but a natural incident that with the close relationship between women's education and the feminist movement, the feminists should join the cry. The following figures obtained in 1928 indicate the slow growth of our women's education compared with our men's, although both forms were started at the same time in early Meiji:

Against 222 institutions of university and college standard for our men, there are only 37 of a similar kind for women. Of the total number of students in the above institutions, 161,430 are men and 14,127 are women. As for our middle schools, there are 1915 for 597,710 enrolled boys; whereas there are 934 for 405,427 girls. With these scanty women's educational institutions, and low academic standards, it is no wonder the Japanese feminist movement should advance so slowly.

Owing to the close interrelationship between the elevation

of women's position and their education, the feminists have been asking for the right of women to study with men in the government universities. But the government has never admitted women, except as "listeners," on the simple pretext that there is no preparatory process for women corresponding with that which takes place at the men's "higher school"—the only educational institution qualifying students to try for the entrance examination of the government universities. By the regulations originally drawn in early Meiji, this higher school is open only to boys. The elimination of the single phrase "for men" in the article would give women an absolutely equal educational opportunity with men. Yet, the government will not bother about it. This is partly due to the government's unwillingness to grant the privilege to women when the educational expenditure at present is running to high figures in the budget, and partly to the old Confucian teaching still exercising an influence on the authorities, making them deny the propriety of coeducation.

"A vote is the key to the happiness of woman!" the feminists declared. "Get the vote! Get a precious vote to move the governmental machine for the benefit of woman too!" Finally convinced that action was imperative, I stepped out from the ivory tower of my institute to join the women's suffrage campaign. In the Alliance of Suffragettes, the leading body in our feminist movement, I was appointed chairman of the finance committee. Like many other movements of this kind in every country, the Suffragettes' Alliance was in dire need of funds. The women's cry for equal legal treatment was strong in the campaign, but their purse was always miserably weak, in contradiction to their voices. We went out and visited women of the upper class asking for contributions. Some said that they didn't care for such an unwomanly business, while others said that they had to ask their husbands' consent for that and almost without exception their husbands gave no funds for the campaign of their rivals, as they regarded us.

Therefore, in order to raise a somewhat substantial sum, I organized a club called "Reijitsu-kai" (Bright Sunshine Society) mainly among those bourgeois women who had sympathy with the movement, yet could not share in its activity on account of their family bonds. This enterprise was successful, gaining sympathy from a great many literary men, artists and journalists, together with their wives, and producing a sum unusual for this kind of organization. With this comparative abundance of money, we could accomplish a large amount of work at least for some time after the men's acquisition of the suffrage, when the extension of civil rights to women was conceived as logical. Our woman suffrage movement reached a flourishing stage in its history, concentrating on the right to local enfranchisement as the first step to general suffrage. I spoke at many public-lecture meetings, I joined men's political campaigns at general elections to ask votes from the platform for candidates who were in favor of woman suffrage. We mobilized our force to petition the Diet. Keisuke Mochizuki, Home Minister of the Seiyukai cabinet of 1927, replied to the delegation who presented this petition: "Go back to your home and wash your babies' clothes! That is the job given to you and there is the place in which you are entitled to sit!" But in spite of this poor comprehension of women's problems by the minister, many of the Diet members of the political parties, Seiyukai and Minseito, were well aware that sooner or later the enfranchisement of women must come in the natural course of the political development of the country. Kenzo Adachi, Home Minister of the Minsei cabinet which succeeded the Seiyukai cabinet, showed himself quite sympathetic with women's movements and made an effort to have the bill for the granting of civil rights to women passed in the Diet. Although greatly revised, this bill did pass the House of Representatives under this cabinet in 1930. How excited we were with this triumph although luck stayed with us but a very short moment! The House of Peers rejected the bill without serious discussion. One nobleman spoke for all when he said: "In Japan there is an admirable ideal of knighthood, made for the protection of the weak. What an impertinence on the part of women to claim their rights when they are under men's perfect protection!" The representative opinion of the House was that woman's intrusion into public affairs would endanger the peace of the individual family as well as the family system of Japan—the foundation stone of the country, as they said. Even though the bill was rejected by the House of Peers, the fact that it did pass the House of Representatives set a significant precedent for the Japanese feminist movement. Thus encouraged, the feminist organizations redoubled their zeal, and this was their most flourishing time.

While bourgeois feminism was attempting to lift the position of Japanese women to the standards reached in the most advanced Western nations, the proletarian women's movement acknowledged itself to be a part of the proletarian class war. Reactionary currents of thought, however, began to rule Japan. And the issue of Manchuria pressing to the fore in September, 1931, changed the entire social and political situation in the country. Even liberal citizens were hushed by the rise of militarism. The feminist movement suffered a great setback.

Though its claim is rational, though its appeal is touching, Japanese feminism at best cannot compare with the type I have observed in Western countries. The difference is too sadly striking. Truly, the feminist movement of a country reflects its women's social status. In my country the pipers play music but women do not line up in a grand following behind the leaders. Even if the feminists succeeded in changing the married women's property rights, where is the property to be inherited by them? Even if the government opened its universities to girls, how would they manage to enter them to enjoy this privilege? The Japanese people as a whole are so poor! In this relation the objectives stressed by the proletarian women's group must be better adapted to the majority of our women. Yet women as a mass do not indorse that brand of feminism either. Feudalism is the point from which we must start our fight for feminism. It is only yesterday that we emerged into the new world of industrialism. And feudalism has clung to us like a leech. The feminist movement elsewhere has kept pace with the democracy of which it is the shadow. In European countries it had a long history of struggle against and final triumph over the power of feudal aristocracy, and in a country like America, whose constitution is based on the liberty of the people, individual liberty is the foundation of social life. But in Japan, where modern capitalism was rashly combined with the deep-rooted feudal forces, all in a flash, liberalism in its complete sense is incapable of free development. Thus feminism with its concentration on women's enfranchisement was obliged to retreat under the sudden rise of the fascist power which grew out of Japan's crisis in her international relations.

XXXI

History of Feminism in Japan

SO FAR I have emphasized my relation to the feminist movement, and its present status. To leave the discussion there would imply that the time depth of this movement is shallow, whereas the truth is that it dates back to the beginning of the Meiji era. This greater time depth is important to understand for, in its long stretch, roots of thought about the position of women in our society so grounded themselves in the social thought of Japanese intellectuals that reliance is still placed on their vitality for eventual flowering.

When I joined our feminist movement there were a number of bourgeois organizations and the proletarian organization too was in a flourishing condition, indulging in some warm controversies over ideologies with the bourgeois women. The outstanding middle-class feminists, the Kyojukai, were Christian humanists. The Women Suffragettes' Alliance was a political department of the Federation of Women's Organizations formed immediately after the earthquake in 1923.

But, as I say, the history of feminism runs back into the nineteenth century when Japan's resistance to world trade was broken down. The new government that came into being in the confusion of the Meiji restoration adopted, almost wholesale, Western ideas for its policies and institutions, and their influence was responsible for liberalism in Japan. Rousseau's natural right of man, Montesquieu's theory of sovereignty, Bentham's utilitarianism, and Mill's liberty and equality were eagerly read and discussed. Among Japanese women, Mill was a radical force with his plea for sex equality.

The restoration government discarded the political and economic phases of the feudal system, and adopted, or was forced to follow, Western capitalistic enterprise. In the social life, it succeeded in abolishing by law a few feudal customs, such as the wearing of swords by samurai, men's peculiar hair-dressing and the discriminating appellations (honorifics) based on class. But the mental and spiritual adjustments of the nation could not take place by fiat alone. The feudalistic conception of woman as man's property still was dominant among the people, affecting the habits of both sexes. Nevertheless, Mill's *Subjection of Women* when introduced into this society had a profound influence. As early as 1876, Koho Dohi threw down the gauntlet for Japanese feminism by publishing a book called *Great Civilized Learning for Women,* based on Mill's perspective. From Tokugawa times, the *Great Learning for Women,* which I discussed in Chapter XXIV, had been held to be the final authority for women's education, inculcating among them the feeling of inferiority to men. And of course it remained the supreme authority for society at large. The vast majority of women were untouched by the revolutionary doctrine of sex equality. In spite of this, with the growth of capitalism and the advancement of bourgeois liberalism, the feminist theories were widely debated and interested men and women began to draw together.

In the middle of the Meiji era, following the discussion of Mr. Dohi's volume, came others: *Women's Rights in the Western Countries,* by Hokichi Yumoto (1882); Naiki Fukama's *On Mill's Equality* (1884); Yukichi Fukuzawa's *On Woman* (1885) and *On Social Intercourse of Man and Woman* (1886); Miss Nao Inoue's *Japanese Women* (1886); Kojiro Tatsumi's *History of Women's Rights in the West and in Japan* (1887); Ko Yoda's *Monogamy* (1887); and Seiu Nakayama's *Japanese Women of Tomorrow* (1888). But alas! only one of these books was written by a woman. Men seemed to be

Reading a prospectus to a group which met to establish a branch office for the birth control movement in Osaka in 1932

Leaving Yokohama on the S.S. Chichibu Maru for my lecture tour in the United States, October 13, 1932

Returning to my work in Japan

the better feminists. The bourgeois view of feminism was definitely established with the publication of *Criticisms on the Great Learning for Women* and *Revised Great Learning for Women*, written by Hukichi Fukuzawa and both published in 1898. In the former the author argued for the elevation of the Japanese woman's position, attacking word by word *Great Learning for Women,* and declared that the old moral code was unjust to our sex.

Meanwhile, the westernization policy adopted by the restoration government had brought some actual changes in the education of women. In December, 1871, a few months after the establishment of the Department of Education (July, 1871), the government issued an edict to the following effect: "The prosperity of each family depends upon each individual's awakening to the sense of responsibility, regardless of sex. Now, while we have educational institutions for men, there is none for women. Hereby we establish a girls' public school by hiring Western women teachers and admitting students whether noble or common, on their presentation of the tuition. Applicants shall send in their applications by January 15, 1872." This was the first girls' public school in Japan.

Together with this government school for girls, a number of private girls' schools were established. Among them were schools founded by the feudal lords for their clans, notably the Izushi, Toyooka, Matsue, Iwakuni, Nagoya, and Fukuyama girls' schools. The Christian missionary schools for girls established about this time were Joshi-Gakuin, Aoyama Jokakuin, and Rikkyo Girls' School in Tokyo; Ferris Girls' School and Kyoritus Girls' School in Yokohama; Doshisha Girls' School in Kyoto; Baika Girls' School in Osaka; and Kobe-Jogakuin (now Kobe College) in Kobe.

In 1874, a girls' higher normal school was established in Tokyo through the initiative of Jujimaro Tanaka, Minister of Education, and there followed the establishment of a number of girls' public schools in the local districts. This surely shows a great public enthusiasm for women's education in the seventies. But there was more evidence. In 1871 five Japanese girls of impressionable ages were sent abroad by the government, accompanying the party of Prince Tomomi Iwakura on a round-the-world trip to observe Western life: Toiko Yeda, aged eighteen; Ryoko Yoshimasu, aged sixteen; Sutematsu Yamakawa, aged twelve; Shigeko Nagai, aged ten; and Ume Tsuda, aged nine. All of them were taken into American homes and three of them went to college in America. Prior to their departure, they were honored with an audience by the Empress, who spoke the following gracious words of encouragement and farewell: "Her Majesty appreciates your ambition to study abroad. As Japanese women's education is in a stage of transition, you will bring yourselves up to be the models for your countrywomen on your completion of the intended study abroad." Miss Ume Tsuda, the youngest of the five, became the founder of the famous Tsuda College in Japan.

Such enlightenment may lead one to expect that a great advance in the actual feminist movement itself followed swiftly. The fact was quite to the contrary, however, for the feminist movement was regarded merely as a minor activity inside the men's liberal movement; the true feminine elements were for some time represented by the activities of Mrs. Toshiko Nakajima and Miss Eiko Kageyama.

The men's liberal movement developed as a challenge to the conservative politics of the bureaucratic government which was made up of the surviving forces of the old feudal regime and rather timid innovators. The immediate demand of the movement was the realization of a constitution and parliamentary government. The bourgeois liberals, forming a political party of their own, sought to propagandize among those members of the bourgeoisie who failed to gain governmental patronage, and among the discontented landowners who were the victims of the advancing capitalism. From 1880 to 1884 the movement took on militant activities, such as leading peasants' revolts, and proved to be a great menace to the autocratic government. Persecuted by the government, deprived of much of its freedom of activity, and finally suffering from internal dissensions, it had, in 1884, to declare voluntary dissolution. This dissolution of the Liberal party restored everything to a smooth surface, in appearance; but in reality, discontent against the autocratic government was smoldering. It was not extinguished.

The government, with a view to revising the humiliating foreign treaties which it had been forced to sign under the circumstances of the restoration, adopted a policy of extreme westernization, as a demonstration of Japanese genius for self-government. It built the famous Rokumei-kan (Reception Hall; later the Peers' Club Building) and held grand dancing parties there. The entire aristocracy and the upper bourgeoisie got intoxicated in the gay imitation of the Western diplomatic manners. Lords and ladies, not long out of their lacquered palanquins, stepped to the lively Vienna waltz in European ball dress! This is what we call the Rokumei-kan period of Japanese culture.

With the approach of the promulgation of the constitution and of the opening of the Diet, which the government had previously promised to bring about in the year 1889, public agitation in many forms became increasingly intense. In 1887 the worried government issued the tyrannical Peace Preservation law, another noteworthy event in the cultural history of Japan. This law completely repressed opposition parties, but in so doing aroused a nationalistic reaction to its extreme westernization policy.

Our feminist movement, which had displayed a precarious existence under the wing of general liberalism, was now almost completely destroyed by the successive unfavorable circumstances accompanying the dissolution of the Liberal party with the issuance of the Peace Preservation law. After this, with the development of capitalism in Japan, labor questions came steadily into being as something inseparable from the economic phases of the new social order. As for the feminist movement, it almost disappeared. The Peace Preservation Law, designed for the suppression of any political and social movement which might arise among the people, explicitly excluded Japanese women from the right to join political parties and to attend political gatherings even in the form of lecture meetings. Thus the early feminist movement was brought to an ignominious end.

However, books expressing new ideas on women's education—particularly those by Yukichi Fukuzawa, although quite aristocratic in temper, were to leave their imprint upon women. Now that political opportunities of any kind were specifically denied, women turned to writing as a way of expressing their insurgency. From about that time Japanese literature exhibited more naturalism and less romanticism. Naturalistic literature taught more Japanese women to be self-conscious, as the themes show: *Home and Myself; Society and Myself; Woman as a Human Being*. North European literature, especially Ibsen's— *The Doll's House, Ghosts, The Lady of the Sea* and *The Weaver*, helped to stir the native women. Ellen Key also provoked thought. Her *Love and Marriage* and *Woman Movement* did not differ much in substance from Fukuzawa's *Revised Great Learning for Women,* but her works, by virtue of their absolute denial of feudalistic morals and the glorification of Love, became a sensation to the Japanese women when they were put into their hands. They now dared to dream of romantic love. And to grow critical of domestic servitude.

The influences emanating from Ellen Key and other North European writers were to be seen later, in 1911, in the organization of the Seito Society, which is the Japanese way of saying Bluestocking Society. This noted young women's movement is now considered to have been the true pioneer in bourgeois feminism. The Japanese Bluestocking Society included among its members and supporters most of the literary women of the time who had hitherto been fighting their battle only with the pen. The declaration, published in the *Seito,* the monthly organ of the society, reads as follows: "Woman in the primitive age was the Sun, a real and just human personality. (The ancestor of the Japanese race is worshiped as the Sun Goddess.) Now she is the Moon, dependent on others for a livelihood; the Moon that borrows light from others, pale like a sick patient. We are to restore the hidden Sun. 'Find the Hidden Sun which is our genius!' This is our constant cry, and the inspiration of our unified purpose. The culmination of this cry, this thirst, this desire, shall lead to the finding of genius in ourselves." This declaration, though short and very poetically stated, is convincing with respect to the earnest attitude manifest toward the issue of women's freedom and emancipation. This bold assertion of "the awakened women" astounded the conservatives of the country, on the one hand; and on the other it stimulated the feminine public to thought and action. Thus feminism revived through the stimulus of literary women. Yet, in spite of its fiery zeal, the Seito Society had to end as a mere literary movement because of lack of funds.

And feminists had to remain cautious. The crushing of socialist leaders on the charge of high treason drove social criticism of every sort underground. However, even in this dark age, the implanted ideas grew in the hearts of the people. From Ellen Key's *Love and Marriage* to Edward Carpenter's *Love's Coming-of-Age* and on to Bebel's works on *Woman,* a movement in thought made its way through Japan.

Toward the end of the Great War, immediately after the Russian Revolution, great new currents of ideas flowed into our country. The "war for democracy," in which Japan had been arrayed on the side of democrats, necessarily stimulated the discussion of woman's status. The fact that the promotion of women's rights has been so slow in Japan, which has seldom lagged in the international industrial competition, indicates to what extent the Japanese are psychologically bound by the leftover feudalistic ideas and practices.

It was about 1920, the time when the movement for men's universal suffrage was approaching victory, that the feminist movement assumed a united front for a universal suffrage not discriminatory in the matter of sex. No longer able to suppress the democratic impulse, the Japanese government granted manhood suffrage. But it stopped short of enfranchising women.

After the grant of manhood suffrage, women took heart anyway. They pushed organization directed to winning political, legal and social rights. They had one victory; they got the right to attend political meetings, almost accidentally, when in 1922 the Peace Preservation Police Act was revised as a result of the spirited protest by laborers against the prohibition of their right to strike. Except for this single privilege, our women are still rightless. They cannot join political parties. In such a situation, it is but natural that spirited leaders should be so impatient to awaken their meek sisters to a sense of woman's innate power and potentialities.

It must be recorded, however, that impatience is all the Japanese women can for the moment know. A nationalist reaction against liberalism has recently swept all else before it in the Island Empire. Fascism with its strong militaristic flavor is no defender of feminism with its strong humanistic flavor. This is the contemporary current of opinion which has caught even women in its high tide.

PART TWELVE
A NEW START

*A*CCUMULATED discontent with the theories and practices surviving from feudalism helped to turn my face toward modernism. And dire need helped to hold my attention to the future. One cold winter day, during my husband's absence which had become habitual through his frequent and prolonged journeys to Korea and Manchuria, the heaps of old art amid which I had been living were assessed by his creditors who threatened to carry them all out of the house to pay off the loan my husband had got by mortgaging them. In this emergency my father came to my financial help and the objects of art were rescued. But the experience taught me how insecure was my economic situation and I realized that I could no longer dawdle—that I must face the future with less of compromise. The education of my sons was now placed squarely on my shoulders. I must earn a living for us three.

Fortunately at this crisis an invitation came from America for me to lecture there. And daring as was this undertaking, considering the state of my English and my competence on the platform, I took the dare! Behind the invitation stood my uncle, Yusuke Tsurumi who was in New York at the time, and the Herbert Houstons who had long been interested in Japan. The Feakins Lecture Bureau was ready to arrange my tour. I was told that I would be expected to speak on Japanese women, the culture of my country, and what was going on in Manchuria. What was more, I must begin the tour without delay. Of course days were spent in the rush and strain of preparing lectures, closing my house, settling my sons in the home of my parents, and practicing English. As my boat left its moorings at Yokohama, my heart was almost bursting with emotions but it would never have done to betray the fact to my family and friends, really as excited as I was, who bowed me off so politely and formally—in the proper Japanese way: fire within, calm without!

How I ever accomplished this bold and hazardous tour in the year 1932-33 I do not know. It ranged from California to New York and back, including communities so diverse as Boston, Palm Beach, and Dallas, Texas. I had to travel alone. I had to broadcast; give difficult interviews at all times and places. There was much banqueting with after-dinner speaking. One evening I addressed a congregation from a pulpit in a Unitarian Church in Canada. Another evening I spoke in a Free Synagogue. An ex-missionary to Japan, Dr. Horace Coleman, was the chairman at a meeting in Boston when angry questions about Manchuria were asked from the floor and I was deeply thankful for his presence. Sometimes there were equally urgent diplomatic adventures which I had to meet unchaperoned, notably one at Palm Beach when a sturdy American patriot and national naval hero sitting at my side burst forth with anti-Japanese sentiments which I had to counter without corresponding passion.

And once there was a rough physical adventure on the street when a sudden lurch of my taxi threw me against the front seat and knocked out several of my front teeth. As a result, I was brought to appreciate even more fully American hospitality and friendship. Dr. and Mrs. Frederick Peterson of New York City kept me in their home for weeks. They engaged a nurse to watch over my diet, build up my nerves, and attend me on my trips to the X-ray specialist and the dentist. While I was recuperating, my hosts were zealous for my comfort, sensitive to every aspect of my plight, and eager to learn all they could about Japan which they had visited but only for a short time. Mrs. Peterson even wanted to try one of the Zen exercises. I performed Japanese dances for them. I enjoyed telling them about our arts, especially since they had studied the Chinese background and possessed some fine specimens of Chinese painting. Through these gracious New Yorkers I met many other Americans some of whom entertained me in turn.

Thus I had the rare delight of visiting Mr. and Mrs. Louis Ledoux whose villa at Cornwall-on-the-Hudson is so refined in its setting and so aesthetic in its restraint that it suggests a Zen monastery. They have been close students of Oriental culture. They own a splendid collection of Japanese prints, paintings and No robes. We talked about Lady Murasaki and Baseo and in these noble surroundings I found it possible to rest and for a time forget the changing world. I was pure daughter of a samurai again.

But I came sharply up against the present through my renewed association with Margaret Sanger the Invincible. In her clinic I studied intently the latest methods of birth control. Together we went now and then to meetings where each of us presented her philosophy with respect to the object of birth control. Mrs. Sanger and Mrs. Ruth Litt introduced me to the group of New York women who aid in promoting this movement and we had chances to discuss ways and means which might be helpful in Japan. In addition to enlightening me, Mrs. Sanger gave me magnanimous personal attention, inviting me to her home and looking out for my comfort in countless ways. Her amazing secretary, "Rose," was all devotion. Feeling that I needed diversion, she bore me off to Coney Island late one afternoon and we had a very lively time there, indeed, running to catch boats and trains, riding on merry-go-rounds, shooting the chutes, and seeing the resort as others see it while enjoying ourselves in similar style.

Always for public lectures and for formal dinners I wore my native costume. It seemed to create the best atmosphere for friendship. Since I wore Western costume at other times I often felt as exotic in my native dress as I doubtless looked to others. However, I felt utterly at home in it during a convention at Chicago which I attended. This had been called by the National Council of Women and women from many foreign lands were present to give it an international flavor. Some of these guests were, like myself, in native apparel. Thus I had the pleasure of feeling rather more dignified than exotic as I sat beside Selma Ekrem of Turkey, for example, who wore her fascinating native dress. She is the author of that important book on Turkish women, *Unveiled*. I was deeply impressed by her skill in handling the English language, by her directness of expression, and by her knowledge. But I did the best I could to represent my race too. Since the general theme set by this conference was "Our Common Cause—Civilization," the speeches all revolved around the idea of women in a changing world. And since they were delivered by such forceful women as Mrs. Carrie Chapman Catt, Jane Addams, and Margaret Bondfield of England, I derived from them a stronger determination than ever to face the modern world courageously and as intelligently as possible.

To aid in my emancipation from the traditional burdens of Japanese housekeeping with a view to saving time for public work, I purchased out of my lecture fees several conveniences such as studio beds and rugs, the rugs requiring less care than straw mats. To interest my young sons in American boys I bought for each of them a silver wrist watch such as the Scouts wear. But I also spent some of my earnings for the most up-to-date equipment for a scientifically managed birth control clinic.

Helped financially by my tour in the West and stimulated mentally and emotionally by the experience, I returned to Tokyo to take up a new life in greater earnest, with stronger conviction. There could scarcely be retreat into the past now for me. I knew that I should have to struggle against spells of melancholia for these had attacked me even during my lecture tour in the United States. There had been some inevitable nostalgia for things once, and indeed, still beloved. I had been overpowered at times by the consciousness of the relative poverty of Japan and America. The larger opportunities for women of the West and their larger numbers of brave innovators made our Japanese life and labor seem too much of a contrast to be borne. I found it hard to keep my eyes fixed steadfastly on the work I must do. In some respects my American tour was devastating to my spirit.

Nevertheless, I understood very well my own inner difficulties and on my return I hurried to prepare for the opening of a clinic in Tokyo which would be scientific in practice and noncommercial in interest. First I had to persuade the police authorities that I was not a dangerous subject of the crown. So I showed them the equipment which I had brought from New York and explained how birth control was handled today in the West. And as I interpreted the movement to them, the austere gentlemen in gold braid, with swords at their sides, nodded slightly and formally from time to time despite their affiliation with a government concerned with an abundant supply of soldiers. These nods enabled me to open in March, 1934, the scientifically operated birth control clinic of which I had dreamed. The Birth Control Movement of Japan supported this experiment. Miss Kawasaki, a prominent newspaper columnist and women's counselor, took it under her powerful protection. Other friends rallied about it.

But there remained the task of convincing the poor mothers-at-large that Buddha would not punish them for entering our clinic. Like myself they face two ways. But civilization is our common cause.

THE END

171 D